FOR THE BEREAVED
The Road to Recovery

EDITED BY

Austin H. Kutscher
President, The Foundation of Thanatology;
Department of Psychiatry, Columbia University

Sandra Bess

Samuel G. Klagsbrun, MD

Mary-Ellen Siegel, MSW

Daniel J. Cherico, PhD, MPH

Lillian G. Kutscher

David Peretz, MD

Florence E. Selder, RN, PhD

The Charles Press, Publishers
Philadelphia

The Charles Press, Publishers
Post Office Box 15715
Philadelphia, Pennsylvania 19103

Library of Congress Cataloging-in-Publication Data:

For the bereaved: the road to recovery / edited by Austin H. Kutscher
   . . . [et al.]. —3rd ed.
     p. cm.
   Rev. ed of: For those bereaved. New York: Arno Press, 1980.
   Includes bibliographical references.
   ISBN 0-914783-32-7
   1. Bereavement—Psychological aspects. 2. Death—Psychological aspects.
3. Grief. I. Kutscher, Austin H. II. For those bereaved.
BF575.G7F67 1989   89-22190
155.9′37—dc20   CIP

ISBN 0-914783-32-7

5   4   3   2

Printed in the United States of America by Princeton University Press.

Contents

Editors vi
Contributors vii
Dedication xi
Acknowledgment xii

Prologue 1
   A.H. Kutscher
Second Spring... 6
   S. Bess
Introduction 10
   D. Peretz

PART I: GRIEF
Why You Should Understand Grief: A Minister's Views 14
   E.N. Jackson
Grief: A Physician-Minister's View 18
   W.B. McCullough
Understanding Your Mourning: A Psychiatrist's View 24
   D. Peretz
Grief in Anticipation of Death............................ 37
   F.P. Herter & J.A. Knight
When a Child Dies... 39
   M.E. Robinson
The Lost Image.. 45
   S. Bess
The Special Needs of Bereaved Children 47
   S. Goodman
To the Bereaved of a Suicide.............................. 50
   E.S. Shneidman
Surviving a Suicide....................................... 52
   D. Lester
Tender are the Scars 56
   M. Jones
Thoughts on My Wife's Death............................... 58
   J.P. Rudin
Rights of Passage—Rites of Passage 64
   M. Siegel
A Lifetime of Preparation for Bereavement................. 68
   A.C. Carr
Lindemann's Studies on Reactions to Grief................. 73
   A. Rosell

A Message for the Living 76
   H. Zinsser
The Second Time Around: Grief Revisited 78
   A.H. Kutscher

PART II: FUNERALS
Grief and Meaning of the Funeral 88
   L.G. Kutscher
Acute Grief and the Funeral 92
   R. Pinette
The Funeral Service 103
   E.L. Post
The Condolence Call 114
   R. Flesch
Children and Funerals 125
   J.E. Schowalter
The Bramble Bush 130
   S. Bess

PART III: THOUGHTS ABOUT DEATH
Judaism and the Experience of Death .132
   I. Blank
Christianity and the Experience of Death 139
   W. DeBold
Superstructure at High Tide 146
   S. Bess

PART IV: THE RECOVERY
Grief: The Road to Recovery 150
   Rev. A. Pangrazzi
Avoiding the Mistakes in Bereavement 159
   J.P. Cattell
Talking Out, Feeling Out, Acting Out .163
   E.N. Jackson
How We Should Mourn 170
   J. Stern, Jr.
The Magic of Time 171
   A.H. Kutscher
Expression of Grief 172
   J. Bess
Transitions for the Bereaved: The Future 173
   C.M. Parkes
Reaching Out: The Library 179
   R.D. Miller

Reaching Out: Education 182
    K.O. Budmen
Renewal 184
    A.H. Kutscher

PART V: NEEDS OF THE BEREAVED
Medical Needs of the Bereaved Family 190
    G.A. Hyman
Why You Need Your Physician Now 192
    J. Bess
Physiological Aspects of Depression 193
    J. Steiner, et al
Opinions of the Bereaved on Bereavement 200
    A.H. Kutscher

PART VI: STARTING OVER
A Doctor Discusses Sexuality and Bereavement 206
    R. Michels
A Practical Guide for Young Widows 207
    T. Ferguson, et al
Finding Fulfillment in Remarriage 241
    D.B. Maxwell
Remarriage: A Psychologist's Advice 243
    R.N. Franzblau
Thoughts about Remarriage 254
    F.P. Herter
Etiquette and Remarriage 255
    E.L. Post

PART VII: FINANCIAL PRAGMATICS OF BEREAVEMENT
Counseling the Bereaved 258
    G. Rosner
The Multiple Roles of the Estate Lawyer 263
    R.H. Bernstein
Family Assistance and the Probate Process 268
    M. Miller
A Confidential Family Checklist 273
    E. Nadel and J.J. Parker

EPILOGUE
Rural Funerals 282
    W. Irving

Editors

Austin H. Kutscher
President, The Foundation of Thanatology, New York, NY; Professor of Dentistry (in Psychiatry), Department of Psychiatry, College of Physicians and Surgeons, Columbia University, New York, NY

Sandra Bess
Poet, Willow Grove, PA

Samuel C. Klagsbrun, MD
Associate Clinical Professor Psychiatry, College of Physicians and Surgeons, Columbia University, New York, New York; Director, Four Winds Hospital, Katonah, New York

Mary-Ellen Siegel, MSW, ACSW
Senior Teaching Associate, Department of Community Medicine (Social Work), Mount Sinai School of Medicine, New York, NY

Daniel J. Cherico, PhD, MPH
Director of Programs and Policy, The Foundation of Thanatology, New York, New York

Lillian G. Kutscher
Publications Editor, The Foundation of Thanatology, New York, NY (deceased)

David Peretz, MD
Assistant Clinical Professor of Psychiatry, Department of Psychiatry, College of Physicians and Surgeons, Columbia University, New York, NY

Florence E. Selder, RN, PhD
Associate Professor, Urban Research Center, University of Wisconsin, Milwaukee; Clinical Associate Professor, The Midwest Center for Human Sciences, Milwaukee, WI

Contributors

Richard H. Bernstein, Esq.
Warshaw, Burstein, Cohen, Schlesinger & Kuh, Attorneys, New York, NY

Joseph Bess, DO
Private Practice of Psychiatry, Philadelphia, PA (deceased)

Sandra Bess
Poet, Willow Grove, PA

Rabbi Irwin Blank, DD
Formerly Temple Sinai, Tenafly, NJ

Karl O. Budman, EdD
Professor of Education, State University College, New Paltz, NY

Arthur C. Carr, PhD
Professor of Clinical Psychology (in Psychiatry), Cornell University Medical College, New York, NY; New York Hospital (Westchester Division), White Plains, NY

James P. Cattell, MD
Assistant Clinical Professor, Department of Psychiatry, College of Physicians and Surgeons, Columbia University; Assistant Attending Psychiatrist, The Presbyterian Hospital in the City of New York, New York, NY

George Crile, Jr., MD
Surgeon (Emeritus), Cleveland Clinic, Cleveland, OH

Reverend Walter Debold
Englewood Cliffs College, Englewood, NJ

Tamara Ferguson, PhD
Adjunct Associate Professor of Sociology in Psychiatry, Department of Psychiatry, Wayne State University School of Medicine, Detroit, MI; Lafayette Clinic, Department of Psychiatry, Wayne State University School of Medicine, Detroit, MI

Regina Flesch, PhD
Eastern Pennsylvania Psychiatric Institute, Philadelphia, PA

Rose N. Franzblau, PhD
Psychologist, Columnist for New York Post, New York, NY (deceased)

Soll Goodman, MD
Special Lecturer, Department of Psychiatry, College of Physicians and
Surgeons, Columbia University, New York, New York (deceased)

Fredric P. Herter, MD
Hugh Auchincloss Professor of Surgery, Department of Surgery, Col-
lege of Physicians and Surgeons, Columbia University, New York,
NY; President, American University of Beirut, Beirut, Lebanon

George A. Hyman, MD
Associate Clinical Professor of Medicine (Oncology), Department of
Medicine, College of Physicians and Surgeons, Columbia Universi-
ty, New York, NY

Edgar N. Jackson, DD
Formerly, Pastor, Mamaroneck Methodist Church, Mamaroneck, NY;
Chairman, Advisory Board, Guidance Center of New Rochelle, New
Rochelle, NY

Marty Jones, RN
Psychiatric Nurse, Veterans Administration Hospital, Houston, TX

James A. Knight, MD
Formerly, Associate Dean and Professor of Psychiatry, Tulane University School of Medicine, New Orleans, LA

Austin H. Kutscher
President, The Foundation of Thanatology, New York NY; Professor
of Dentistry (in Psychiatry), Department of Psychiatry, College of
Physicians and Surgeons, Columbia University, New York, NY

Lillian G. Kutscher
Publications Editor, The Foundation of Thanatology, New York, NY
(deceased)

David Lester, PhD
Professor of Psychology, Richard Stockton State College, Pomona, NJ

David B. Maxwell
Formerly Associate Protestant Chaplain, The Presbyterian Hospital
in the City of New York, Columbia-Presbyterian Medical Center, New
York, NY

Rev. William B. McCullough
Formerly Resident, The Presbyterian Hospital in the City of New York

Robert Michels, MD
Chairman and Professor, Department of Psychiatry, Cornell University Medical College, New York, NY

Milton Miller, CPA
President, Miller and Company, CPAs, New York, NY; Former Chairman, Estate Planning Committee; Chairman, Financial Planning Committee, New York State Society of CPAs

Roy D. Miller, Jr., MS
Chief, Division of History, Biography and Religion, Brooklyn Public Library, Brooklyn, NY

Edwin Nadel, CLU
General agent, The Nadel Agency, New England Mutual Life Insurance Co., New York, NY

John F. O'Connor, MD
Associate Clinical Professor of Psychiatry, Department of Psychiatry, College of Physicians and Surgeons, Columbia University, New York, NY; Assistant Director, Vanderbilt Clinic, The Presbyterian Hospital in the City of New York, New York, NY

Rev. Arnaldo Pangrazzi

John G. Parker, Esq.
New York, NY

Colin Murray Parkes, MD, DPM
Senior Lecturer in Psychiatry, Department of Psychiatry, London Hospital Medical College, London, England

David Peretz, MD
Assistant Clinical Professor of Psychiatry, Department of Psychiatry, College of Physicians and Surgeons, Columbia University, New York, NY

Raoul L. Pinette
Past President, National Funeral Directors Association; Funeral Service, Lewiston, ME

Elizabeth L. Post
Editor, Emily Post's Etiquette, Funk and Wagnalls, New York, NY

Mary Evans Robinson, PhD
Director, Chronic Illness Project, Research Foundation of Children's
Hospital, Washington, DC

Alan Rosell, D.D.S.
New York, NY

Gerald Rosner, ChFC, CLU
Chartered Financial Consultant; Executive Director, P.M. Planning
Company, New York, NY

Rabbi Jacob Philip Rudin, DD
Temple Beth-El, Great Neck, NY (deceased)

John E. Schowalter, MD
Professor of Pediatrics and Psychiatry; Associate Director of the Yale
Child Study Center, Yale University School of Medicine, New Haven,
CT

Edwin S. Shneidman, PhD
Professor of Thanatology and Director, Laboratory of Study of Life-
Threatening Behavior, Neuro-Psychiatric Institute, University of
California, Los Angeles, CA

Mary-Ellen Siegel, MSW, ACSW
Senior Teaching Associate, Department of Community Medicine (Social Work), Mount Sinai School of Medicine, New York, NY

Jerome Steiner, MD
Assistant Clinical Professor Psychiatry, College of Physicians and Sur-
geons, Columbia University; Assistant Attending Psychiatrist, The
Presbyterian Hospital in the City of New York, New York, NY

Rabbi Jack Stern, Jr.
Westchester Reform Temple, Scarsdale, NY

Lenore O. Stern
Research Assistant, Department of Pediatric Psychiatry, Babies Hospital, Columbia-Presbyterian Medical Center, New York, NY

Hans Zinsser, MD
Physician, Scientist, Author (deceased)

To

Joseph Bess
Charles Koplin
Helene W. Kutscher
Dr. Harvey Goldberg

Acknowledgment

The editors wish to acknowledge the support and encouragement of the Foundation of Thanatology in the preparation of this volume. All royalties from the sale of this book are assigned to the Foundation of Thanatology, a tax exempt, not for profit, public scientific and educational foundation.

Thanatology, a new subspecialty of medicine, is involved in scientific and humanistic inquiries and the application of the knowledge derived therefrom to the subjects of the psychological aspects of dying; reactions to loss, death, and grief; and recovery from bereavement.

Prologue

The results of most efforts reflect the motivations and impulses which originate and sustain them. Viewed in perspective, this book owes its meaning to the impelling force of its origin. It came into being a few weeks after my young wife's lingering death from cancer, while I was confined in the solitude of a hospital room because of complications following minor surgery. Such were the circumstances surrounding the formative stages of the book, the concept of which was furthered by the contemplative tendencies of the editor and a lifetime devoted to academic pursuits and endeavors.

For The Bereaved was approached as a "labor of love," and as a much-needed effort: an original and definitive multi-contributor book on the subject of *recovery* from deep grief and personal loss.

I knew from my own quests that no book covering both emotional and practical problems had been published to serve as an aid to the grief-stricken person in his recovery from bereavement. There are essays in periodicals, pamphlets, or monographs, and even many excellent compilations of literature in book form (such as *A Treasury of Comfort* by Dr. Sidney Greenberg). There are, as well, extensive and learned books for professional counselors (such as *Understanding Grief,* by one of our contributors, the Reverend Edgar N. Jackson). Other books have certain relevant passages or chapters, profoundly moving in their spiritual quality, such as those by Joshua Loth Liebman in his memorable *Peace of Mind.* And innumerable articles on bereavement are scattered in the psychological, medical, and social science literature, but most of the scientific sources deal with the subject on a professional level and are of little practical use to the bereaved because of their technical nature, their inaccessibility, and the understandable inertia that would preclude the bereaved's seeking them out.

The outline for the book emerged from weeks of conscious and unconscious effort, from reflections which were crystallized and recorded note by note, minute by minute, day by day, and only thereafter placed into sequence. And, because of my professional background, which had included the editing of three multi-contributor scientific textbooks, I conceived of this endeavor as a multi-contributor multi-disciplinary book which would bring together the counsel of as many authorities in their respective fields as possible.

The decision to proceed was markedly influenced by the interest shown in this project and the encouragement offered by the Reverend Robert B. Reeves, Jr., Chaplain of the Presbyterian Hospital at the Columbia-Presbyterian Medical Center, and the "blessings" be-

1

stowed by Dr. Lawrence Kolb, Professor of Psychiatry and Director of the Psychiatric Institute, Columbia University College of Physicians and Surgeons, who granted me permission to solicit the assistance of members of his staff and who, in addition, volunteered the names of a number of individuals outside of the university who he thought had an interest in this area and might serve as a further nucleus about which to build.

Some contributors were asked to address themselves to the spiritual, or philosophical, or medical needs and problems facing the bereaved; others, to the practical problems of everyday existence; still others, to ways in which to reduce or temper mental, physical, or pecuniary complications; others, to a prophylactic or therapeutic, psychologic or psychiatric prescription designed to lessen the incidence of depression or maladjustment.

It was understood from the outset that different circumstances, different persons, different ages, different bereavement relationships, as well as many other factors, all combine to result in a most complex individual picture, but we have firmly held to the belief that there are certain basic premises which can be used as points of departure for the making of decisions on many, if not all, problems. Thus, the principal goal of the book is the development of a more mature, useful, forward looking, and hopeful understanding of the problem of deep grief and, along with it, the synthesis of one or a number of practical and workable approaches to what, when, and how to do what can, should, or might usefully be done. We set out to provide a multicontributor book which deals with reasoned authoritativeness with the disposition of the innumerable problems of the bereaved.

It should be pointed out that the information presented has been buttressed by the results of an extensive consensus survey of contributors and professional consultants. Virtually the same survey was completed by a large group of widows and widowers. Since these latter individuals had had the personal experience of intense bereavement, it was felt that they would have developed a distinctive and informative point of view—one which had actually evolved from their former despair and hopelessness. Because these widows and widowers were able to view their experiences in retrospect, it was felt that they could offer realistic and valuable answers and advice. Much of the information thus compiled proved to be of inestimable value in further assuring the authoritative qualities of this book.

The outline went through constant revision. Suggestions were made by many contributors and consultants to whom the editor turned for the benefit of their wisdom and understanding. I could only pose the questions. Little did I know at that time how profoundly important this effort, in its entirety, was to be in "working

2

my own way through grief," a concept with which I was only familiar theoretically; of how important it was that these energies were being devoted to a cardinal therapeutic concept, that some form of creativity be coupled to the mourning process.

Long after the inception of this book, and long after many of the contributions had actually been received, an extremely important facet of the problem was brought into clear focus: the fact that relatives and friends, although personally involved, are not in as unbiased and detached a position to give constructive advice to the bereaved as are the professional experts in the many and diverse fields of human care and relations whose views are presented here. Relatives are themselves undergoing a reaction to loss, are themselves grieving, and hence are in a state of bereavement also in relation to the same loved one.

Gradually, as work progressed, the importance of understanding grief came to be appreciated. This concept was to become one of the basic tenets of the book, and one which it is necessary to comprehend in order to recover from grief. A bridge must be built over the painful ground of grief and mourning, a bridge which will lead to understanding; then, ultimately, through understanding, to a release from many anxieties and much despair. This concept is not easy for the bereaved to appreciate; nor is it one which he is prepared to accept in the initial stages of acute loss.

As the weeks passed, weeks devoted to studying submitted manuscripts and preparing the final manuscript, the preoccupation of many contributors with the dying patient himself became apparent. It appeared logical and necessary to them to explore for the bereaved the reaction of the ill patient to his illness and its prognosis, as well as the relationship of the dying patient to those to whom he is bound by love.

In the same frame of reference another area of concern was found to be somewhat elusive in relation to its importance and to the rewards to be derived from understanding it. This is the extent to which an aura of bereavement makes its appearance prior to the death of the chronically or terminally ill patient—when the outcome has been unmistakable for a period of time. There appears to be a timetable of grief, oriented to the date of the onset of a fatal illness as well as to the date of death of the loved one. This timetable, somehow built within us, is one for which we should indeed be thankful, for it sequentially relates the period of bereavement to a somewhat finite period of time.

A great complexity of influences affects the intensity of despair and the difficulties of recovery. There are specific differences to be noted which apply to recovery from grief in relation to death following prolonged illness in the young adult, sudden death (the heart attack or accident), or suicide. Singular problems and differing time-tables are also encountered in the case of lingering or sudden death in childhood as well as in old age. Grief differs with the age, resiliency, reserve powers, and vigor of the bereaved; also with the age of the loved one who has died; and, perhaps most importantly, with the relationship between the bereaved and the one who has died.

Doubtless, nearly everyone who has experienced deep bereavement will agree that no amount of warning or grieving in advance will do more than temper the death event when it comes, but one should expect the reactions of the bereaved to differ significantly on this basis. To the extent that the bereaved can be brought to appreciate this, he will have taken a valuable step in his attempt to recover from bereavement.

And so great stress has been placed on understanding death and understanding grief, on dying, on grief in advance of death, and on the relationship between those who care for the dying and the bereaved. If not of immediate value in the recovery from acute paralyzing bereavement, these concepts should be found, in retrospect, to be of some comfort. At the same time, it should be noted that the comfort and benefits to be derived from such an understanding will be dependent upon the events which transpire, their timing, the coloring which they impress upon the life of the bereaved, and what the bereaved undertakes to do with his life.

In addition, and of much relevance, the discussion of bereavement had to be broadened to include the profoundly important question of remarriage, certainly a matter of critical concern to the bereaved spouse or to the parent who has been left without a partner.

One more hue should be added to the tapestry: hope for the future. The editor has remarried. Formerly, two bereft families existed as best they could, as fragments, not as a whole; now they share with each other the inexpressible blessings of renewed hope and love. The families have united in loving perseverance to see this entire project through to completion and even to incorporate the Foundation of Thanatology, which is devoted to the furtherance of the objectives of this book and the medical text already mentioned.

Two quotations seem to me to embody the theme of this book: understanding death and grief so that the spirit may recover. They express the epitome of the understanding of both death and life. The first is attributed to Mrs. Colin Kelly, the widow of the Air Force hero of World War II, who at the time of her remarriage commented: "Of course you can never forget the past and the past will always color the present. But I do not think that you should let the past affect the present so much that there can be no future."

The second quotation was written by the eminent Cleveland Clinic surgeon, Dr. George A. Crile, Jr., in his moving book, *More than Booty*, a memorial to his wife who had died of cancer. It is reproduced here as his contribution to this book:

We are gathered together in memory of Jane Crile. If you seek her memorial, look about you in the hearts of her family, in the faces of her children, in her writings and in her home. Life has been given and life has been taken away. Life and death are one, even as the river and the sea are one. Death is only a horizon and a horizon is but the limit of our sight.

It is now more than a year since Jane died. For the first few weeks there was numbness and obsession with sorrow. Some of it may have been because of insecurity. Through the years I had become so dependent on Jane that it did not seem I could find a way to live without her. But gradually I found I was competent to do or arrange for many of the things Jane had always done for me. Interest in my work returned. I began again to find pleasure in people.

As is often the case with those who have been deeply in love and the husband or wife dies, I married again. A new life began, filled with new interests and with a continuation of the old.

I still live in the same house. Many of the same birds, the wood ducks and the swan, are still in our back yard. Many of the relics that Jane and I collected in our travels are about our house. But there are no ghosts. Memories that for a time were inexpressibly sad have once again become a source of deep pleasure and satisfaction.

Since we know nothing of death except that it comes to all, it is not reasonable to be sad for the person who has died. The sorrow that once I felt for myself, in my loss, now has been transformed to a rich memory of a woman I loved and the ways we traveled through the world together.

In order to complete the details of my personal odyssey rather more than to provide new revelations, these pages should reflect that I have, since the death of my first wife (Helene, to whom the first edition was dedicated), lost through death from cancer my second wife (Lillian who was so largely responsible for both the first and second editions of this book). The saga of this second great loss is chronicled in the chapter *Grief Revisited* which describes my reimmersion in, work of, and recovery from grief. It was, indeed, this revisitiation which provided the crucible for this 3rd edition. It is meaningful to further relate that I have since married again and can affirm—with certain added personal perspective and academic comfort in doing so—that the processes detailed throughout this book, when followed once again, gratefully proved to provide for me, in the main, proper and positive approaches to successfully regaining the pleasures of living—once again.

A.H.K.

Second Spring

SANDRA BESS

With a breath
that was hushed
and a smile
that would rush
the stars down to earth,
you fell
with the brightest leaf
into golden October.
You fell into death
as the last
petal
falls
from
the
rose,
And Winter's birth
came cold,
came bare,
came sober.
Came heavy with
the grief that grows
that tortures and enfolds
the heart
and dares it break.

I search out the night
to find you
amid the waking
and the tossing times.
I search out the day
to find myself...
to find the
me
so
lost
and
narrow;
the me that makes
no rhyme
without you,
How do I measure
the distance
between
us?
What is near?
How long is far?
How do I measure
what is little
in a day
and what is much?

Everytime
I touch
the things
you touched,
all time and space...
all reasonings and riddles
all rights and wrongs ...
rise
with
the
grace
of a wondrous song
to
be
where
you
are.

But,
when my heart
hangs tough;
and
I've had enough
of the tears
and the pain
that pinch the past
beyond endurance,
I will start
the
second Spring
of my life.
I will take
my bereft soul
and fill it
with the love
and
the happy years
you left me.
In the solitude
of our altogether dreams,
I will feel
again
the stirrings,
the longings,
the whisperings
of things ...
without pain,
without sorrow,
without regret...
for all we shared
and cared about
remain.

Bound
by your love,
I will borrow
from the past
and yet
will keep the present
close at hand.
In that Spring...
I will gather

the
scattered
leaves
of my withered world
and
one
by
one,
place them back
upon the trees.

In that Spring...
as a seedling grows
and turns
towards the sun,
I
too, will run
to meet the day,
and
surrounded
by your love,
will learn
to gently
put
the
petals
back
upon
the
rose.

Introduction

DAVID PERETZ

For The Bereaved has a unique place in the literature on bereavement. In 1966, Dr. Austin H. Kutscher—"Bill" to family, friends and colleagues—found himself in the midst of his own grief, following the death of his beloved wife, Helene. He realized his own need for information that could assist him with both the emotional and practical aspects of recovery from grief. He found, to his surprise, that there was little material available either for the lay person or the health professional. Although everyone undergoes the first hand experience of bereavement at some point in life, bereavement was then largely neglected as an area of study.

Bill, a skilled, compassionate practitioner at Columbia University and the author and editor of numerous books, articles, and journals in the field of the health sciences, set out now to enlist a number of collaborators in various disciplines to prepare a volume of readings for the person—or the family and friends of the person faced with or in the midst of loss and grief. Some of us who were contacted initially by Dr. Kutscher became the nucleus for a team effort that would expand into research, teaching, the publication of 90 books to date, four journals, and the convening of more than 70 symposia directed toward health professionals and others in various allied disciplines who work with the dying and bereaved.

After 20 years, what were once considered "taboo topics"—death, dying and their consequence, bereavement—have become subjects of serious discussion in hospitals, schools, the media and within families as well.

We later revised the original text of *For The Bereaved* for a second edition, and more recently in 1989 for this, the Third Edition. In doing so, we found that many of the articles have withstood the test of time—still affording the reader useful information about what to expect during the days, weeks, or months following significant loss. To these, new articles have been added. The present edition calls attention to the problems confronting the bereaved at a time when the ability to cope is taxed by anxiety, fear, depressive affects, anger, and guilt, among other feelings.

Bereavement is a time of profound change: change in social role, of change in status in the social system of economic threat but most of all, a change in the security system comprised of our relationships to those we love—parents, children, spouses. By the time they reach adulthood, most individuals have formulated their own typical solutions to painful circumstances. Some try to "look on the bright side of things," some lose themselves in their work, some seek friends with whom to share their feelings, some seek to rationalize the event. The experience of profound loss may disrupt the usual solutions, and certain individuals may find themselves open to developing a deeper awareness and new solutions. This may account for the emotional growth some experience after having gone through a significant loss and a grief reaction.

When a person we love dies, we become bereaved. In fact, for many, bereavement begins in a state we have come to call anticipatory grief. When, in the course of a long illness (or even a brief one), we recognize the inevitability of the loss, we may begin to grieve as if the loss has already occurred.

Whether or not anticipatory grief occurs, there is a wide range of potential experiences such as: sad feelings, tearfulness, numbness, shock, tension, psychic pain, surges of anger, self-reproach, depressed mood, trouble with sleeping, changes in appetite and bowel habits, loss of sexual interest, restlessness, early awakening and even hallucinatory experiences (believing that we hear the footsteps of the lost loved person, or their key in the lock). There are many others as well. Each person experiences some, but not necessarily all or the same as those of another member of the same family or a friend.

Between these experiences following loss and the "solutions" to these experiences lies an intermediate step: *the interpretation of the experience*. This interpretation may be more or less objective, depending upon the individual, but also upon the information brought to the experience. Some are evaluated or interpreted as good, others as bad. For example, a bereaved person who is very tearful may regard crying as a good means of releasing sorrow, while another may see crying as reflecting weakness or self-pity. Thus, the latter person has not only the sorrow to deal with but also the self-interpretation that this is a "bad" reaction. One individual may find tenseness and sadness intolerable, another views it as natural. One bereaved individual may worry over trouble falling asleep, and another be accepting of it as inevitable and short-term.

The articles in this Third Edition offer information about these experiences in bereavement which can clarify interpretation. Several authors also describe solutions that they, or the bereaved individuals with whom they have worked, have found helpful. It is the hope of the present editors that careful reading will contribute to greater recognition of the profound impact of bereavement upon our lives, and allow those who wish to help to distinguish between offering

11

their *own* solutions, and offering *support* while the bereaved individuals work out *their* personal solutions.

With information available about what may be expected, it is hoped that both bereaved individuals and those involved with them will be less frightened and critical of the experiences of grief, and see them instead as inevitable, usually relatively brief in duration, and part of a process by which one gradually adapts to the changes that result from loss. Guildelines are also suggested as to when, in the course of bereavement, professional consultation should be considered.

Part One
GRIEF

Why You Should Understand Grief: A Minister's Views

EDGAR N. JACKSON, D.D.

It is important for us to know what grief is and how it works, for we have discovered that it is a major source of illness and distress to body, mind, and spirit. Research in psychosomatic medicine shows that some forms of illness are the means by which the human organism acts out its grief. Admissions to general hospitals are higher among the grief-stricken than among the general population. Admissions to hospitals for those with mental and emotional ailments clearly indicate a form of depression that is related to grief. Among the grief-stricken, spiritual crises develop marked by a loss of meaning for life and active despair. The percentage of suicides, both actual and attempted, among the grieving is above average. These things emphasize the importance of understanding what takes place in grief.

Grief is often camouflaged. This in itself presents a problem as the grief may not be expressed through the usual and more easily identified forms of behavior. In some it may appear as a subtle change of character. In others it may take the form of increased dependence on sedation, tranquilizers, or alcohol. In still others grief may be acted out as aggression and hostility or dependency and indecision. It is important to realize the variety of ways by which grief may manifest itself, for the human being is complex and brings into each new experience all that he is and has been in the past. With his response thus modified, variations, as numerous as the individuals involved, are produced.

The problem of coping with grief in contemporary culture is also somewhat different from what it was in the past. In the first place, grief is an experience of acute deprivation. In an affluent society, there is less experience in adjusting to deprivation, and thus there is less preparation for the injured personality to manage the new and disrupting experience of death.

In the second place, our culture is not only affluent but also largely death-denying and death-defying. It tends to isolate and leave the grief-stricken emotionally unsupported; the natural and usual feelings that come with grief seem to be rejected as inappropriate. Even the social devices which support the sound expression of emotion are being modified to conform to the death-defying mood and thus the bereaved person is doubly denied at the time when his need is most acute.

An implication of the general mood of denial is that it limits the opportunity both to talk out and to act out the deep feelings. If the general level of the nature and impact of acute grief could be understood, it would make significant communication more prevalent, and this in itself would have therapeutic value. And the importance of acting out deep feelings through rites, rituals, and ceremonials has special value when dealing with emotions too intense to be put into words.

It is important to understand that some emotions are often misinterpreted because there appears to be no direct relationship between the effect and the cause. Some of the unfortunate emotional responses show up in the unwise "falling in love," which is the way some people try to handle the emotional capital they are obliged to withdraw from the lost love object, but cannot wisely reinvest. Thus persons establish unwise or ill-advised love or dependency relationships to physicians, pastors, or others who happen to be on the scene during a period of emotional crisis.

With grief there is almost always guilt—real, neurotic, or existential. This grows from the ambivalent nature of love itself, with its balancing of responsibility and privilege, sorrow and joy, benefits and deprivations. When death comes, life is rethought, and the bereaved tends to think of what might have been if he had been different. Some persons are overwhelmed by their feelings of guilt and try to punish themselves by using a variety of techniques of self-injury, self-deprivation, and self-rejection. Remorse is as unfruitful an emotion as self-pity, and when understood can often be relieved.

Wisely, funeral practices provide methods by which people can quickly work through their guilt feelings. Sometimes this is done by the final gift for the deceased, a casket, or by gifts to the bereaved. Gift-giving is a generally employed device for acting out guilt feelings, for it serves as a symbolic form of retribution when real retribution is no longer possible because of death.

On the more positive side, it should be noted that the person in grief needs a philosophical base from which to operate in sustaining the value of life. The whole idea of the rites and ceremonials at the time of death is to verify these ideas in the grieving individual and in the supporting community, which needs to assert its viability.

Other positive ideas are found in certain concepts—a concept of purpose that is adequate to give a significant meaning to a person's life and the lives of others; a concept of man as a being with sustaining spititual value; a concept of God as essential goodness; a concept of death as relative; a concept of historical continuity; and a concept of an undying quality of some portion of what he may call his own soul. These ideas would be an achievement of the individual and would bear the marks of his own needs and the qualities of his own personality. For all practical purposes, these would be the elements of the faith he would live by. Often confrontation with death stimulates the building of a more positive philosophy of life.

Sometimes the person in grief is so puzzled by the feelings and physical symptoms that possess him that he feels he is becoming emotionally disorganized. It is important to realize that grief has the characteristics of a normal neurosis; hence, for a short period of time the bereaved may well show symptoms and suffer feelings out of the ordinary.

Physically, these symptoms may involve the breathing apparatus, with shortness of breath, choking up, sighing, crying, and sometimes hysterical reactions. On a short-term basis this is quite normal and nothing to be alarmed about. The digestive system may also be affected by nausea, loss of appetite, loss of sphincter control, or compulsive eating and drinking. These symptoms, too, are quite within the range of the normal on a short-term basis. Also, there may be generalized responses, with weakness of the large muscle systems, dizziness, faintness, and an over-all feeling of distress. This, too, is quite within the range of the normal on a short-term basis.

The abnormal tends to show up when the normal responses are prolonged over extended periods of time, or when they do not show up at all. The person who shows no feeling may be in more difficulty than the one who does. We do not choose whether or not we have feelings, but only how they will be managed. When feelings are so powerful that they cannot be coped with, they are apt to be repressed, denied, or detoured into other behavior forms that act out the feelings through the body in illness, through the emotions in personality change, or through the mind in disruption of the basic value structure of the individual.

The seriously disturbed person, who is unable to function normally in meeting his own needs or in his basic relationships with others, needs special help and should have the benefits of treatment by those who are qualified according to accepted professional standards. Grief can be a most painful emotion, and for people to remain in that state for long periods of time is unfortunate and usually unnecessary.

Grief work is the natural process by which the emotions reorganize themselves to cope with the loss and re-establish healthful relationships. The essential processes of grief work are, first, the facing of the physical reality with all of its implications; second, the recognition and expression of the emotions that are relevant to the physical event; third, the process of working through the emotions by talking them out in visitations and family events or with trusted counselors, and also by acting out the deep feelings through appropriate rites, rituals, and ceremonials. These tend to create an atmosphere of acceptance of the emotions at the same time as they confirm the reality of the event. Fourth, is the acceptance of emotional support from the general community, the religious or spiritual community, and the supportive family. The grief-stricken are probably more dependent emotionally than at any time since early childhood. To deny this may create emotional hazards. To accept the fact and the feelings as well as the emotional support provided may be a major resource in hastening the process of wise grief-management.

Grief work may have its negative manifestations, and thus there are some things to guard against. We may try to blot out the natural pain by drugs. This usually does not serve a therapeutic purpose, but only postpones feelings that will then have to be dealt with at a less appropriate time and place. Unless there is a special medical problem, it is usually best to face the painful facts as quickly as possible and let the wisdom of the organism work itself out. Perhaps one of the soundest of the procedures for resolving psychological denial is the traditional practice of "viewing the remains." Here the basic fact of death is spelled out so that there is no longer any basis for psychological denial. This often produces a breakthrough of denied feelings and hastens the grief work.

An understanding of the meaning of grief as a profound emotion, and the other side of the coin of love, gives a sounder base for interpreting the meaning of life itself as well as for a significant structure of values for living. Furthermore, an understanding of grief supports a kind of courage that is not afraid to live because it is not afraid to recognize that life must be lived within mortal bounds. A wise reexamination and an imaginative development of resources may make it possible for us to understand clearly and to manage wisely the powerful emotions of grief so that life grows through the process rather than being destroyed by it.

Grief: A Physician-Minister's Views

REV. WILLIAM B. McCULLOUGH, B.D., M.D.

I have talked with those who have lost a loved one, both as a minister and as a physician. Death sets an awesome task before the bereaved adult, for his life has been radically changed. He feels a strong responsibility toward the one who has died, and yet there is also a great responsibility toward himself. Things are happening within him that are difficult to understand.

The purpose of this chapter is to offer insight into some of the conflicts that the bereaved faces. It is based on the belief that as the mature individual comes to understand himself and his world, he will be able to find significance and joy in it, and to fulfill his obligations to those who depend upon him. It is also based on the belief that many experiences that are new to the individual are common to mankind and, in times of crisis, the bereaved will be able to draw upon the discoveries and resources of others to enable him to grieve deeply in his loss, but not to lose.

After the initial paralysis, when one is without direction and feeling, the numbness to all that is happening changes to disbelief. Particularly toward the unexpected death, the bereaved reacts with denial. "It can't be true." "There must be some mistake." Disbelief gradually gives way to a developing awareness of the loss. The transition may take minutes or hours or sometimes days. But usually, the full impact of what has happened settles slowly into consciousness. As one begins to become aware of the loss, the bodily sensations of distress are quite uniform.

These symptoms come in waves and appear as one is becoming aware of death as a reality. They may return later during the period of bereavement. For the full impact of the loss of a spouse or parent or child to be realized requires days and often weeks.

The religious ceremony usually takes place in the midst of developing awareness of loss and it can help to make the loss objective. Friends and relatives, by sharing grief or by their concern, provide comfort for the bereaved. The ceremony is also a symbolic sharing with the deceased in his death. The religious services offer to many people contact with a source of strength beyond their own. And they can strengthen the faith and religious values that a person held before he faced bereavement. A few may find faith that was not present before. But one should not chastise himself if he finds no meaning in the services. The numbing and withdrawal of the early reaction may contribute, in many instances, to such a lack of significance. The lack of meaning should be seen as a phase that is common to believer and nonbeliever alike. Because of guilt, one must not deny it, for it may be the beginning of a gradual discovery of genuine faith that can provide strength to face life in a way that is richer, more rewarding, and more significant.

The early experience of disbelief and the developing awareness of loss are thrust upon the bereaved. He is the one to whom these things happen; he is the recipient, not the cause. As the third stage of mourning begins, active participation is required on the part of the bereaved. This is the time of restitution or "grief work," the time of working through one's memories and feelings about the deceased. It is the time when one relates the past and the future. It is the time when one begins living again in a way that is changed radically but yet not changed. It is the time when one picks up a book such as this to seek new directions and patterns. Comfort, which up to this point, has been so important, is now not enough; one must accept the pain of bereavement. Most authorities agree that the work of recovering from bereavement requires six to twelve months.[1] This is a time of paradox; at the same time it is work and yet it is not work. The memories of the deceased are both sweet and painful. The future is frightening and challenging. For most people the task cannot be undertaken alone. It is essential that the bereaved have someone with whom he can talk—someone who will be able to listen. A sympathetic friend who is filled with advice but unable to be silent and listen will not do. The listener may be a friend or relative who shares a special closeness with the bereaved, or who himself has experienced deep grief. It may be a clergyman who is able to listen. It may be a psychiatrist or pastoral counselor who can be of inestimable help. A word of caution must be said to the parent of older children who has lost a spouse. Although openness between parent and child is essential, one should seek another adult in whom to confide his deepest feelings. The child needs the parent as a confidant. The parent needs another adult.

There are some specific areas where conflicts are faced in these weeks of grief work and restitution. They include loneliness, anger, guilt, weeping, asking why, and the future.

LONELINESS AND SOLITUDE

Everyone who faces the death of a person whom he has loved feels profound loneliness. This is to be expected, for every death means parting, separation, and isolation. It is an event in which we cannot participate. The loneliness is painful, and one's natural reaction is to avoid it at all costs. It is painful not only because of the profound loss of the person one loves; it is also painful because this loneliness touches the essential aloneness of man. For it is the destiny of man to be alone and to know that he is alone. It may well even be true in some way beyond the dimensions of time that death is the first introduction into an existence where one is not alone.

The word "loneliness" describes the pain of being alone. But there is also another word for being alone: "solitude." Solitude expresses the glory of being alone. The transition from loneliness to solitude is not clear-cut. But both states often exist together in the same experience. One requires the courage to face loneliness, to dare to be alone. It is the experience of many that to face the intensity of loneliness and its true pain is to change loneliness into solitude; the power of loneliness is destructive only when we run from it. To experience it fully is to change it into solitude. In solitude we come to meet ourselves as we truly are. It is in moments of solitude that something happens to us.[2] The experiencing of the power of loneliness is at the heart of mourning. "Blessed are those who mourn, for they shall be comforted."[3]

ANGER

At the very time one needs and can benefit from "talking through" one's feelings with a close friend or relative, there is a genuine tendency to avoid people, often a withdrawal from friends and relatives. Most bereaved people experience a disconcerting loss of warmth in relationship to other people.[4] The irritability that the bereaved person feels is surprising and often inexplicable to him. But the anger should be recognized and not suppressed. It is neither right nor wrong, but appears to be a part of bereavement. When it is expressed, most people will accept and understand it—especially those who have themselves experienced acute grief.

GUILT

Frequently the bereaved is overwhelmed by a feeling of guilt. The possibilities of rectifying past errors or of carrying out our basic desires for a person are suddenly ended. Certainly prolonged and paralyzing feelings of guilt should encourage the grief-stricken person to discuss them with a professional counselor. But guilt is often resolved in knowing that these intense feelings are a common experience in facing the death of a loved one.

Our closest relationships are never perfect, and there is always a valid basis for guilt. We must deal with this genuine guilt in the light of forgiveness, which is a part of any love relationship. The highest love of man, like the love of God, accepts us as we are, demanding nothing of us but to be what we are. The experience of basic guilt and the grace of forgiveness were expressed most profoundly by the late Paul Tillich:

> Grace strikes us when we are in great pain and restlessness. It strikes us when we walk through the dark valley of a meaningless and empty life. It strikes us when we feel that our separation is deeper than usual... when despair destroys all joy and courage. Sometimes at that moment a wave of light breaks into our darkness, and it is as though a voice were saying, "You are accepted". You are accepted, accepted by that which is greater than you, and the name of which you do not know. Do not try ... to do anything now; perhaps later you will do much. Do not seek for anything; do not perform anything; do not intend anything. Simply accept the fact that you are accepted!" If that happens to us, we experience grace.[5]

WEEPING

At the very heart of mourning is weeping. It has a basic value which helps us to deal with sorrow and grief and appears to be an indispensable means for the sorrowing human being to regain emotional stability. In our society, crying is generally natural for women, but not for men. The culture in which we live usually dictates the way in which we weep. Some cultures expect loud lamentation, whereas others shun public displays of grief. To the extent that we are products of these cultures, the expected responses may well be ours also. But often a person has moved away from the culture to which he returns at the time of bereavement, and his own make-up requires different expressions of grief from those demanded by the culture. It is important for the bereaved to express freely his own form of weeping. He must avoid the rigidity of behaving only as he is expected. Sometimes it is necessary to seek actively for the place— alone or with understanding friends or with a counselor—where he can yield to the inner tensions of grief in a way that comes from the depths of his own being.

ASKING WHY

There is no doubt that we cannot answer the personal "whys" of the death of a child or a young man or woman or one "in the prime of life." Our reasoning, even at its highest, reaches an impasse. Yet there is something within us which hammers at the closed door. Save for the aged, whose lives "have been lived," death comes as a tragedy. The physician often turns off or tones down his feelings because he is confronted with death day after day. The clergyman, all too often feeling the need to provide an answer, misses the depth of the tragedy. The bereaved finds himself on the battlefield where tragedy and hope fight each other without victory. The psalmist can exclaim, "Precious in the sight of the Lord is the death of his saints."[6] The Psalms also abound in human despair and unanswered questions. Perhaps the reason for the lack of answers is that every human way of thinking reaches embarrassment at every point. Perhaps the beginning of understanding is this human despair. Perhaps it is only here, standing empty-handed, throwing away the straws we have grasped, that we can hear a voice from a dimension other than that in which we ordinarily live. Here, where reason has been exhausted, we can be open to a deeper and higher dimension of life. It is in despair that we meet faith as it comes to us "from without"— faith as a gift.

The experience of many is that the acceptance of death as a tragedy which we cannot explain does not cast them into despair, but rather gives them new strength. In facing tragedy, something happens to such people to give them meaning and a drive toward the future. What one calls this experience is of secondary importance. What is primarily important is the assurance that in the helplessness of despair, something happens to you. St. Paul expressed this: "O death, where is thy victory? O death, where is thy sting?"[7] The ancients described the phoenix arising from the ashes. Biblical theology talks of death and resurrection. What they describe is a real event which happens to those who look for it—hope in the midst of despair, comfort in the depths of loneliness. It is a gift. It is grace. This event is not a sudden experience. But gradually, often at first imperceptibly, the bereaved experiences renewed interest and direction, and realizes he has been granted the gift of the work of mourning.

THE FUTURE

Said Edna St. Vincent Millay, "Life goes on ... I forget just why." From this point the bereaved begins. A great part of the work of grief involves the sorrowful and joyous recalling of past memories, in thought, in discussions, even in dreams. It is to those who do this work of sifting memories and emotions that the future belongs. The desire to be with the deceased is replaced by a desire to fulfill his finest aspirations and wishes. "Time heals all,"not in *the sense of an anesthetic*, but in the use of the time of mourning lead the bereaved to a new life and new relationships, enriched by a positive identification with the lost person. "We experience only what is built into our life, has become an element in it, and is surpassed by the drive toward the future; for life is the drive toward the future."[8] The work of grief leads us back into life. We are changed, deepened, more able to offer solace to others, more able to live significantly and, in the best sense, joyously.

In the Gospel according to Matthew, Jesus invited one man to follow him. The man agreed, but said, "Let me first go and bury my father." Jesus replied, "Leave the dead to bury their own dead."[9] There is here no disrespect for either the person who has died, nor death itself. Rather there is a more profound respect for living and living to the fullest.

Often religious persons consider the prolongation of grief a spiritual duty. Nothing could be more false. To pick up and move on at the right time is an essential part of the truly religious life. Indeed it is only the genuinely religious man who can mourn, and then, out of the sadness and richness of his grief, enter fully into active life. It is he who has faced loneliness and seen it become solitude, who has accepted his anger and guilt. This is the one whose weeping has made him free, and who, without answers to his "whys," is again able to enter fully into the living of each day. He can now plan a meaningful future and enjoy rich human relationships. "Blessed are those who mourn, for they SHALL be comforted."

REFERENCES

1 Engel, G. L. *Psychological Development in Health and Disease*, Philadelphia: W. B. Saunders Co., 1962. Noyes, A. P. and Kolb, L. C. *Modern Clinical Psychiatry*, Philadelphia: W. B. Saunders Co., 1963.
2 Tillich, P. "Loneliness and Solitude" in *The Eternal Now*, New York: Charles Scribners Sons, 1963.
3 Matt. 5:4.
4 Lindemann, E. *American Journal of Psychiatry* 101:141.
5 Tillich, P. "You are Accepted" in *The Shaking of the Foundations*, New York: Charles Scribners Sons, 1948.
6 1 Ps. 6:15.
7 1 Cor. 15:55.
8 Foss, M. *Death, Sacrifice and Tragedy*. Lincoln: University of Nebraska Press, 1966.
9 Matt. 8:21, 22.

Understanding Your Mourning:
A Psychiatrist's View

DAVID PERETZ, M.D.

Each of us will at some time face the pain of personal bereavement. Our first experience with it may be when a loved one or friend is bereft and we must share their pain; or we may be struck more directly and ourselves feel the brunt of pain. Bereavement refers to that state of feeling, thought, and activity which is a consequence of the loss of a loved or valued person. An individual who has experienced such a loss is said to be bereaved, deprived of someone important. The deprivation may be gradual, as in the case of old age or chronic illness, or sudden as with a traumatic death or an acute coronary attack; a human equilibrium which has included the loved or valued person is upset within the bereaved.

There are a variety of bereavement states, all of which may be viewed as illnesses. Each represents a significant departure from the bereaved person's usual state of feeling, thought, and action. Each state has a cause, an onset, symptoms and signs, a course and an outcome. As with any illness, the preferred outcome is a return to health or that physical and emotional state which existed prior to the illness. Recovery would then imply that when the bereavement state is over the individual will have no new symptoms or disabilities, and his capacity to deal with his own feelings and his environment will not be reduced. As with any illness, recovery may be total or partial. The bereaved person's reaction to the loss may be likened to the reaction to a wound or an infection. For some, the wound or infection is minor, for others, major. For some, healing proceeds in a smooth, predictable way without complication, but for others, healing leaves serious scars which later interfere with function.

Bereavement states are often limited in degree and duration. These states require no specific medical advice or treatment. As when afflicted by the common cold, these bereaved persons heal within a certain period of time with or without the help of a doctor. Time, environmental support, and the natural resources of the bereaved combine to permit recovery. This type of bereavement state is known as grief.

Other bereavement states are more maladaptive. These are not limited, and do not run a direct course toward recovery. They are more exaggerated or more persistent, more crippling or more disrup-

24

tive to the bereaved, his family, and his friends. They may last for many months or years rather than days, weeks, or several months. Certain bereavement states appear most adaptive. An example would be an individual who denies his grief and proceeds to act as if nothing important has happened, or who exhibits only a minimal response. When this occurs in circumstances where the lost loved or valued person was an emotionally important current figure in the life of the bereaved, the absence of a grief reaction or of any significant symptoms of bereavement suggest the potential of a delayed or future maladaptation.

The more serious bereavement states include depression, hypochondriasis, certain worsened symptoms of pre-existent bodily illness, and absence of bereavement, to name a few.

LOSS AND COPING

Loss is an integral part of human experience. It occupies a central position in normal growth and development, as well as in the precipitation of illness. Loss has profound consequences for each of us from birth until death. Certain losses are necessary; others are predictable. Birth itself may be viewed as the sudden loss of the relative security of intrauterine life for the more hazardous situation of neonatal life. The newborn infant must accommodate itself quickly to the profound changes which accompany the loss of one position and the circumstances of the new one. Weaning represents the loss of a particular form of gratification. Temporary separations from parents are inevitable but are nonetheless losses that can evoke significant responses. Other losses are haphazard and unpredictable. Such losses include loss of health, loss of position, loss of affection, and permanent loss of loved ones.

These losses provide repeated stressful challenges which are met by the development and organization of techniques of coping which become part of one's personality. We learn from loss even as we are painfully traumatized by it. Death represents the ultimate loss and therefore has a particular capacity to arouse powerful emotional states in each of us. Each time we confront death, we lose not only the loved or valued person but a portion of our own wishful sense of immortality. Death is a cruelly recurrent reminder of the limits of our power: our power to save another or our power to save ourselves from the same fate. It is a great threat to our psychological economy. The more closely we are identified with the lost loved or valued person, the more threatened we are. The threat may be experienced as a fundamental threat to survival (how will I be able to live without the other person?), or as a threat to patterns of personal satisfaction which we may not feel confident to achieve on our own or able to establish with someone new.

Coping includes dealing with the feelings and emotions that loss or the threat of loss arouses, as well as with the objective meaning of the loss. The bereaved may have lost an economic provider and has to face the real problems that this poses. Simultaneously, the bereaved must cope with the inner apprehension, fear, or anger that this new responsibility or burden evokes. And this single example is never the entire story. Each time we lose a loved one or a valued person, many qualities and attributes are lost. The lost loved or valued person may have been a source of great tenderness, warmth, comfort, support, sexual gratification, and pride; or, a painful burden and a cause of frustration; or, as is so often the case, a combination of these positive and negative qualities. Because of the varied qualities and attributes which are lost, multiple feelings are aroused. The feelings and emotions aroused by the loss of a loved or valued person include mental pain, yearning, anguish, sorrow, dejection, sadness, depression, fear, anxiety, nervousness, agitation, panic, irritation, anger, disappointment, guilt, shame, helplessness, hopelessness, despair, disbelief, denial, shock, numbness, relief, emptiness, and lack of feeling. Some of these feelings may at times conflict with others. The conflict between expected and unexpected or acceptable and unacceptable feelings generates new emotional states which must be coped with. The bereaved may find it difficult to cope with a mixture of sorrow, yearning and anger. Unable to accept being angry with the lost loved or valued person, the bereaved may experience shame or guilt. Then these painful feelings become a problem in their own right to be dealt with in the state of bereavement.

Individual personality characteristics and coping techniques vary tremendously. Because we are human and grow up in the same society, we are more similar to one another than to an Arapesh tribesman. However, within that broad similarity lies tremendous diversity. Each person carries unique hereditary and temperamental equipment which interacts with a unique environment. Each of us has a typical style of perceiving, problem-solving, thinking, feeling, and acting toward others and toward ourselves. This psychological style will be a powerful determinant of the type of bereavement state experienced.

A series of rhetorical questions about individual personality can shed light on the potential ways in which the personality influences the bereavement state.

Does the individual accept feelings of yearning, fear, anger, tenderness, disappointment, and other internal emotional responses readily? Does the individual deny feeling and try to appear strong at all times? Does the person generally deal with strong internal feeling states by seeking to escape them through some substitute form of gratification? Does he blame others for his own misfortunes or painful feelings? Does he feel capable of managing his life without someone else playing a central role in it? Does he feel lovable, worthwhile and valuable in his own right, so that he can conceive of making a new relationship? Is he trusting, hopeful, and optimistic, or wracked with mistrust, hopelessness, and pessimism?

These are but a few aspects of the psychology of the bereaved which will contribute to the nature of the bereavement state.

The nature of the relationship between the bereaved and the deceased loved or valued person also has a significant influence upon the bereavement state. What kind of relationship was it? Was it parent and child, husband/wife, sibling, friend, employer, neighbor, extended family? Was the relationship an important one recently, or had it been more intense in the past? The relationships must be appreciated not in terms of our assumptions about which relationship should be most important but in terms of the meaning to the participants. A current relationship between very close friends which culminates in the death of one may precipitate a more profound bereavement state than that which occurs when an adult, who has developed considerable autonomy, loses a parent.

Was the bereaved actually very dependent upon the deceased person for pleasure, support, or esteem? Were the areas of individual or mutual dependency realistically acknowledged by both without shame, guilt, or resentment? Did the bereaved feel helpless without the lost person when enforced separations occurred? Does the bereaved have other important relationships which may provide a measure of support or fulfillment?

Were there considerable feelings of tenderness, affection, tolerance, and mutual respect with occasional disappointment, hurt, and irritation? Or was there considerable disappointment, bitterness, and resentment with less warmth and close feeling? Was it a highly ambivalent relationship with much affection at some times, much angry, hostile feeling at other times, and frequent alternation between the two states? Was the relationship neutral with little strong feeling in either direction? Were the feelings in the relationship overt or covert? Was guilt a prominent feature of the relationship prior to the bereavement? Were there special problems or circumstances during a chronic or terminal illness? Answers to such questions provide indicators of additional influences upon the bereavement state.

Each society has a prevailing system of values. These include guides to human conduct. The values may be apparent, explicit, unitary, uniformly respected by the majority of people or covert in a state of rapid change or conflict. The values and belief systems of a society will be reflected in the day-to-day structuring of family relationships and will thus be incorporated into the personality of growing individuals by identification with the important people in their lives. Within any society which is heterogeneous, there will exist values which grow out of ethnic, religious, class, vocational, or professional identifications which may be at variance with the society as a whole, or provide aspects that the society neglects.

Our current society tends to provide little framework of support for the bereaved. Grief, rather than being encouraged, seems to be viewed as less than desirable. Admiration is offered for those who appear strong and limit their expression of emotion. This is particularly true of the masculine role in our society. In contrast, the bereaved in many other societies is identified for a long period of time as a special person with singular status and particular needs. Social and religious rituals during bereavement, such as funerals, wakes, prescribed periods of mourning with organized prayers for mourners, modes of dress, condolence observances, visits by clergy, cards, and indulgences can provide considerable support and encouragement for the process of grief. Certain groups within our society, in touch with their religious or ethnic heritage, still subscribe to these practices. These groups not only provide a clear role for the bereaved with definite expectations and practices but actually encourage the open expression of grief. This can be helpful for many, though it should be recognized that even with support from the subculture, the bereaved may find himself at odds with the dominant culture. The opposite can also happen; a bereaved person elects to fulfill the dominant value and transgresses against the customs of his family and subculture.

The tendency dominant in our society is to expect that the bereaved individual will quickly pick up the pattern of his life, return to work, family responsibilities, and socialization within the community, and be rather quiet about his grief. With this set of social values, there may be little support from family, neighbors, and friends. Family dispersal in an urban society can add to the problem. Time and time again, physicians see patients who are relieved to discover in discussion that someone not only appreciates their feeling of loss but encourages them to express grief.

The problem of denying or diminishing grief is not simply a function of the complex nature of our society and the breakup of the family unit which characterizes urban life. There is a strong need in most of us to flee from the reality of death. Our funeral practices, the metaphors we use to discuss the dead, our failure to educate children to its place in life, all attest to the anxiety which death provokes in us. Frequently, friends and relatives unknowingly withdraw from the bereaved person (just as they may have from the terminally ill or dying person). This leaves the bereaved isolated and alone at a time when the knowledge that there are those who care and are prepared to share the painful feelings can be crucial. Withdrawal from the bereaved may occur because the friend or relative feels uncomfortable with the anxiety, pain, and sadness of grief; does not know specifically how to "help" (failing to realize that his presence alone, without words, may be of great comfort); or feels that the bereaved would rather be alone. Were the bereaved persons in our daily midst to wear black and to show grief for a prolonged period of time, it would serve as a constant reminder of the reality of death and the pain of grief, thus increasing our discomfort. As a result, we encourage "occupational therapies" rather than the expression of feeling.

At times the bereaved flees from his own painful feelings by selecting that aspect of social values or expectations which permits him to terminate the bereavement prematurely. In our society, symptoms of physical illness, being more acceptable by presumably being out of our control, can become substitutes for the expression of feelings.

The bereavement state can be seen then as the outcome of an interaction between the highly personal characteristics of the bereaved—the kind of relationship that existed between the bereaved and the dead person—and social values, which may support certain bereavement states and discourage others.

Bereavement states may begin to be experienced before the death of the loved or valued person. This is particularly true when there has been a chronic illness with a downhill course, or briefer illness with certain fatal outcome. When the bereavement state begins weeks or months before the actual loss, there may be little evident reaction or no prolonged state after the death. In some circumstances, wherein pain and suffering have been prominent, the bereaved may experience an appreciable sense of relief or release.

Absence of emotion in the period immediately following the death may represent temporary shock, numbness, or denial. There may be postponement of grief until it can no longer be avoided (as at the funeral service or burial). This may be seen when the bereaved feels that there are tasks with which he must immediately cope, such as in wartime, or where provision must be made to protect other more vulnerable bereaved persons.

Another situation in which there is no evidence of apparent bereavement involves the individual who hides his grief. This person grieves secretly in the privacy of his home or room and thus is limited in the degree to which he can express grief or receive support. These individuals consciously control themselves in public or rationalize their pain by indicating that the deceased person is better off and free of suffering. They are ashamed of feeling as deeply as they often do about the deceased loved or valued person. There is frequently a hidden need to deny the reality of the loss because of close identification with the deceased. These people tend to be seen by others as strong but not cold. They often express their feelings by caring for others. Their sadness is felt by those close to them, though their actions seem to belie the feeling. If the family physician recognizes the problem, he can encourage the bereaved to express grief or he can suggest that it be shared with a few close friends or relatives.

People who experience the above group of bereavement states are in contrast to those individuals who neither show their feeling in response to loss by expressions of weeping, sadness, and pain nor are even aware of feeling deeply. These individuals think a variety of unhappy thoughts but seem defensively to isolate the feeling state. They suffer from an inability to grieve and may be guilty or ashamed of this. They are often seen as "cold fish" by family and friends, which tends to increase their emotional aloneness and stirs up further anxiety, thus necessitating further defensive isolation a vicious cycle. Techniques used by these people to support their isolation of feeling include busy-work, involvement with details, cleaning up, or some other form of ritualized activity. Their behavior has a compulsive quality. Much ideation may be expressed about whether this or that should have been done for the dead individual. These people tend to fear strong feelings in themselves and move away from them. They may develop delayed reactions to the loss many months or even years later. They are not usually defined as ill by those in their environment because their kind of adaptation is often socially utilitarian. They are more often seen as difficult to get along with and unpleasant to live with, and the defensiveness of their behavior goes unappreciated.

Individuals who have experienced considerable painful grief in the past over the death of loved or valued people, may experience milder states of grief with future losses, and this should be considered in attempting to account for the relative absence or minimal nature of a bereavement state. Symptoms of insomnia and loss of weight appear to be more prominent in those bereaved individuals who show few emotional responses to the loss.

Unlimited mourning or bereavement refers to individuals who arrange their post-loss environment to reflect no change in life pattern. The home is not changed an iota. It becomes a shrine and awaits the return of the deceased person. This may represent a way of denying the reality of the loss as a means of protection against the intense suffering it would engender. It is a defense against grief though it appears as a prolongation of grief.

GRIEF

Grief is characterized by intense mental suffering or distress, sharp sorrow, and painful regret. The intense mental suffering includes painful recognition of what has been lost and frequent thoughts and memories of the deceased. Shock, numbness, and the loud denial that it cannot be true alternate with bewilderment and the weeping, despairing, confrontation with the truth of the loss. In the initial stage, the bereaved soon feels exhausted, has little appetite, and frequently has difficulty sleeping. There may be agitation with wringing of the hands, restlessness, and an appearance of confusion and puzzlement. There is a marked tendency for the emotional state to come in waves, at frequent intervals at the beginning of the period of bereavement and less frequently as it progresses. Painful yearning and loneliness are prominent. Any mention of the lost loved or valued person can precipitate episodes of sobbing and expressions of pain. Tearless sobbing may occur, paralleling a sense of emptiness associated with the loss. There are, when the waves of powerful emotion subside, increasing periods in which the bereaved appears to be himself. There is some retention of the capacity for pleasure from the beginning, and the capacity to laugh, though temporarily reduced, may be revealed at an early stage. Sexual interest tends to be diminished in the first weeks or at times months of bereavement. Physical complaints may be present and involve various systems (i.e., cardiac, gastrointestinal, muscular, etc.).

The bereaved often have dreams of the deceased and these are frequently described as comforting. The deceased person may be visualized in the dream as younger than at the time of death. At times, the bereaved may experience terrifying nightmares in the first days or weeks.

The bereaved in a state of grief may experience illusions. He may think at times in the days and weeks following the death that he hears the footsteps of the lost person in the hallway at a time when they would ordinarily return from work. There may be a momentary, very real sense of the deceased person's presence and even the false perception that he is seen. The bereaved is sometimes able to realize that these experiences are illusory.

Withdrawal from social activities and even from family and professional responsibilities is to be expected in the state of acute grief. Gradual return to activities occurs over a period of weeks or months.

Feelings of numbness may reflect a deep identification with the lost person and for a brief period give the impression that the grieving person has experienced a deadening of feeling. He will, however, respond to people in the environment who reach out to him. A sense of helplessness may be experienced initially. This may be defined in terms of not having been able to do anything to save the lost person or where the prospect of continuing to live without the loved one seems unbearable. The bereaved may feel that he would be better off dead or that it should have happened to him.

Anger at the deceased person may be felt for leaving the survivor burdened, for not using his power to stay alive (when the loved one was seen as all-powerful), for withdrawing gratification, or for other reasons. It is often difficult for the bereaved to accept anger in himself, or to talk about it with relatives or friends. It may become the source of guilt in grief. Guilt may be part of the state of grief. Most relationships are ambivalent to some degree (with disappointment and anger as well as love and affection); thus a seedbed for guilt is present in each of us. Guilty self-reproach should not be extravagant, and reassurance usually offers some relief in contrast with depressive guilt. Old guilt feelings which may have little to do with the real relationship to the deceased person can also be activated in the bereavement state. This can be seen when there has been a previous loss which was never fully worked out.

Feelings of shame may occur in the period of grief. The shame may be related to a sense of failure with regard to some personal ideal: not having done enough for the deceased or showing too much or too little feeling.

Some bereaved individuals tend to blame others for the loss as a way of coping with their painful feelings. This is usually amenable to reason when the family or friends point out the inaccuracy of the statements. If it occurs in this manner, as part of a state of grief in which other feelings are being expressed, such as sadness and dejection, it is not serious. When other elements of grief are absent and the bereaved is not amenable to reason and persistently blames others, the condition is more serious.

The duration of grief as a bereavement state is variable and may range up to six months or a year. One way of judging the grief process is by whether there is a steady increase in the capacity to function as the bereaved had functioned before the loss. It is to be expected that when faced with highly personal reminders of the dead person and their relationship (pictures, songs, places), temporary upsurges of strong grief feelings will occur. We look for an upward slope of improvement in the feeling state and whether other relationships are being re-established or interest expressed in them. Particularly important for recovery from grief is the return of full capacity for pleasure without shame or guilt.

The period of grief, whether brief or extended, will consist of conscious and preconscious experiencing of memories and feelings about the deceased loved or valued person. This appears ultimately to permit healthy loosening of the original tie to the lost person and the creation of potential for establishment of new ties.

DEPRESSION

While many of the symptoms and signs of acute grief described previously are seen in depression, the two conditions differ significantly and qualitatively. The grief-stricken person will, within a reasonably short period of time after the loss, show shifts from the grief state to a more normal state within the same day and from hour to hour. They will usually be responsive to words of reassurance and support, and will be able, after a time, to laugh a little. The depressed person will be more persistently downcast (though there may be a lifting of depression toward evening each day), gloomy, and pessimistic. The more depressed the state, the greater the feelings of despair, hopelessness, unresponsiveness, and withdrawal. Whereas the grieving person responds to warmth and reassurance, the mildly depressed person may respond to pressure, promises, and urging, and the most seriously depressed will not respond at all. Restriction of pleasure is markedly persistent in the depressed.

The depressed person, if listened to carefully, will seem much more preoccupied with himself than with the deceased loved or valued person. This self-preoccupation may be in a negative, self-reproachful, self-deprecating way. The depressed individual will at times express considerable overt shame and guilt. The shame and guilt will seem, however, to be related to the depression rather than to the personal relationship with the lost individual. These persons are likely to berate themselves and figuratively, if not literally, beat their breast about how they should have done more, should be doing more now, how inadequate or worthless they feel, how they have no future, will never get better, and are ruining others by their illness. These ideas and feelings may not be expressed verbally but are the wellspring of silent preoccupation. These ideas or statements will be at variance with periods of irritability, criticism, and complaints directed toward others. Open anger or hostility will not be prominent in the depressed person.

Among the complaints of the depressed person will be lassitude, inability to get started, lack of energy, trouble in concentrating, and not thinking clearly. Whereas the bereaved in a state of grief may feel that the world is empty and experience a temporary sense of personal emptiness, the depressed person tends to feel the inner emptiness more persistently and intensely.

Physical complaints are frequent among depressed people. Severe insomnia with early morning awakening (4, 5, or 6 A.M.), and inability to get back to sleep, poor appetite, dry mouth, constipation, considerable weight loss, decreased sexual ability or impotence or decreased menstrual flow can occur singly or in combination; headache, back pain, and palpitations are also experienced. There is a frequent tendency to hypochondriasis in this group, and this will be discussed separately.

The depressed individual has difficulty in weeping, often expressing the wish that he could cry and the conviction that he would feel better if he did. Suicidal feelings and ideas can occur in depressed persons. This is a serious symptom. Warning signals include (1) suicidal threats, (2) deepening depression or beginning improvement from profound depression although considerable depression is present, (3) prominent guilt still as a symptom, (4) a history of suicide in the family, (5) increasing tension associated with tendency to an early morning insomnia pattern. Active suicidal ideas, threats, or gestures should indicate the need for prompt medical evaluation.

Where depression is mild to moderate, the person may deny feeling depressed and instead focus on the physical complaints. The family member or friend may find that *he himself* feels depressed rather than sad when with the bereaved. This can be an empathic clue to depression in the bereaved.

Depression may occur as the dominant feature of the bereavement state. It may develop almost immediately in response to the loss, occur gradually during the days, weeks, or months following the death, or may appear after an apparent recovery from grief. It may also present itself after a prolonged period during which there have been no prominent signs of a bereavement state.

Differentiating depression from grief in the bereaved individual permits early medical consultation and treatment. Since specific treatments ranging from antidepressant medications to brief psychotherapy are now available for the depressed individual, early intervention may permit earlier mobilization, prevention of crippling disability, and hope of return to the pre-bereavement status.

HYPOCHONDRIASIS AND WORSENED SYMPTOMS OF PRE-EXISTENT AILMENTS

Hypochondriasis refers to a state of exaggerated, worrisome preoccupation with some form of dreadful illness. The person obsessively believes he is ill with some potentially fatal disease. In contrast to worrisome complaining, there is often a reluctance to seek medical consultation. When finally checked out medically, there is no demonstrable basis for the preoccupation—a mountain has been made out of a molehill (i.e., symptoms of a tension headache have led to the conclusion by the bereaved that he has a brain tumor; arthritic shoulder pain is interpreted as heart disease; constipation becomes a symptom of a malignancy). Rather than reacting to a symptom in terms of its likeliest source, a remote probability is made the only or major possibility.

Hypochondriasis may occur transiently in grief, may be an important symptom of depression, or may exist independently as an illness in its own right. The fantasied disease may be an elaboration on genuine symptoms associated with either grief or depression. Loss of appetite is experienced as a symptom of tumor; weakness or nervous tremor is interpreted as evidence of severe neurological disease; palpitation becomes coronary disease. There is a tendency at times for the illness to be similar to that which caused the death of the loved or valued person.

Medical consultation should be obtained to (1) attempt to mobilize the underlying feelings of bereavement, (2) rule out the presence of serious illness, (3) treat what illness may be present, (4) clarify the emotional components of the state.

Discussion with a physician may lead to (1) emergence of underlying anxiety, grief, or depression, (2) shifting to another hypochrondriacal complaint, (3) persistence of worrying with a feeling that the examination failed to reveal the illness or that the doctor was not sufficiently thorough.

Hypochrondriacal complaints should not be confused with an increase in the extent of specific physical symptoms of *pre-existing ailments* as a prominent feature of bereavement. The gastrointestinal system is a frequent focus of increased symptomatology during bereavement. Persons with hiatus hernia, ulcer, duodenitis, or colitis complain of increased discomfort (vomiting, nausea, pain, constipation, diarrhea). Often, their overt sadness, mental pain, and suffering appear focused less on the loss than on their physical illness. When careful examination reveals no change in the status of the physical problem, the physician may be helpful by relating the "pain" to the "pain of the loss" and indicating that anxiety, tension, and yearning as well as depression, can aggravate symptoms of physical illness.

There are circumstances in which the stress of the bereavement actually appears to contribute to the precipitation of physical illness in a person so predisposed. In contrast to hypochondriasis, the person with physical illness which appears intensified during bereavement does not demonstrate an increasing preoccupation with the belief that his worsened symptoms mean a new and terrible disease. These persons will tend to explain any anxiety or depression they experience as secondary to the worsened physical symptoms. "If only my stomach didn't hurt, everything would be fine." The statement denies the fact that the loss of the loved or valued person would still have to be coped with.

The bereaved individual who experiences his grief by complaining of worsened physical symptoms is often characterized by exaggerated independence, difficulty in showing feelings to others (though they may be very much aware of them internally when someone else defines them), and difficulty in accepting help from others. Physical symptoms appear to be a more acceptable route to the expression of painful feelings and the receipt of support. The physician may play an important role in consulting with such people in that they often "open up" with him if he presents a sympathetic ear and encourages the expression of emotions. Several visits may afford considerable relief of worsened physical symptoms and allow grief to proceed more directly.

Some individuals deal with strong internal feeling states by action. They get up and go rather than experience the pain of bereavement. Instead of feeling yearning, loneliness, and sadness, they attempt to satisfy the yearning (and diminish the sadness) by flying into the arms of another person, immediately finding a substitute for the deceased loved or valued person. They may find a series of substitutes and behave promiscuously or find one substitute and rapidly remarry. Other individuals flee the bereavement state by denying the pain and yearning through immersion in job, travel, hobby, etc.

Drug dependence may be a problem for some persons in bereavement. They may substitute drug dependence for human dependence. These drugs include tranquilizers, barbiturates, stimulants, or, most frequently, alcohol. Each has its place in the management of various aspects of bereavement, but should not serve as a narcotic against feeling or memory. There will usually be a history of prior usage under stress or else moderate past usage becomes excessive. Sudden new usage of drugs may also occur. Persistence of changed patterns of drug or alcohol usage should alert those close to the bereaved that something is amiss and that emotional reactions are being dealt with self-destructively.

Preexistent mental illness and organic mental states (senility, chronic arteriosclerosis) may be worsened after an important loss. Any of the major forms of neurotic or psychotic behavior may be precipitated by profoundly important loss. The overtness of their symptomatology makes it unnecessary to describe them in detail in this section.

SUMMARY

In conclusion, bereavement states vary according to (1) the personality of the bereaved, (2) the relationship between the bereaved and the lost loved or valued person, and (3) the values or institutions of the society in which the bereaved lives. Bereavement states are usual following a significant loss, and attempts to block or inhibit bereavement feelings and activities may lead to more serious maladaptation. Expression of feelings of grief is not only appropriate after loss but is to be encouraged. The development of certain states during bereavement clearly indicates the need for medical consultation. These states include depression, hypochondriasis, worsening of symptoms of previous bodily illness, alcoholism or drug dependence, and neurotic or psychotic behavior. Absence of symptoms or signs of a bereavement state or extremely minimal signs of bereavement also require evaluation. Under certain circumstances lack of reaction is to be expected and appropriate, while at other times it may betoken hidden emotional conflict.

The physician is increasingly aware of the signal importance of loss and bereavement and can provide considerable advice, support, or treatment where it appears essential.

Grief in Anticipation of Death

FREDERIC P. HERTER, M.D. AND
JAMES A. KNIGHT, M.D.

Grief following long-anticipated death presents special problems of its own. There is no initial shock phase. Preparations have already been made in detail. Friends and relatives have long since been informed of the impending end. Expressions of sympathy and acts of support have already been conferred. Grief has found its fullest expression long before death and has been gradually replaced by a re-

37

signed acceptance of the facts. The life alone has already begun and the attendant adjustments in thinking made.

Death, under these circumstances, comes anticlimactically, without drama. A transient resurgence of grief may ensue, but it is dulled by long months of anticipation. More often, the end is marked by a sense of relief—of release from a protracted phase of anguish and suffering into a new life of relative normalcy. It is not unnatural that this suppressed relief should be accompanied by feelings of confusion and guilt. To the outside world, a posture of grieving must be assumed out of proportion to the actual sense of loss. In our culture, any overt expression of relief is inappropriate. Hence, honest emotions are sublimated to a degree, and a charade is played out.

Whatever conflicts may arise can be lessened significantly by a simple awareness of their nature, and once again the physician can play an important role by anticipating this reaction and preparing the family for it.

There is a final area of anticipatory grief which many bereaved and even some workers in the field fail to understand and appreciate. This concerns the extent to which grief is experienced in advance of the actual death of a loved one and is especially true if he has been sick for a long time and is now terminally ill. Here, bereavement is imminent; the inevitability of coming death has been faced over an extended period. At the same time that the approaching loss is profoundly affecting the bereaved-to-be, the situation is further complicated and compounded by evidences of grief in the patient himself related to his illness and fear of death.

There appears to be a timetable of grief, oriented to both the date of the onset of a fatal illness as well as the date of the death of the loved one. This timetable of grief, somehow built within us, is one for which we should indeed be thankful, for it sequentially relates the period of bereavement to a finite period of time.

No amount of foreknowledge or grieving will do more than mitigate the event of death when it comes. But the presence of grief in anticipation of the loss alters its subtle progression; the inevitable change has foreshadowed one's feelings; one is powerless, and a measure of resignation has crept in. A sorrowful reality is about to ensue; actual death comes as an affirmation of our pre–knowledge. Sharp grief has already been experienced, but the sharpest edge of grief comes at this time. However, because of his anticipatory grief, the bereaved more readily finds his way back to peace according to the dictates of his own situation and the ensuing circumstances. Those about him should somehow be brought to the same realization, so that they will understand all the bereaved's reactions to the ultimate event and will become better able to assist, rather than hinder him in working through his grief.

Thus, without recognition of the influence of anticipatory grief, no consideration of the complexities constituting the transcendent emotional and physical state of bereavement would be complete. Hence, once the bereaved and those about him become aware that grief in anticipation of the death of a loved one does, in fact, occur, a giant stride toward recovery will have been made.

When a Child Dies

MARY EVANS ROBINSON, PH.D.

The death of a child is always an agonizing experience for the parents, but when it comes after a long period of illness, it will have a special meaning for them. While maintaining hope, they have been living with the knowledge that the child's illness could or would end in death. They have anxiously watched his progress, possibly through periods when he has seemed much improved, only to have his condition worsen. They have talked to doctors, read exhaustively about the illness, and undoubtedly sought out others who have undergone the same experience. Often they have worked hard in caring for the child at home and have experienced the emotional and financial strain of repeated hospitalizations. When death comes, they are often emotionally and physically drained.

When it has been known for some time that a child's illness will end in death, the parents may go through a process of "anticipatory mourning" in which they begin to accommodate themselves to the idea of losing him soon after his condition has been diagnosed as fatal. Such a process is a normal protective device by which the human mind gradually prepares itself for a loss that it will not be overwhelmed by the final reality. When death does come, it represents the end of a long road, the greater part of which the parents have already travelled. Death ends not only the child's suffering but the parents' suffering for him. Thus, some parents find that while continuing to care lovingly for their child in the last few months of his life, they have emotionally begun to pull away from him, and at

39

the end they often find themselves beyond tears. Although this is a normal process, parents may often feel guilty about "not feeling any worse," and relatives and friends may express disapproval of the parents' apparent coldness. Sometimes this anticipatory mourning does not take place; if the parents have never completely believed that their child would die, the shock of his death may be particularly painful.

Close, meaningful human relationships, including those between parents and children, are characterized by what the psychologists call ambivalence. This means that no matter how much we love someone, there are times when we feel irritated, resentful or angry toward that person. Should that person die, however, we find ourselves dwelling on the things we should or should not have done, had we known that we were to lose him. But what is important and painful is the guilt we feel about angry feelings we have had. Young children, like primitive people, believe that they can cause a thing to happen by wishing it. Even adults are often unable to rid themselves of this atavistic belief. Such an idea is particularly painful to the parents of a chronically ill child, for it is virtually inevitable that, exhausted by the physical and emotional demands of caring for the child and longing to end their own suffering as well as his, they will have openly or secretly wished for his death.

In addition, parents often have feelings of guilt about the part they might have played in causing their child's illness. When told that the child is seriously ill, it is only human for the parents to ask, "What could we have done or what should we not have done to prevent this illness?" Should they have prevented him from going to the swimming pool? For it was after that that he developed rheumatic fever. Should they have suspected sooner that his paleness, fatigue, frequent bruises, and minor physical complaints signaled the onset of a blood disease? When one doctor said the symptoms were not important, should they have consulted another? The tragedy of this self-accusation is that the parents blame themselves for situations which could not possibly have been predicted; they blame themselves for overlooking symptoms which either could not have been recognized earlier or, even if recognized, would not have changed the course of the disease.

When a child is ill, he frequently becomes demanding and irritable. He may resent many of the medical procedures to which he must be subjected, and he becomes angry at his parents for not protecting him from these experiences. Sometimes the home care of the child may require that certain unpleasant things be done to him, and he develops the feeling that only a parent who hated his child would do such things. The parent, caught between his desire to do his best

40

to maintain his child's life and his desire to have the child love him, may become quite angry at the child's demands. This does not mean that he is a bad parent but only that he is human.

At best, the care of a chronically ill child makes demands on all members of the family, particularly the mother. But in some instances the illness becomes the focus of all family activities, and the family has little life that is not centered on the sick child. In such a situation, the death of the child can only mean relief from pressure for the whole family; yet the parents may be overwhelmed by guilt feelings because they are glad that "it is finally over."

In the face of personal tragedy, it is human to ask, "Why did this happen to me?" When a child has a fatal illness and doctors say, "Sometimes these things happen and we don't know why," parents will often go to great lengths to convince themselves that their child's death resulted from something they did or did not do. Such a reaction may be the expression not only of the guilt feelings discussed above, but of the feeling that it is less painful to accept personal responsibility than to accept the fact that in a world of chance and hazard, children can be struck down by illness.

When a child dies, parents must deal not only with their own grief but that of their other children. One of the most difficult things can be to let his brothers and sisters talk about his death and the feelings it has aroused in them. Some people have the idea that "children forget so quickly" or "children are so heartless." Often it is assumed that a child will always express his feelings. It is difficult for many adults to realize that a child can often suppress his feelings, particularly his fears. But it is extremely important that the surviving children have an opportunity to talk about what they feel. Although an attitude of "let's not talk about it" may work for a while, more often it only appears to work, and the fears and anxieties of the child remain cloaked beneath a surface of silence. Thus, the child is denied the support and help he so desperately needs. In adults, grief is a highly personal and individual experience, and so is it also with children. Their feelings and expressions of grief must be recognized and respected.

The relationship between brothers and sisters, like that between parents and children, is characterized by positive and negative feelings. However, children cannot control or understand their emotions the way adults do, and in their relationships with their brothers and sisters they are often in competition for their parents' love. In the minds of children, parental love is expressed primarily by parental attention. Thus, any child resents the time and attention given to the other children. This resentment often becomes intensified when for a long period a sick child has received the major share of attention.

41

Even when a child is old enough to understand that such a situation is unavoidable, he may still resent it. There are also situations in which the parents, because of their grief over the illness of one child, actually do make an emotional investment in him which surpasses his real need for care and which shuts out the needs of the healthy child. Parents find themselves deferring to the ill child, making fewer demands on him, punishing him less often and less severely, and being more indulgent because they feel he has enough to bear. Sometimes they feel that by making demands on the child, they will make him more ill. In some families, particularly when more than one child has the same chronic illness, the well children may openly envy the others, feeling that to be healthy is to be outside the circle of family warmth and concern. In this case, the parents must be prepared to face the fact that the well siblings are going to be envious and angry about the situation. This will often take the form of wishing that the sick child would die.

In view of the resentment which he has felt toward a brother or sister who has died, it is extremely easy and astonishingly common for the surviving child to conclude that it was his angry thoughts which caused his sibling's death. In such a situation, he desperately needs to be reassured that his bad wishes did not do so. Even more, he needs to be reassured that his parents understood them and that he was not bad for having had them.

The death of a brother or sister inevitably causes the other children in the family to have fears about their own death. In general, parents can reassure them that they are well and that there is no reason to feel that they will die. However, this explanation is inadequate in those situations in which the disease or condition which killed one child is present in other children in the family. In such instances, it is essential that parents let the surviving children talk about their concern and tell them that they are not as sick as the child who died; that doctors are constantly finding out more about this condition and may soon discover an effective treatment.

Sometimes children react to the death of a brother or sister in ways which the parents find it difficult to understand or to accept. They may be appalled that, upon being told of the death, a child will not cry at all, or only briefly. Sometimes he may express resentment because the death has interfered with his plans, or within the first few hours after death he may ask for some long-coveted possession of his brother. In Tad Mosel's play *All the Way Home*, a little boy who has been told of his father's death dances around the room chanting, "My daddy's dead, my daddy's dead," yet the chant ends in tears.

42

Understand these reactions, parents must appreciate what death means to a child. First of all, most young children under five years have difficulty in comprehending the finality of death. In games they "shoot" a playmate with an imaginary gun, saying, "Bang, bang, you're dead"; yet they fully expect the playmate to return to play. Perhaps they feel that death merely means the deceased is away for a while but will soon return. Thus, all the commotion seems strange to them.

Even if the child is old enough to comprehend the finality of death, he does not have the emotional resources of an adult. He may seem quite casual in his reaction to the death of a sibling because he must protect himself from the full impact of his feelings of loss, guilt, and fear about his own death and that of his parents.

Another concept which children have difficulty in understanding is the reason for death. Like adults, they are puzzled by their feelings toward the deceased and are unwilling to accept the idea of a world in which death comes by chance to children; they are even willing to believe that they caused the death. More disturbing for the parents is that such children often believe that their parents were somehow responsible for the sibling's death and may also cause them to die. Although many parents are shocked by this, it is only by open expression of this notion that the child can win reassurance from the parents, and find himself able to cope with it.

Often parents cannot accept the fact that there is no perfect way to deal with this question of how to prevent or eliminate the anguish, the fears, and the feeling of loss after death. Older children, who feel secure in their relationship with their parents, who are able to accept and express their feelings, and who in the past have been able to cope with emotional stress, often do a relatively good job of adapting to the death of a sibling. Other children, particularly the very young, who feel unsure in their relationship with their parents, who have difficulty in expressing their feelings, and who are sensitive and vulnerable to stress, may show signs of disturbance for an extended period. These signs may include difficulty in going to sleep, nightmares, fears, thoughts of their own death, overconcern about minor illnesses, clinging to their parents, or a regressive return to immature behavior. When this reaction persists over a period of several months, the parent should seek professional help. Without such help, many children develop a serious emotional illness which persists into adult life.

Even after the immediate period of mourning has passed, parents may find complications developing in their relationship with the surviving children. If the dead child had endured much during his illness, parents may be extremely impatient with the everyday demands of the surviving children. When a child cries over a scraped knee, they are tempted to say, "Your brother had a lot more pain than that and I never heard a whimper out of him." Obviously, this is grossly unfair to the child, who at that moment is experiencing real pain and looking for comfort, only to be made to feel guilty about expressing his own honest need.

Another problem which may arise in relationship to the surviving child or children is that they will be made to feel that they must personally compensate the parents for the loss of the dead child. A little boy may be told, "Now you'll have to be a really big boy since you're the only boy left," or he may be made to feel that he is obligated to distinguish himself in school or a career as perhaps his brother did. Thus, he feels he must live the life of his brother as well as his own, in terms of emulating a model. This is too much of a burden to be carried by anyone. Each child needs to be respected and appreciated for himself, and no child should be expected to compensate for the death of another.

Often parents find it difficult to re-establish the family's life after the death of a child who has been ill for a long time and where much of the family's existence has been centered on his care. However, it is extremely important that this be done as soon as possible. Only then can the parents begin to realize that through their experience with the child who has died, they have had the opportunity to become more sensitive to the feelings of their other children, to the feelings of people outside their family, and to the feelings of each other.

Parents who best survive the grief experience are those who are able to accept and express their own feelings while supporting the emotional needs of their surviving children. They know that human beings are fallible and that there is much about certain illnesses which is simply not known. They are able to derive comfort from knowing that they did everything possible. They respect not only their own grief but that of their children.

Grief is an honest emotion which lends dignity to human relation ships. If these relationships have been meaningful, their termination cannot help but be painful. Parents do themselves and their children a great disservice unless they acknowledge the pain of their loss and encourage their remaining children to do this also.

The Lost Image

SANDRA BESS

someday
I will return
to the lost
image of my childhood
how much has it cost
me to earn
the title of man
I walk now
head down
with a plan
over the road
which I ran
head up
not knowing how
to stop
and think
of what is bad
and what is good
I was both
a poet and a clown
in one hand
the world in the other
a toy
the day and I
shared our growth
and brought joy
to each other
someday
I will feel again
the timelessness of
my childhood
when everything
will be real again
to sing about
to hold
to love
and all the
lilies of the field
will bloom for me
and yield
their soul

and I in turn
shall make it
part of mine
I in turn
shall take it
and be glad
there will be
no more good or bad
I shall know
the whole
again and relearn
that life lives
all
in space and time
now there's much
that doesn't rhyme
now there's much
to stand or fall
but when there's
no more
should or shouldn'ts
when there's
no more
could or couldn'ts
I will be a child
the wild
wild roar
of the lion will say
to me come
come out to play
and I'll take you
home

The Special Needs of Bereaved Children

SOLL GOODMAN, M.D.

How willing is one to think about death, to try to understand for oneself what it means, what it entails, and the consequences when one is actually confronted with it? Above and beyond ourselves, how pre pared are we as adults to deal with the situation when our children come for explanation, support, and assistance so that they, too, might live through the experience with the least amount of emotional up heaval and trauma? Surely, the adult is not justified in leaving the child to muddle through as best he can.

Because we are reluctant to think about death, we avoid conceptualizing the process that occurs when life no longer exists. This is particularly evident when a child asks his parents what happened when someone they had known has died. How euphemistic are the parents, how vague and how confusing when they tell the child that "Uncle went away." How lame and how feeble are the explanations when the inquisitive child persists in asking questions about where the person has gone and when he will be coming back. How inadequate are these explanations, how confusing is the picture to the child, and, consequently, how mistrustful does the child then become of all of the parents' subsequent explanations. How insincere and inadequate these explanations are. If the child thinks that his father or mother has merely "gone away," he will continue to wait for their return; he will picture their being somewhere else. Or a sense of being observed, watched, and looked down upon follows the explanation that the person who died went to Heaven, is sitting up there with God, and is looking down upon us here in this world. Such a youngster constantly feels that he is being watched; he cannot do certain things for fear that he will be caught. The struggle with his impulses often be comes highly intensified, and under some circumstances such a child may come to hate vehemently the loved one who died.

The question arises constantly about what we should tell a child when death occurs. Should we avoid acknowledgment that the person has died? Should we, as intimated previously, present the idea that the lost one has "gone away"? Should we suggest that he became ill and had to go away to a hospital or to some place where he could recuperate and become cured, hoping that, by this continued

47

absence, his memory would gradually fade away and the child would come to accept the absence as being the norm? All of these evasions merely indicate the uncertainty which the adult has about the child's capacity to deal with reality situations. It also attempts to encourage the child to develop the capacity to "forget about things." This ill prepares a person to deal with realities.

It is possible to explain to a child that the process of growing up and dying, as one sees it repeated in flowers, in trees, through the spring and summer seasons, only to be followed by death in the fall and winter seasons, is a phenomenon that occurs throughout nature. The child is able to grasp this concept and to recognize that the same sequence occurs in plants, in animals—and in human beings. The manner in which the adult presents these facts determines how the youngster will accept the explanation. If the adult is reassuringly direct, simple, and clear in his descriptions, without being lurid, gruesome, or terrifying, the child can accept the phenomenon, knowing full well that there is adequate support from the person who is explaining it, knowing that there can be support from others in the immediate family and in the related families. One should be alert to the concept of reincarnation since in nature perennial flowers return each year.

What is most important is the reassuring aspect that death is not imminent, that statistically, adults usually live to a reasonable age. One can demonstrate, by pointing out people whom the youngster knows, that there is a certain longevity, and that only under unusual circumstances is a life span shortened or terminated abruptly. It is the reassurance and the support that is most essential. It is the unpredictability and the aspect of imminent death, and the uncertainty, the feeling of helplessness and the lack of preparedness, that bring on anxiety, apprehension, and fear. Death is associated with a feeling of loss. Mourning and sadness are appropriate emotions to this loss. The more meaningful the relationship, the more genuine the feeling of loss. However, the reassurance of the presence and the support of the remaining members of the family counteracts any fear of destruction of the family, of disintegration and of lack of survival. These are the ideas which must be nullified, and this can be accomplished by a direct approach and a quiet, calm reassurance. The degree of adult involvement can counteract the acute feeling of a void. Encouragement to broaden interests also tends to counteract this feeling provided it is not for total escapist or denial purposes.

The development of concepts, ideas, and attitudes about life and death, love and hate, the relationships of one human being with another is a long-term, gradual process. Concepts such as these can never be evolved quickly; neither can they have much sincerity or meaning unless small, piecemeal fragments of ideas are taken in, thought upon, dissected, rejected, refined, and temporarily resolved, only to be reconsidered in the light of ever-changing circumstances. Youngsters are capable of grasping only fragments of ideas, and therefore exposure and repetition must be never-ending processes. Under proper circumstances all of these concepts would come in for comment and discussion during the course of everyday living. Hopefully, the ideas concerning death should have been talked about long before the child is exposed to the actual experience of the death of someone close to him. It would seem important, therefore, that parents use natural opportunities to broach such subjects so that they are not totally foreign and totally unexpected.

In the case where there is a chronic or a lingering fatal illness, it would seem important that one of the parents should introduce, in a mild manner, the concept that, under certain circumstances, chronic illness leads to death. Whether or not the afflicted adult is aware of his condition determines how much one might tell a child, since it is always possible that the youngster, in an unthinking moment, might convey the prognosis to the adult in question. In some instances it has been possible for the child himself to broach the subject to the sick one. In those instances where the afflicted adult can reassure the child and can demonstrate that he has no fear of the consequences, the child has been helped to have a more realistic and less apprehensive attitude.

There are those who advance the concept that, in order to orient a child as completely as possible to reality, one must present the facts of death in a simple, direct, unreserved fashion. There are those who would propose that the youngster see the dead body so that the reality of the death is concrete and any illusion or fantasies about the adult's possible return are completely nullified. It is my opinion that some of these procedures, while advanced in the name of reality-testing and reality-orientation, are, instead, more destructive and can adversely affect the youngster's capacity to prepare for and to accept the idea of death. Before describing or elaborating on the death process, one must consider the capacity of the particular child to understand and to absorb various phenomena. It would seem that any youngster younger than an adolescent ought to be spared some of the more startling, gruesome facts and exposures, if possible. One can explain the funeral to a child without his necessarily having to attend and participate. In fact, talking and describing help to develop the capacity for conceptualization which is necessary for understanding.

By the same token it is also important to convey the idea that one can retain the memory of someone who has died without having to visit a particular plot of ground and witness a particular piece of stone.

To feel sad or melancholy when one has lost someone who is close is not abnormal or unusual. One should help the child to recognize that these feelings are within the norm and that they can be experienced and tolerated without fear of dissolution or irremedial depression. One should not deprive the youngster of learning that he can tolerate this experience by sending him off to a holiday spot or to activities that would completely negate or deny reality. By the same token, however, it is important that he be supported so that the experience is not an overwhelming one. Much, of course, depends upon the attitude of the remaining adult and how he himself reacts to this loss. It is extremely important to the learning process and the youngster's development that he recognize that one can have a loss, be saddened by it, and not "go under." One must learn that he can master emotional catastrophes. This knowledge permits a person to be able to live through everyday situations rather than feel the need and the urgency to run away from them.

If the adult continues to maintain an intense relationship with the lost partner, refuses to establish new relationships, and continues to live in the memory of the old one, the youngster will grow up with the concept that there is a single marriage relationship that is established in life and that none can take its place. Thus, the manner in which the adult demonstrates his handling of the lost relationship plays a strong role in determining how the child will subsequently relate to others.

To the Bereaved of a Suicide

EDWIN S. SHNEIDMAN, PH.D.

When should help to the suicidal person or those connected with him be given? Logically considered, there are, in relation to suicide, three specific points at which help can be provided: before the act, i.e., by prevention; during the crisis, i.e., by intervention; or after the fact in an attempt to forestall recurrence of a suicide attempt, or, in the case of a committed suicide, to offer relief for the emotional

50

perturbation felt by the survivors; i.e., by postvention. A comprehensive national program of suicide prevention must address itself to all three of these areas.

Local suicide prevention facilities should provide services not only to modify grief but for drawing off, handling, exploring, ventilating, and repressing the negative side of grief's coin—shame, anger, guilt, and hopelessness—in those bereaved by suicidal deaths. Only in this way can we practice prevention against next year's or next decade's inner ravages of tormented souls.

The recovery from bereavement as a result of suicidal death should take advantage of the principle that use of professional help creates the best possible augury. The bereaved person (like the suicidal person) has limited focus, a kind of "tunnel vision." His mind does not present him with the full picture of how to handle such a problem. His first need may often be his need for help to get help. In this respect, his physician, his pastor, priest, or rabbi, his attorney, or other knowledgeable friends can guide him to the resources within the community where he can receive appropriate psychological assistance. The potential helpfulness of the psychiatrist or clinical psychologist, seen even on a limited basis, should not be underestimated. For the survivor, the period immediately following a suicidal death is a very special one in which forgotten memories, repressed wishes, and tabooed thoughts can run riot under the stress of shock. In a few days, they are usually repressed, especially if professional help is sought. In his own best interests and in the interest of his other loved ones (the children, most often), the important survivor (the spouse) of a suicidal death would do well to reveal his deepest anguish and fear some burdens in the sanctuary of a psychotherapeutic consultation.

In a curious way, the question of "rights" intrudes early in a full discussion of suicide. Some individuals, who either cannot understand or who deny the nature and the burden of suicide, sometimes ask, "Does an individual who wants to kill himself have a right to do so?" A mature comprehension of this issue revolves around understanding the words "wants" and "rights." From studies in the last decade, we know that individuals who "want" to kill themselves "want" to do this for a relatively brief period of their lives. Individuals are acutely self-destructive for a matter of days or hours—not weeks or months. If one can give a suicidal individual effective sanctuary or surcease for a very short time, his active suicidal impulses will pass. The question, then, is why attention should be focused on a minute portion of an individual's life with disregard of the much larger extent of his normal existence. Further, and even more importantly, practically everyone who is self-destructive is deeply ambivalent about his own self-destruction. It is perfectly possible, and indeed almost always true, that an individual can drive toward his own suicidal death, involving active plans for killing himself, and at the very same time have the strongest yearning for intervention and for rescue. The paradigm of suicide is the paradigm of ambivalence, where one can cut his throat and cry for help at the very same time. A society that claims to be benign ought to know the cry is there. Justice Cardoza said, "A cry for help is a summons for rescue."

As to the rights of man, what would be considered the most important human right? On a complete list, one may or may not have included the right of an individual to commit suicide. But what of the right of every individual to lead an unstigmatized life, specifically, a life unstigmatized by the tabooed suicidal death of a parent, spouse, of progeny or a sibling?

We now can see the "right" to commit suicide in the same context as the "right" of an individual to drive his automobile on the wrong side of the road, or to yell "fire" in a crowded theater. It is a social right with a built-in deterrent: the inevitable disaster embodied in its exercise. In the case of the would-be suicide, the deterrent is the inevitable scarring of his survivors. The survivor of a suicidal death must recover psychologically on a different level from that of people who have suffered a more natural bereavement. Natural, accidental, or even homicidal deaths elicit deep feelings of loss, emptiness, sorrow, loneliness, disbelief, torment, yearning, anguish, and heartache; in the case of suicidal death, these emotions are intensified and aggravated, sometimes to unbearable proportions, by the grim additions of shame, guilt, self-blame, and hostility. The suicide raises the question of "Why?" and "What might I have done to have prevented it?" The survivor often is obsessed by the thought that the death might have been prevented, and sees himself in the role of the potential rescuer and intervener who has failed. Thus the suicidal person places his psychological skeleton in the survivor's closet.

Surviving a Suicide

DAVID LESTER, PH.D.

All deaths are hard for the survivors. But the problems faced by the survivors and the emotions experienced by the bereaved differ for particular causes of death. In suicide, the deceased chose to take his or her own life. This has implications both for the deceased (for example, Was he mentally ill?) and for those who survive him (for example, did his family contribute to his death?).

UNEXPECTEDNESS

Many suicidal deaths are unexpected. Although experts can often pick up indications that a person may be close to suicide, most of the friends and relatives of the suicide are caught by surprise.

Most suicides are psychiatrically disturbed and, in particular, depressed people. However, the majority of depressed people do not kill themselves. Similarly, though we read about and may know of people who killed themselves when they discovered that they had terminal illness, when they experienced a divorce, or during some other crises do not kill themselves. (In fact, only about ten people out of every one hundred thousand kill themselves in the United States of America each year.)

The unexpectedness of the suicide creates similar problems to those faced by survivors of sudden natural deaths, accidents and homicides. Survivors may be left with unresolved feelings toward the deceased and possible guilt because there was no time to atone to the deceased for the wrongs done them.

However, not all suicides are unexpected. The alcoholic may have been making suicidal threats almost daily for months or years. (Alcoholics do in fact have a higher than average suicide rate, but suicide is still relatively rare among them.) Although the suicide of such a person may not be unexpected, the spouse and other close relatives may have been wishing for his death for a long time and may have experienced a great deal of anger toward him, resulting in feeling of guilt after the death.

NEGATIVE FEELINGS TOWARD THE SURVIVORS OF A SUICIDE

It has been noted frequently that people in the community often feel quite negatively toward the survivors of a suicide. They act as if the bereaved drove the person to suicide or did not respond caringly enough when he was alive.

When the friends and neighbors of the survivors of a suicide blame the survivors, this adds to the stress of the bereaved and reduces the degree of social support available to them. The survivors of a suicide are less likely to receive comfort, reassurance, and practical help in daily affairs. In extreme cases, the bereaved may be driven out of their community by gossip and ostracism.

A focus on mental illness as the cause of the suicide (rather than interpersonal stress from the survivors) changes the focus of the stigma for the family from "see how they drove him to it" to "I wonder if the madness runs in the family."

Stigma also affects the family directly. They have the same concerns as their neighbors, although their ways of defending against the feelings aroused by the stigma may differ. For example, they often seek to deny responsibility for the suicide in order to avoid a sense of guilt. They may turn to mental illness as "the cause" of the suicide for the same reason, but then they too may worry whether they will follow suit. (Some cases of this are well-known. For example, Ernest Hemingway's father shot himself thirty-three years before Ernest shot himself).

DENIAL

One result of the additional stress created by a suicidal death is that everyone connected with the deceased may try to deny that the death was indeed a suicide. Such denial was not surprising before the 1950s, when the study of suicide and suicide prevention began to assume importance in the field of mental health. However, denial remains quite common even today.

Denial is especially dangerous for the children of a suicide. Any death of a parent is traumatic for the children, and a suicidal death creates additional stress. However, if the family is denying the suicidal nature of the death, the child has no one to turn to discuss his or her fears and thoughts about the suicide. Furthermore, while the family may be denying the suicide, the peers at school and in the neighborhood have no reason to support the denial and may even taunt the child with the facts of his parent's death.

Denial is often manifest in a mild form as a "conspiracy of silence" in which people will not talk about the suicide. This may hinder the normal mourning process, especially the resolution of irrational and rational guilt and the angry reproaches toward the suicide for killing himself and abandoning his family.

REJECTION BY THE SUICIDE

In some ways, the more disturbed the suicide person is and the more stress he was under, the easier it may be to cope with his suicide, for it seems that there was little the bereaved could have done to prevent the suicide. Typically, however, suicide implies a rejection of the survivors. The suicidal act seems to say "You could not help me. You were of no use."

The suicidal act may even have been planned by the deceased in order to express his anger toward the survivors. Karl Menninger has classified the motives found in suicides as anger at others, anger at oneself (especially manifest as feelings of guilt and depression) and the wish to escape from physical or psychological pain. He may shoot himself in the head, leaving his spouse and children to find his body. (When Ernest Hemingway's father shot himself, his thirteen year old son, Leicester, was home and discovered the body. Some fifty years later, Leicester too shot himself.) He may leave a suicide note in which the anger felt toward the family is clearly expressed.
For example,

"Bill, I do hope you'll suffer more than I have done."
"I wish you'll die in a beer joint."

The guilt experienced by those who survive a suicide may, therefore, be much greater than those surviving a natural death.

OFFICIAL REACTIONS

Finally, the reactions of officials may be harsh for those who survive a suicide. The police must investigate and convince themselves that the death was not murder. Insurance representatives may look for ways to avoid paying the death benefits. Ministers may refuse to conduct typical burial services and refuse burial in church grounds.

In many ways, the official agencies in the community serve to remind the bereaved that the death was not a "natural" one and to create unpleasant experiences that the bereaved are ill-equipped to cope with.

Tender Are the Scars

MARTY JONES, R.N.

The pain is gone. When did it leave? Who knows?

It is now four years since my husband was killed in a car accident. Time heals all wounds? Perhaps, but the scars remain. Somehow I thought that if I could just get through one year I would be all right again. I set my jaw and held on. At the end of the year I suddenly found myself almost more miserable than on the day my husband died.

What a fool I had been to expect an instant cure at the end of a year's widowhood! There can be no set time for the agony to disappear. But it does go—gradually—almost without your realizing it. One day it dawns on you—"I can breathe again I can smile and mean it. I can laugh and feel it. I can even recall the memories, pleasantly now, without hurting." Maybe you won't have found happiness, but at least you will have some degree of peace and contentment with life. There is that to be thankful for. There are many other things to be thankful for.

The blessings are different for each of us. For me, even as they were telling me the news, "He was killed instantly," I thought, "Oh, thank God, thank God, he didn't have to suffer!" He was on his way home from work—happy, successful, healthy—and then, gone. No illness, no incapacity, no aging. He was so lucky. And I was glad for him. And I envied him!

What else could I be thankful for? Oh, yes, the day before the accident. It was a Sunday and, as though it were planned, it was one of those rare, perfect days when the entire family was in complete harmony from the time we awoke until we kissed goodnight. There are other things: family, friends—even strangers—all being helpful. Concentrate hard on all the little blessings; none of them will dull the pain, but they will make it easier to bear.

Above all, don't feel guilty! There is no one who can't dig up some small event to feel guilty about. Maybe you fought the day before—you wouldn't have had a normal, close relationship if you hadn't fought sometime. Maybe, like me, it occurred to you that you might have been able to prevent his death. (My husband had phoned that evening and asked me to meet him in town. Maybe, if I had—if I had been driving, or just with him ...) "If I had done this ... If I hadn't done that . FORGET IT. Such guilt is just another form of self-pity.

What else helps? Work. Lots of work, and the sooner the better. I was lucky. I'm a nurse, and working to help others seems to be the best way to blot out personal misery. Also, being a student of human behavior, I tried to "get out of myself" and observe my feelings clinically. I examined my every reaction. And I wrote out all the wild horror that engulfed me which was too stark to say to anyone. I sought out people who would talk about him as he really was—not in any hushed, hallowed reverence as though by dying he had become a saint but laughing and joking and making his memory alive.

Some things I had to shut out completely—to run from. Silly, little things: "our song," his pipes, grocery shopping (of all things!)—insignificant everyday things, that for one reason or another had had special meaning for us alone. Even now as I write this, after having felt safe from the pain for quite some time, it makes me uneasy to unearth these tiny treasures.

My soul aches to find some word—some formula, some magic pill—to help those who are going through this thing, this wretched, clinging thing called bereavement. I think the most important "lifeline" is accepting the reality of it. Face the facts. It is done. It is over. Your loved one is dead. He was not perfect and would not want you to make a martyr of him, nor waste your life mourning. Let him go in peace, and do him the honor of making the best of what you have left, with perhaps just an occasional smile of memory.

Big brave words? No. What headstone, shrine, or monument could begin to honor his memory as much as your having a life as rich and full as possible? Which would please him more—to have you bring flowers to his grave with tears in your eyes, or to give your love to others with joy in your heart?

Marry again? I hope I can! We had a good marriage—perfect balance of loving and fighting, understanding and misunderstanding. He was a great husband, and he thought I was a great wife. He wouldn't want me wasted on widowhood. I don't want myself wasted on widowhood! So far, I haven't been lucky enough to meet the right man. Maybe I won't. The odds are against me at forty-two. That's another reality I must face.

I went through a period of frantically looking for another husband. That was most frustrating, and I soon gave it up. Now I live my life enjoying what I have: family, friends, work, hobbies, health, and all the lovely gifts mother nature gives us—beautiful sunsets, rainy days, changing seasons. If "he" should come along someday, I will know I have received more than my share of good in this tough old world.

It is tough and, at times, lonely. Sometimes I wonder how it would have been if my husband had lived. Of course, it's easy to think it would have been better. But I don't know that. It could have been worse! It's not for me to say. All I know for sure is that I had a fine marriage that I can always remember and be grateful for, and that it was more than worth the suffering its ending cost me. There is no time for self-pity. I have to go on and make the best of what's left—for myself and others, as well as for him. Life will never be the same, but there must be some purpose for my still being here. That purpose can only be fulfilled by looking forward—not back.

God grant all the strength to do the same.

Thoughts on My Wife's Death

RABBI JACOB PHILIP RUDIN

I would not presume to deal with this theme, "Concerning Life and Death—Some Questions and Some Answers," a theme which obviously grows out of the tragedy which has come to me and to my family, were I not quite certain that my sorrow, devastating though it be, has certain overtones which transcend the strictly private and the personal.

For life, into which we are born, is a miracle; and death, into which we all go, is a mystery. This is forever true: life born in our midst is linked with life born a thousand miles away; death touching life here is the same death that touches life in a far corner of the earth. Men are joined in the majesty of newly given life; they are encompassed, as well, in the dread circle which death sets implacably around all the living.

This is true when men are not known to each other—strangers. It is driven home more poignantly when death comes to one who is familiar to many and held by them in true affection. Then the private sorrow becomes public grief and the personal tragedy overflows from one heart into many hearts.

And so one dares to speak, because one senses that there is identity with his words, and a kinship in the bleak hours that mark one's melancholy. If I speak then, out of myself and, in a very deep way, to myself, I speak, I trust, also to you.

Here was a beloved one, gracious and lovely, devoted to the word of God and to the ways of man. A dread disease, the worst we know and in one of its worst manifestations, strikes her, and for seven years pain gnaws and suffering eats away the quiet meanings of every day until it seems that pain is the only meaning and suffering the only reality; and when finally there is release in death, loving eyes are still filled with the sight of brave but hopeless struggle, and loving hearts are still numbed by the blows which the relentless hammers of the cruel minutes and days and weeks have ceaselessly dealt. Then, at last, it seems altogether reasonable and altogether right to shake one's fist at the universe, and to shout to the remote heaven "Why?", and to say with Job (16:9):

He hath torn me in His wrath, and hated me; He hath gnashed upon me with His teeth; Mine adversary sharpeneth His eyes upon me.

It seems proper to ask the old questions.

"Why did it happen to her who was so good and so faithful, whose life was devoted to her people, her community, her sanctuary?"

"And if," as Rabbi Gittelsohn asked in his eloquent and moving eulogy, "and if it could happen to Elsie, what is the meaning of all that we are and of all that we do?"

"And where is the justice in the world? Elsie stricken down at 53; and others whose lives are devoid of works such as hers and of inspiration and leadership such as hers, and, indeed, lives even less worthy—these others live on into golden years, rich in the harvests of serenity and peace?"

These are the questions the shattered heart asks. These are the bitter queries that grief plunges like daggers into our empty, tear-drained spirits.

Are there answers? Is there any reply which makes sense, which suggests pattern and wholeness?

There are some answers, I believe: not complete answers, but more than fragmentary answers, nonetheless; not total answers, because life itself is not totally clear. Who fully understands himself and his life? Who comprehends the miracle which life is, or the wonder of love, the infinite possibilities of man's mind, the reach of man's spirit? No one does. But mature people, humble about themselves in God's world, can find out.

So the questions I have posed are natural questions; but natural though they be, they are not the most helpful questions, and their answers will not sustain us greatly in the face of the tragedy which death brings. They are not good questions, because they do not make the right assumptions about life.

What are the right assumptions then? Let me try to state them. Life isn't a matter of comparisons: my life in terms of someone else's life; nor a series of measurements: the number of my years versus the number of somebody else's years; nor a contrast in human values: my joys against another's joys, my sorrows against another's one way of death against another way of death.

The judgment of a life is not in the mathematics of the years nor in the sum of birthdays and anniversaries. It is not saying anything important to say that a life is longer than another or that goodness has been rewarded if the years are many and the manner of death gentle, as in a sleep.

No life can be equated with another life. Each person belongs, first of all, to himself. He is a person within himself. He reaches out from within himself, and he touches lives around him. But the brightness of the outgoing light depends upon the intensity of the flame within, and the strength imparted to another derives and flows from power created inwardly.

One life is not to be evaluated in terms of another life. The goodness of one life is not greater because the goodness in another life is less. The glory of one life is not less incandescent because the glory of another life is brighter. The fulfillment in one life does not depend on, nor is it to be measured by, the fulfillment in another life.

So Elsie's life was not short, because the life of another person may have more years. Nor was her life less blessed, because her passing was through the gates of pain.

God must not be reduced to a cosmic Bookkeeper Who doles out the years, so many to one person, so many to another. His justice is not to be reckoned in terms of His generosity with years bestowed: proclaimed a God of goodness if the years are many, or a God of wrath if the years are few and the road difficult and filled with the stones of heartbreak and the boulders of despair. God is not in the measurement nor in the comparison of life with life, reward with reward, blessing with blessing, hard death or easy death.

Where, then, is He? Where was He in Elsie's life? Where is He in anyone's life? How does He declare Himself? How is He manifest?

These are the right questions. They are right because they have validity in terms of life and in terms of the meaning of life. And there are answers to these questions, for me, at least.

We are not masters altogether of what comes to us in the years of our pilgrimage on earth, not masters wholly of the joys nor masters of the sorrows. Who, much in love and much loved, has not in some quiet private moment asked himself, "What have I done to deserve this deep and abiding joy?'' And who, in a sorrow, has not asked, ''Wherefore this night through which I must walk?''

But to give meaning to the joy and to give meaning to the sorrows: that is something else again.

Elsie was grateful for joy, and she never took it for granted. I heard her saying it each day to the very, very last day: ''How blessed I am.'' She lifted the cup of gladness and she drank of it, savoring its sweetness gratefully.

So she met sorrow and pain, too. She accepted it. She fought it when there were weapons with which to fight back. She endured it when there was no defense. But she had too high a respect for her own spirit as a human being to give that spirit over unto defeat. A disease enslaved her, but it never conquered her. It dominated her, but it never vanquished her.

These were the manifestations of God in her life. They are for every life: that we take our joys humbly and gratefully; that we meet our sorrows nobly and courageously.

Edna St. Vincent Millay was the favorite poet of Elsie's younger years, and she often turned to her verse. In her poem ''The Harp Weaver,'' Edna St. Vincent Millay wrote:

> She sang as she worked
> And the harp-strings spoke;
> Her voice never faltered,
> And the thread never broke.

That's where God was, and that is how He showed Himself. And that is what Elsie's life means. God was in the quiet gratitude of her joys. He was in the victory of her courage.

He was also in her humor, which never forsook her.

In one of her last days on earth, when the burden was becoming intolerable and the light began to flicker, we, her dearest ones, were gathered in her hospital room and I made some remark. From her bed, eyes closed, she said, ''Jack, you're talking too loudly.'' Then she opened her eyes and there was a sudden roguish look in them as she said, ''You always talk too loudly.''

What blessed gifts: gratitude for joy, strength for trouble, and laughter for them both.

These are the answers to life and to death. These are the values. Here is where they are to be found, and not in the number of years and not in comparisons with other lives and other's gifts and destinies.

Was her life rich? Was God present? Who can doubt it?

But there are other ways and there are other answers, in other places. I said that life begins within itself and depends upon itself. But it goes beyond, if it be a God-consecrated life. There is the person, and there is the world.

But the world is never the same. The world varies. Sometimes it is the world of home and parents; sometimes the world of school and college and teachers and books; sometimes the world is love and marriage, the making of a home of one's own; sometimes the world is the synagogue and friends.

Sometimes the world is a hospital room with nurses and doctors and pain and hope, suffering and despair.

Elsie's world and our world, in the days of conclusion, was a hospital room. And God was there.

A hospital can be a necessary world, but a world as clinical and as antiseptic as a scalpel. It can be spotlessly clean and very efficient, possessed of the newest scientific equipment. All these things, being present, can create a great institution. But all these things will not make a hospital. For a hospital is quite different from an institution. A hospital is a world for those who seek it out because they need it. No one can live in a world that is made up only of spotlessness and of regulations and of the best equipment. The world needs something else, or it isn't a world.

The hospital was not an institution for us. It was a blessed hospital because it had within itself those characteristics which transformed it from institution into hospital, from a place into a world of understanding and of sympathy and of caring.

I haunted that hospital for weeks—morning, noon and night. It was not a hospital for us and an institution for others. I saw the same kindly understanding which was given to us, shown to everybody by the doctors, by the staff, from the greatest to the least, by the wonderful volunteers.

Patients were people. They weren't merely manifestations of a disease or postoperatives or special diets. Is this not God in the world: hearts reaching to hearts, the well helping the sick, the human being regarded as a person for whom a hospital was built so that in his hour of need it would be there to help him?

God was in that hospital world for us, as He was in the world of the doctors who became a world, too. These men brought us endlessly great skill, the endowment of their minds, the experience of their years. They brought these gifts to us, as they do, nobly, day after day, to every one to whom they minister. I saw the spirit of God at work in them and through them. I saw enormous respect for life, a sense of humility toward the essential quality of life, so that even when they knew that their efforts could not triumph nor their

62

work succeed, they continued to try, using their wisdom and their knowledge to aid life, so that the dignity of life never left the room nor the person nor the hospital.

They were doctors. But they were first friends, serving not in an institution but in a hospital. So they ceased to become practitioners of a profession and they became the defenders of the spirit of life against the legionaries of death. And I believe deeply that in the world of that hospital and in the world of these doctors, God dwells; and no human being who respects humanity and the decent things of the heart and of the mind can do less than stand at the doorway of these worlds in awe and in gratefulness. For those doors lead us to the love of fellowman and to the knowledge that we belong together, that the weak need the strong, the sick the well, the ignorant the learned, the frightened the brave, that life is a common gift and death a common end.

So, in a wonderful way, when a life is right, within itself, death does not conclude the matter. Surely, there is the pain, and the ache of separation, and the long, dark hours of the night when sleep is absent and time is a deep loneliness. But there is more than pain and more than ache and more than loneliness. There remains, at the end, when all has been said, the simplest and most beautiful of things. A good life is a good life. Good of itself, because the person living it was a good person. And it isn't to be measured in terms of anything except itself.

Life is a victory in itself, a victory that death can only crown, but cannot crush. Because life is an inner thing and death an outer. Life grows with life. Death dies with death.

So there are some answers: not complete answers and not whole answers. But no life is complete, nor whole. There is always something beyond, something unfinished, for another life to complete, for another life to fulfill.

This is how God gives us immortality, by giving us memory and by giving us love.

Concerning his play, *J.B.*, Archibald MacLeish observed: "... man can live his truth, his deepest truth, but cannot speak it." It is for this reason that love becomes the ultimate human answer to the ultimate human question. Love, in reason's terms, answers nothing. We say that *Amor vincit omnia*, but in truth love conquers nothing certainly not death—certainly not chance. What love does is to arm. It arms the worth of life in spite of life.

Archibald MacLeish is right. We must face the mystery of death and we must forever turn to incompleted life again. Turn to it in love, which means to turn to it in gratitude to God for courage, for faith, for a hospital, for doctors, for a sanctuary, for friends, for people.

Because we are all as one; and love, in life and beyond life, teaches us that it is so.

Rights of Passage—
Rites of Passage

MARY-ELLEN SIEGEL

In every society and culture there are certain "rites of passage." Many of these rites represent a coming of age. When was it that I felt really grown up—when did I really "come of age?" The day I graduated from high school? Got married? Had my children? Finished college? Watched my oldest daughter walk down the aisle? Finished graduate school? Held my father's hand at my mother's funeral? Asked my father to send out the invitations when I remarried? Had my first grandchild? (Yes these things have been arranged in proper chronological order.)

These, like many other events, were rites of passage. But it took a single event on a cold December day in 1982—in my fiftieth year— for me to truly come of age.

Let me tell you the story. It is the story of a rite of passage and of the *right* to passage.

After celebrating Hanukkah with my husband's family, we walked into the house as the phone was ringing. It was the phone call I always knew, but never really believed would come.

"Your sister has been trying to reach you," the caller said. "Your father has had a stroke and they are on the way to the hospital."

Please, please, God, I silently prayed, don't let him survive. And then, a minute later, my husband and I were on our way to the suburban community hospital where they had gone. And during the half hour drive I talked incessantly.

"It's amazing what they do now," I explained to my husband. "I've seen so many stroke patients make a great recovery. Sometimes

64

they even can get back to work. I'll bet Dad will come through this just fine, and he'll be back to his office in no time.''

"He's eighty-six,'' my husband said gently.

"You know, maybe it wasn't really a stroke. Maybe it's just a little TIA. [transient ischemic attack] My sister always likes to be on the safe side so she's taking him to the hospital.''

And the silent voice was screaming in my head, Let go, let go!

As we pulled up to the hospital I composed myself and strode into the strange, sterile atmosphere as if I had the power to make it all work out right.

Dad was still in the emergency room, and he looked so old and frail. The admitting physician looked incredulous when we gave his history:

He's eighty-six. A urologist. No he's not retired. He has an active practice. I guess we'll have to call his office and explain he won't be in tomorrow. Yes—had a heart attack almost twenty-five years ago. He's been fine since, except for prostate surgery. Oh, and he has an indwelling catheter. His urologist? Well, he changes it himself monthly.

And please, Doctor... be careful when you speak in front of him. He may understand you, and even if you speak in medical terms, he can understand. If you don't mind, Doctor, I would like a sign over the bed explaining he's a doctor, so folks will be careful what they say. I remember...how upset he once got with some residents who talked about an aphasic patient in front of him, and later they found out the patient understood everything.

They admitted him, tried to stabilize him, and then did a CAT scan. We heard the result but didn't seem to really hear it. We made an appointment with the director of rehabilitative medicine. "We know if you get started early, the results can be more favorable,'' we said. The doctor told us, I remembered much later, that based on this first CAT scan we shouldn't really expect him to get back to work.

So while we sat over the fourth cup of coffee in the hospital cafeteria, we talked about what would happen after Dad recovered. If he couldn't work, what would he do? We came up with a number of ideas and thought all of them worthy of implementation.

But in the meantime Dad's condition was worsening. He suffered a number of small strokes, and it was getting harder to pretend he recognized us. But we were still trying to convince ourselves that he was resting, mobilizing his strength to recover.

But his condition and the time we needed to assimilate the impact of the stroke converged, and at last we knew. Another CAT scan proved he had deteriorated still more since admission.

And then we began to talk to each other about so many things. Like the wonderful family parties, especially his eightieth birthday, when we each wrote a little "piece" telling him how much he meant to us. My sister and I talked of the times he closed his office on a busy afternoon to teach us how to ride our new two wheeler bikes: would sit patiently through endless school and camp plays waiting for us to recite our one line, and was always there when we needed him, even when we didn't know we needed him but did.

And we remembered the wonderful gifts of words that our children gave him for that eightieth birthday. Teens and young adults they were, and they looked back at the years. They talked of football games, bicycle rides, and one told about the way he held her hand when she was wheeled into an operating room. And all told of unequivocal mutual love.

And then shortly after that eightieth birthday our mother took ill and died. Then too, there were special words that we wrote for the funeral. Among them was: Dad always knew that the nicest thing he could say about us was, "They learned that from their mother."

Those were the special family memories. But there were others too. The way he assumed his role as a physician was so much a part of him. And when I decided to become a social worker after having brought up three children, it was Dad who was one of my staunchest supporters. And he gave me the same advice that had been given to him by one of his teachers at Bellevue back in 1919.

"Care, feel, and really believe that that patient is the only one you have when you are standing next to his bed," this nineteenth-century-trained physician told my father. "Try to maintain some optimism, when possible, but if things are hopeless, and the patient knows it, let him know you care and are saddened. You will be no less a physician if you demonstrate to your patients that you are a human being. But when you turn to the next patient on the ward, wipe the grief from your eyes, lest he think he too is hopeless. And when you leave the ward, leave your feelings behind, or you will be of no use to the next group of patients."

And Dad shared other feelings with us. About letting go when there was no hope for a patient. In the days before life-support systems, sometimes that meant doing nothing but just watching. Sometimes it, meant hastening the end with extra doses of pain medication.

And sometimes the patients were dear friends and colleagues. And he would speak with love and pain—his pain watching an older colleague whose mental deterioration was advanced. "I wouldn't want to live like that," he would tell us over and over.

And I remembered another cold day many years ago when we sat together at the bedside of a beloved family member a physician like himself. The man had suffered many strokes but was stabilized at home with nurses. This time he had a massive stroke, and Dad supported the family decision not to call an ambulance and have him moved to a hospital.

And after this physician was pronounced dead, Dad turned to us and said, "I hope there will be somebody around to make this decision for me when my time comes."

And I promised.

But still, I thought, he would live forever.

And so, as my sister and I sat in that little hospital waiting room, we saw two young members of the house staff go in to see our father.

We followed them in, and one of the young house officers said, "I'm glad you're here. We are just about to move him to the Intensive Care Unit."

"The Intensive Care Unit?" I stammered. "Why?"

"He's taken a turn for the worse," the young man said.

"But," I replied, "we learned from the neurologist that there is no chance of any reversal hat he is never really going to respond any more than he does now. He doesn't know us, or anything," I said, choking back the tears.

"This must be very hard on you," said the other young doctor.

My God, I thought. This doctor doesn't even look old enough to shave, and he knows to say things like that. But he doesn't really know anything, or he wouldn't want to take my father to an ICU. Not my father.

In real life these things don't happen, I thought. A lifetime of memories doesn't really flash in front of your eyes or resound in your ears. But it's happening now. I'm hearing Dad saying over and over, "I don't want to live like that." And I'm thinking over and over I thought he would go on forever.

Without even a word between us, just an exchange of looks and some tears in our eyes, we made our decision.

We asked those young doctors to sit down. And we explained to them how until a few days ago Dad had been busy in his office, had patients in the hospital, and had climbed the two flights of stairs to have dinner at his grandson's house the young man whose law school graduation he was so looking forward to attending. And that he had spent the last few months attending a granddaughter's wedding, attending two Thanksgivings, and enjoying life to the fullest.

I told these young doctors, Boy Scouts, as my father used to refer to house staff that our father had many times stated his feelings and philosophy. I told them of that vigil some years back when the decision was made not to transfer a family member to the hospital.

And I told them how Dad said he hoped that someday there would be somebody to do that for him.

"Someday is here," I said.

The young doctors understood. And the promise was kept. He died the next day, peacefully, in bed.

Our cousin, Judge Berman, gave the eulogy.

Notwithstanding his remarkable span of productive years, his death comes as a shock. Somehow, so many of us came to look upon him as being almost immortal. But our sadness can be tempered by the knowledge that he lived his life and met his death just as he always said he wanted it...swiftly and without pain or suffering.

For years we had given and received from our father wonderful tangible and intangible gifts. Now it was time for that final gift—the right to passage.

With it had come my rite of passage. With the pain of shock, anger, denial, and finally the acceptance and the decision, I had come of age.

A Lifetime of Preparation for Bereavement

ARTHUR C. CARR, PH.D.

As a response to the loss of a loved person, grief is a universal reaction experienced by all individuals at some time in life. As one's interdependence on others grows, particularly through familial ties, the likelihood increases that one must also face separation, loss, and death, which elicit intense feelings of grief or mourning. The capacity that makes one capable of warm, satisfying relationships also leaves one vulnerable to sadness, despair, and grief when such relationships are disrupted.

Intense grief is easily recognized through signs of sadness and depression which bear a temporal relationship to major separation or loss of some kind, frequently that of death. During such an experience, the sympathy and attention of others are important supports which make the loss more tolerable and continued living more possible.

Generally not recognized, however, is the degree to which throughout life we are continually subjected to separations and losses which are so subtle or so well disguised that they may never be recognized or acknowledged. To a surprising degree, we are confronted with and tested by loss and separation throughout life. In many instances, such experiences, or the reaction to them, may be barely apparent even to the person himself. In other instances, they may be keenly experienced but custom or pride may preclude the possibility of the person sharing or expressing his sadness.

As ordinarily described, growth and development are pictured in positive terms. In the change from childhood to adulthood, from helpless dependency to maturity, from childish naivete to wisdom, from physical smallness to full development (changes which are normal and taken for granted), growth is ordinarily conceived of as becoming, in the sense of something developing or being added, something more or other than existed previously. Very seldom does one consider that loss, whether it be of a possession, a function, a value, an ideal, or a relationship, also is part of development and contributes to it.

From the time of birth, the growing child has constant experiences with loss. Perhaps the most significant one, which is generally emphasized by authorities, is that represented by the experience of weaning when the mother is no longer automatically available to gratify the infant's needs. At a time when the child has not developed full awareness of the distinction between what is his and what is not, what is subject to his control and what is not, weaning can be an experience of great consequence. How this separation and loss, a positive growth step, are integrated by the child determines his future capacity for coping with frustration and deprivation. This experience establishes the model for the way in which all later losses are handled: his basic optimism or despair, his passive resignation or the angry unwillingness to "let go," his assumed benevolence or malevolence of "fate," these and other significant attitudes may stem from this early loss.

But loss and separation are the recurring themes of human existence and development, quite apart from such major events as weaning. The first haircut, even when responded to with anticipation and pride by the child and the family, is an early experience of a separation from the body of a part that is one's own. At a time when the child's growth and development command interest and attention in the family, the child is also losing teeth, hair, and baby possessions— dolls, toys, dress, the cradle, and even the license to behave as a child. All of these are viewed by others as no longer appropriate for the "big" boy or girl. The child's increased motility, which opens new avenues for exploration, at the same time deprives him of the continuities and sameness that were previously available. Bowel training, while adding to his sense of independence, focuses on possessions which were in and of the body but which are now removed and disparaged as objects to be rejected. With each step forward, there is an experience of loss accompanying the change.

In the course of growing up, there is a continued experience with separation and loss. Important values, real and symbolic, are associated with the body. One's conception of and perception of his body—the "body-image"—become important aspects of how the child feels about himself and how he relates to others. Changes in the body which occur throughout life must be integrated into this image, both in regard to the reality of the change and in regard to the feelings about it. It would be unhealthy and most difficult to deny such changes.

Since the body is an important mediator between the external environment and the self as a psychological entity, it is natural that one would experience mourning and depression when an individual body part is removed through accident or surgery. The loss of an arm or leg, for example, presents a difficult problem of adjustment in which actual mourning for the removed limb may be experienced. Hence, doctors have learned that to prevent unnecessarily painful reactions and to facilitate recovery from and adjustment to such a loss, it is beneficial to prepare the patient and to help him understand that the loved part of the body will be handled with respect and dignity.

But in contrast to such obviously traumatic separations as those that occur with loss of a limb are less dramatic occurrences, ones that are assumed to be happy experiences but that, in reality, are as real a loss and as real a disruption to one's body-image as the loss of a limb. Childbirth, for example, represents a loss of a part of oneself that to the pregnant woman may have symbolic or real values which pre determine a mourning reaction when the child is delivered. In the elation which may surround the birth, the separation and loss, not only of the baby but also of the position of importance and attention that must be relinquished to it, may be denied. Postpartum depressions, commonly seen several days after the birth and referred to as "the blues," are much more frequent than hospital records suggest.

Old age confronts one with increasing losses concerning the body and its functions. With a rapidity of change similar to that occurring in childhood, the aged person experiences changes in function, if not actual loss, of body parts. Changes occurring in the texture of the skin, in the quality and quantity of the hair, in energy level, and in sexual prowess are all examples of losses which are real and common place. "Change of life," involving loss of ability to have children, may be a particularly painful experience. For reasons of pride, "good taste," or "custom" many of these losses are not to be reacted to openly in our culture. The individual is not given the opportunity to express sadness, for there is a stress on everlasting youth and beauty which makes the realities of aging difficult to accept. "Maturity" may have positive connotations, but "growing old" is usually viewed as a misfortune.

As in the changes occurring in the body, the history of one's relationship with people is replete with experiences of loss and separation. Aside from the dramatic separations brought about through death, most people are constantly experiencing partings and separations, both temporary and permanent. As one passes from childhood into adulthood, friends, lovers, and often family members are separated. Changes in residence, occupation, or place of business often entail separation from associates with whom one has developed strong ties of affection. Even important successes in life—promotion, graduation, marriage—at the same time confront one with separation and loss. Crying at weddings and sentimentality about leaving "the old school" are common expressions of the reality of loss.

Many losses take on importance because of their symbolic meaning, thereby making the reactions to them appear out of proportion to reality. Even the loss of a symptom can be mourned, necessitating as it does the change of self-image which now no longer holds. Not generally recognized is our experience of loss in regard to fantasies and hopes. Loss of a hope may constitute a more significant loss than that of much more tangible possessions. As one becomes older, the awareness of "what could be" or "what might have been" frequently confronts one with the feeling of loss around which there may be unrecognized sadness and grief.

It is natural and normal for individuals who lose a loved one to experience feelings of sadness, loneliness, grief, and perhaps despair. Sometimes the depression may be partially masked by complaints of feelings of weakness, lethargy, poor appetite, inability to sleep, weight loss, physical discomfort, and irritability.

71

It takes time for the mourner to accept and integrate a significant loss and to achieve renewed feelings of optimism, interest, and vitality. Such "working through" often includes efforts to retain a link to the lost person through fond memories, recollections, and perhaps through symbolic representations of the person in the form of preserved possessions. In the course of normal mourning, the mourner may adopt certain mannerisms or characteristics of the dead person, in an unconscious effort to perpetuate the loved one. Such "identification" serves a useful function in adjusting to a profound loss.

However, if feelings of guilt or loss of self-esteem become too prominent in reacting to a loss, there is the possibility that something has interfered with the normal mourning process. This may happen if the mourner is unable to recognize that in the relationship with the lost person there were negative feelings, as well as those of love. Most relationships are characterized by both love and hate (ambivalence), although these feelings may be particularly difficult to accept. When such awareness cannot be tolerated by the mourner, normal adjustment to the loss is more difficult. In the reparative efforts which then occur, the "identification" may be with the loved one's illness rather than with his loving characteristics. The frequency with which certain physical disorders develop after the person has experienced a loss or separation has been explained on this basis by many investigators. Also, when the mourning process goes awry, unusual reactions (anniversary reactions) may be experienced on the anniversary of an event important in relation to the deceased. At such a time, the person is not consciously aware of the temporal relationship between the past event and the present reaction.

Regardless of how effective the mourning process is, adjustment can be made only through the passage of time. Often such events as birthdays, anniversaries, and holidays must be experienced at least once after the loss before adjustment can occur. One by one, once shared occasions or celebrations are experienced without him or her and, in time, permit the gradual withdrawal of emotional investment in the past. The expressions "it will take time" or "time heals all wounds" thus have intrinsic wisdom. Inherent in such expressions is the recognition that a period of mourning is a normal reaction to loss or separation.

If mourning is accepted as an understandable, normal response to loss or separation, it suggests that to some degree we are always in mourning, although not necessarily clinically depressed. Losses, specific and nonspecific, are constantly presenting themselves and must be dealt with, if only on the periphery of our awareness. Because he is constantly experiencing losses, the individual is routinely struggling with the task of integrating them. Mourning is thus a relative and continuous process associated with all events which entail some type of loss, separation, or withdrawal of emotional investment.

What, then, are the implications of this thesis? It would seem that the individual brings to any major crisis a backlog of experience which does not leave him unprepared for integrating a present tragedy. Awareness of the success he has demonstrated in the past should help the individual to recognize the strength and resiliency dormant within him. Likewise, a present reaction may sometimes seem more bearable when it is made explicit that the person who is reacting to recent loss is reacting as he did to previous separations. Frequently, the intensity of such a reaction becomes meaningful only when one understands his earlier losses and separations. Present reactions which may seem unusually intense even to the person himself become more understandable when he realizes that he is reacting not only to the present loss but to earlier losses as well. Increased awareness of the mourning processes which are ever present within one's self can also greatly expand one's capacity for sympathy and compassion for fellow men who are in the more extreme stages of the continuum of mourning. Confronted with the recognition of "the you in me," all people could make mourning a meaningful experience, with both present and future benefits for living.

Lindemann's Studies on Reactions to Grief

ALAN ROSELL

Dr. Erich Lindemann carried on an intensive study of grief based on the experiences of many people who lost relatives or close friends in the unfortunate Cocoanut Grove fire in Boston.

There are four main points which this study tries to clarify:

1. Acute grief is a definite syndrome with psychological and somatic symptomatology.

2. This syndrome may appear immediately after a crisis; it may be delayed; it may be exaggerated or apparently absent.
3. In place of the typical syndrome, there may appear distorted pictures, each of which represents one special aspect of the grief syndrome.
4. By appropriate techniques these distorted pictures can be successfully transformed into a normal grief reaction, with resolution.

The investigation consisted of a series of psychiatric interviews with 101 patients. The records of these interviews were analyzed in terms of symptoms reported, and the observed changes of the mental status throughout the series of interviews.

SYMPTOMATOLOGY OF NORMAL GRIEF

There is a uniform picture seen in persons suffering from acute grief, the most striking characteristics being: (1) a marked tendency to sighing respiration, especially when the patient was made to discuss his grief, and (2) a complaint about lack of strength and a feeling of physical exhaustion, accompanied by such digestive symptoms as inability to eat, repugnance toward food, or abdominal discomfort.

The bereaved may demonstrate a sense of unreality and detachment from others, and there may be an intense preoccupation with the image of the deceased. Feelings of guilt about what they should have done and what they neglected to do for the lost person are common among the bereaved. Often there may be a loss of warmth and friendship for others and a tendency to respond with irritability and anger. These feelings and actions are often disturbing and interpreted by others as a threat of approaching insanity.

The bereaved person often shows restlessness, inability to sit still, aimless movements, and a search for something to do but at the same time displays a lack of initiative. He follows a daily routine but finds it an effort and sees little significance in it. The duration of grief seems to depend upon the ability of a person to readjust to the environment from which the deceased is missing, and upon the formation of new relationships. Some try to avoid the intense distress and the emotional expression of grief. Others are able, as soon as the grief is accepted and the memory of the deceased can be dealt with, to find relief of their inner tensions and hostilities.

MORBID GRIEF REACTIONS

Morbid grief reactions represent distortions of normal grief patterns.

The most common example of this is *delay* or *postponement* of mourning. The person may show little or no reaction to the loss for weeks, months, or even years, if the bereavement occurs at a time when the patient is confronted with important tasks or concerned with maintaining the morale of others. Patients in acute bereavement over a recent death may actually be pre-occupied with grief over a person who died years ago.

In other cases the bereaved may show alterations in conduct of several types as follows:

1. Overactivity without a sense of loss.
2. Acquisition of symptoms belonging to the last illness of the deceased (hysteria or hypochondriasis).
3. A recognized disease of psychosomatic origin; including ulcerative colitis, rheumatoid arthritis, and asthma.
4. Alteration in relationship to friends and relatives with progressive social isolation.
5. Furious hostilities against specific persons, e.g., doctor or surgeon may be bitterly accused of neglect of duties and 'the bereaved may assume foul play has led to the death.
6. Repression of these feelings of hostility and complete absence of emotional display.
7. Lasting loss of patterns of social interaction in cases where there is a lack of decision and initiative.
8. Engaging in activities which are detrimental to his own social and economic existence. Such persons give away belongings, are easily lured into disastrous economic dealings, lose their friends and professional standing and by a series of stupid acts find themselves without family, friends, social status or money.
9. Deterioration into a state of agitated depression with tension,

agitation, insomnia, feelings of worthlessness, bitter self-accusation and obvious need for self-punishment. Such people may be dangerously suicidal.

MANAGEMENT

Proper psychiatric management of grief reactions may prevent prolonged and serious alterations in the person's social adjustment as well as the onset of potential medical disease.

The psychiatrist can be an aid in helping break the bond to the deceased and finding new patterns of rewarding interaction. Although religious precepts are helpful in providing comfort, they do not provide adequate assistance in overcoming the person's grief. The psychiatrist can help the bereaved to accept the pain, review his relationship with the deceased, understand his fears, express his sorrows, verbalize his feelings of guilt and find an acceptable formulation for his future attitude toward the memory of the deceased.*

A Message for the Living

HANS ZINSSER, M.D.

Dr. Hans Zinsser, a prominent bacteriologist, was stricken with leukemia at the peak of his career. Although he lived his remaining months with full knowledge of his condition, he did not at any time diminish his diversified creative activities. A few lines from a series of sonnets written by him during this period are quoted herewith:

---

*From Lindeman, Erich M.D. Symptomatology and Management of Acute Grief. *American Journal of Psychiatry* 101:141–148.

When I am gone—and I shall go before you—
Think of me not as your disconsolate lover;
Think of the joy it gave me to adore you,
Of sun and stars you helped me to discover.
And if at night in dreams my spirit hovers
And shadows of the memorized past enfold you,
A merry ghost will sit upon the covers
And tell again some flippant tale I told you;
Will sing again some long-forgotten song,
Some artless, tender rhyme I wrote about you,
When moments spent with you made sweet the long,
Slow, desolate days and nights I lived without you,
Then all on earth that Death has left behind
Will be a merry part of me within your mind.

Now is death merciful. He calls me hence
Gently, with friendly soothing of my fears
Of ugly age and feeble impotence
And cruel disintegration of slow years.
Nor does he leap upon me unaware
Like some wild beast that hungers for its prey.
But gives me kindly warning to prepare
Before I go, to kiss your tears away.
How sweet the summer! And the autumn shone
Late warmth within our hearts as in the sky,
Ripening rich harvests that our love had sown.
How good that ere the winter comes, I die!
Then, ageless, in your heart I'll come to rest
Serene and proud as when you loved me best.

The little book of sonnets closes with these lines:

How cold your hands are, Death,
Come warm them at my heart.'

REFERENCE

Zinsser Hans: *Spring, Summer and Autumn*. New York: Alfred A. Knopf, 1942.

The Second Time Around: Grief Revisited

AUSTIN H. KUTSCHER

DWELLING PLACES

Lillian lived almost her entire life in Mount Vernon, New York, and Scarsdale, New York—more precisely, in houses in these two communities. During her final year of illness when, for various reasons, she first lived and later was homebound in a New York City apartment, both of us often wondered about the pros and cons, within the context of chronic illness, of living in an urban dwelling place as opposed to a suburban or more rural setting. As the severity of Lillian's illness deepened, this was on our minds from time to time when we thought of the days ahead, if those days were to be her last.

Clearly, it would take less energy to manage the necessities of life in an apartment than in a large suburban house with flights of stairs separating living quarters from kitchen, kitchen from laundry, and so forth. On the other hand, the ease of getting around in the suburbs cannot be equalled in the city unless one travels exclusively by taxicabs, and then one still must contend with the variability of those vehicles, as well as their drivers. Of course, a home is a home is a home, wherever it is. The Medical Center always seemed closer in the city than in the country, although it was not, really—it was just that when we were in the suburbs, the Medical Center was farther away than the community hospital. But still, we missed the open countryside. We mused on these subjects often and at length. I believe that such issues do need to be considered seriously.

DENIAL

In time it became clear that there was no way to return to the house, with all its demands—not for the time being, anyway—even if it would cost significantly less than living in the city.

We were using phrases like "if the days ahead were to be her last" and "for the time being." *Denial*, that oft-cited psychological defense mechanism, served us well indeed. Lillian edited eighty books before her death from breast cancer, including, perhaps, as many as fifty chapters on dying; she was editing a book on chemo-therapy when she died. So what if we did spend nearly all the days of her terminal illness in the denial that permitted or facilitated fun and function? We acknowledged more than enough acceptance to assure that she received any and all forms of treatment that were offered or available. I would not now change one moment of the time spent in denial. Indeed, the denial was highly functional, allowing us the best quality of life possible. It was no game we played, but rather the means of maintaining, to the end, styles of life and work that were both comfortable and comforting.

Denial, it has long seemed to me, has received an undeservedly poor press, both academically and in the news—sufficiently poor, in fact, that Lillian and I both felt that a book on the subject was war-ranted. That project has been set in motion. For the moment, how-ever, I must conclude that even if there were no other reasons for a reconsideration of "denial"—and there are, indeed, many other reasons—it is necessary that Elisabeth Kubler-Ross' theory of the five stages of dying, like all new theories that move us far forward, be re-examined to determine which of its aspects, most notably denial and acceptance, can stand as originally delineated, and which need to be modified or revised.

SUDDEN DEATH DURING A PROTRACTED ILLNESS

The suddenness of Lillian's death, months before any expectation of that event, placed my grieving in a peculiar time frame. Afterward, I pondered the relatively uncharted effects on bereavement of a *sudden death* in the midst of a *prolonged illness*. I was struck by the fact that this kind of death has so many aspects in common with the sudden, unexpected death which—indeed it is. Then, by coinci-dence, Theresa Rando, speaking at our Symposium on Unrecognized and Unsanctioned Grief, described cases of this kind of death and suggested the need to recognize the response to it as an additional and intermediary type of grief. I wholeheartedly endorse her call for such study: I perceive that these deaths are not at all uncommon and, based on my personal experience, I know that the grief they engen-der includes the best and the worst aspects of love and loss encoun-tered in the grief response to both acute death and prolonged dying.

PERSONAL FINANCES

This is a factor in the recovery from bereavement that has not been fully considered. It is discussed, of course, in relation to the needs of the dying patient and the ability to provide the patient with special kinds of care, including loving, tender care. However, there has been little discussion of personal wealth as a factor in anticipatory bereavement and grief. Everyone would guess that it may be somewhat easier to recover if monetary concerns are not of the greatest moment. In all likelihood, that hypothesis is correct, but it leaves unanswered the questions of why various concerns are eased, how they are eased, and how much they are eased by unrestrictive financial resources; it also fails to identify those factors that are not particularly relieved by the availability of those resources. Perhaps a major area for consideration is how deeply the bereaved should delve into his or her financial reserves to obtain the benefits that money secures, as well as when and how doing so might merely be self-indulgent and counterproductive.

RECURRENCE

We have all heard a great deal about how we cope with serial misfortunes and losses. It has often been noted that we do so in the same ways we have found to be successful in coping with previous losses of a similar nature, or at least of comparable consequence. The second time around offered me an opportunity to examine approaches to coping with the *recurrence* of bereavement.

Close scrutiny of recurrence is needed, whether the suffering arises through living under the sword of recurrent disease, from recurrent losses in the normal course of life, or sustaining recurrent losses like those that occur in families with cystic fibrosis or muscular dystrophy. Similarly, we need to examine our approaches to coping with recurrent losses, whether of love or other essential elements in our lives, to determine which of these approaches have or have not stood us in good stead, to attempt to define their particular nature, and to assess the success with which we have employed them.

THE VALUE OF THE HUMAN/COMPANION ANIMAL BOND

After Helene, my first wife, died, twenty-one years before Lillian died, the only future event that I allowed myself to look forward to was the purchase of a puppy. We had been without a dog for some years because of family allergies. However, our allergist approved the purchase of a poodle, and the family spent two months purposefully trying to find one.

80

Hope was her name—a black mini-poodle—and for many reasons she came to be a pivotal factor in my early and ongoing recovery, helping me to regain pleasure in living. Fifteen years later, after Hope and her offspring had died, Lillian and I were living in the New York City apartment with my ninety-year-old mother, whose health was failing. We decided not to get another dog—we would wait until we returned to Scarsdale. It was, again, a case of wishful thinking one moment, denial the next, and reality the next.

After Lillian died and I did buy another mini poodle, Elle; the whole family adopted her. From the time we first saw her in the kennel, and she had picked us out, there remained two weeks before we could bring her home. For all of us, those were weeks of continued grieving, mingled with intimations of anticipation. After she came home, there was little time for "doom and gloom" or prolonged periods of unproductive brooding: there was Elle, always in need—of me, of us, of warmth, of companionship, of play; always a tugging on one's clothes or one's bedspread; always the request to be fed, watered, walked, talked to, or touched; always the need to be loved. How many of the basic needs of the human during grief are just those! Our experience was not only an affirmation of the bond between human and companion animal, but also a demonstration of its appropriateness in regard to recovery from grief.

THE CHRONOLOGY OF LOSSES

Lillian's death preceded my mother's death from her five-year bout with a chronic neuromuscular disease by a little more than four months. There was ample time both before and after Lillian's death to examine the feelings that surface when the normal chronology of death is set upside down. This proved to be a difficult experience of grief, and one that differed from that more commonly encountered, when a young child or an adult child dies before a parent or grandparent. The unreality of this inversion is profound, and the feelings it engenders are difficult to cope with.

DYING AT HOME

Much has been written, and appropriately I am convinced, of the validity of making it possible for a loved one to die at home. Both Lillian and my mother did. Little has been said, however, of the impact of this decision on the immediate and long-range recovery from bereavement in regard to the physical surroundings in which the deaths take place and in which the bereaved intend to continue to live.

THANATOLOGISTS' RESPONSES TO PERSONAL LOSS

Another question is how well so-called *thanatologists* do during their own periods of bereavement and thereafter. For me, this was another issue of recurrence: when my first wife died, I did not know that I would find myself categorized as a *thanolologist* until a major part of the bereavement period had passed. And yet, even then, it was clear that the work of grief and the renewal of loving were remarkably influenced by my work in thanatology—both before and after my remarriage. Would it prove thus again? I believe that the answer has been the same, probably even more so because of the courage of my own accumulated convictions and the learning and teaching experiences of others.

Yes, my coping with Lillian's dying was facilitated, and I have much reason to believe that hers was also. Thus, I would like to conclude that the presumably obvious was, in fact, experienced. Yet this observation turns out to have pertained only to the pre-terminal state of a protracted fatal illness—what if it had gone down to the final hours? And, in contemplating my own death, I am not at all complacent or at all sure that my experience in thanatology will lead me then to early acceptance or a substantially more positive outlook. I have the feeling that when that time comes, I will do my best to make one or another aspect of *denial* functional again. I believe that for those of us who are involved in thanatology, our experience in this field helps us immensely in coping with grief; when it comes to our own dying, I am not nearly so sure.

REMARRIAGE

My recent experience has also reaffirmed the concept of *remarriage* without the loss of profoundly fond and loving remembrances and without ghosts. Considering the myriad emotions that are involved in grieving—depression, denial, loss of control, guilt, anger, and so many others—I firmly believe that the capacity to regain the pleasures of living and loving and the need for companionship are enormously important at both individual and societal levels.

It should not be necessary to wait another generation, or even another decade, before offering those who are grieving society's sanctioned confirmation of the appropriateness of their resumption of any positive aspects of living, that they can muster, especially remarriage.

I often had pause during this "second time around" to ponder again the question of whether or not grief is, indeed, an illness. Definitions should not be allowed to impede reliable studies of this phenomenologic issue. The substance is very real, and the consequences of bereavement are potentially hazardous to individuals' emotional balance, security, and stability, and even to life. The work done thus far on grief and its sequelae in all the contexts of illness, disability, mental disturbance, and other kinds of loss still does not impress me as being adequate either academically or, far more importantly, When viewed from the perspective of the needs and imperative of the bereaved. Considering how wrenching to mind, body, and soul this experience is, and how often many of us must go through the grieving process, is it not essential to know what threats to personal and societal health are inherent in acute grief and bereavement and to learn what to do about these threats?

Perhaps we can finally look further into the beliefs that confuse all too many of the bereaved—beliefs for example, that relate to precise specifications of an appropriate period of grief for the individual beliefs that look askance at "too short" or "too long" periods of bereavement. Although the extrapolation of something akin to the five stages of grief is conceptually useful in our caregiving, we must beware of placing bereaved survivors who are behaving normally in the straitjacket of a rigid time frame of recovery. It may be entirely appropriate for some individuals in *their* specific circumstances to experience the onset of recovery, or even substantive recovery at an earlier date than might be expected. By the same token, it may be just as appropriate for other individuals in *their* specific circumstances only to achieve *"clinical" closure* at a later time than might be expected. My review of the literature indicates that we are not yet flexible enough in this regard. Certainly, one major research area that is in need of support is examination of the time frame of substantive clinical recovery from the loss of love. My best guess is that thorough studies such as Van Pine's will reveal a far broader time range for individuals' overall healthy recovery than is currently believed to exist. With respect to specific aspects of bereavement for specific individuals, it is likely that a far broader spectrum will be found than that which is currently perceived societally or even professionally. It is important to note that, after all, it is society that the bereaved must usually deal with over the long run rather than the professional community. I feel certain that if properly targeted and well-designed studies are performed, we will find healthy patterns of lifetime bereavement that will also force us to revise some of our present beliefs concerning the far end of the time range. I urge particularly that those who have themselves suffered major bereavements be accorded important roles in planning this greatly needed research effort.

PREVENTION

It is almost axiomatic that we only respond to a need when pressed to do so. When a second child or third is killed at an intersection, the community looks into the problem and installs a traffic light to avoid yet another tragedy. Such an approach at traffic control has many of the built-in aspects of prevention. Although prevention is not nearly the "buzz word" that it once was, it is still eminently applicable to all kinds of general health issues and to mental health issues specifically. Prevention is best accomplished through *education* of all persons, beginning in kindergarten and continuing through secondary school and college, as well as through pre-professional professional, and post-professional schooling. It is, after all, the students of today—both children and adults—who will become the caregivers of tomorrow: those whom they will encounter as patients and survivors are also today's students. It is easy to hypothesize that everyone would profit from a common early educational background in thanatologic issues. But no matter how attractive we find the hypothesis about the need for education as a precursor of prevention, it may be difficult to prove. Nevertheless, this task must be addressed, and will require thorough longitudinal studies. [This all sounds strangely familiar as we ponder AIDS education and prevention in the schools. However, the success of AIDS education may well depend on a grounding in thanatology in our schools.]

THE RELATIVE SEVERITY OF DIFFERENT LOSSES

There is great need for formal examination of the *hierarchy-of-losses* and grief, not just as an academic exercise and not just because it is important to determine whether the death of a spouse is more or less traumatic than a bitter divorce and its attendant losses, but because the more we know of the relative extent and magnitude of different losses, the better we should be able to deal with them— what modalities of care, what resources, and what intensity of care and concern would be most appropriate. To be sure, each person and the specific set of circumstances surrounding each loss preclude a uniform approach to all categories of losses, so many of which involve the loss of love. Nevertheless, appropriate approaches to care ought to be available, based on comparative norms of need in relation to loss and grief, as well as responses to different interventions.

FUNDING, STUDY DESIGN, AND THE FUTURE DIRECTIONS OF THANATOLOGY

The first time around the circuit of grief, I compiled twenty-five single-spaced typed pages of issues, fifty issues per page, that I hoped to answer for my own peace of mind—a mind that was just beginning to function in the field. The cataloguing of these questions was important to my grief work, my work on love and loss. It turned out to be among the most effective kinds of grief work—creative grief, as such efforts have come to be known—and from it were born our own efforts in thanatology, both personally and in regard to the Foundation of Thanatology. Since then, two decades of work by countless students of loss and grief and death and dying, so much of it powered by love lost, have shed light on some of these issues. I feel certain that if I had many lifetimes still to work in the field, there would never be an end to the need for approaches to information gathering and research.

Part Two
FUNERALS

Grief and the Meaning of the Funeral

LILLIAN G. KUTSCHER

Both grief and the funeral are components of a sequence of events that follows the death of a loved or significant person. A death provokes emotional reactions among those who have been bereaved and, at the same time, initiates activities which mark it as a community event. Within a limited number of hours after a person has died, principal survivors must observe certain procedures specified by law for the well-being of the community at large; they must conform to the rites and rituals of an ethnic, cultural, or religious nature observed by the smaller community of family and friends; and they must simultaneously take the first painful steps toward the restoration of normal patterns of living.

It is therefore customary for society and the bereaved to respond to a death with activity, despite the paralyzing emotions of acute grief. The nature of this response is shaped by the legal requirements for disposal of the body and by the structured activities which comprise the psychosocial and pragmatic aspects of grief. In most situations, the ceremony of a funeral service, which terminates with the interment or cremation of the deceased's remains, is involved. The funeral then becomes, and gives, a focus and a setting for experiencing one of the most profound and complex of human emotions, acute grief. And it is this emotion that gives functional validity to the funeral, which in and of itself serves as the mechanism for those who mourn the loss to share and ventilate emotions and thoughts with their family, friends, and community.

Preceding, during, and following the funeral rites, the grief reactions are not only respected but also are granted a very special sanction for almost unrestricted expression. Traditionally, society has recognized that the mourners—should be comforted and made to feel that their loss is being shared. A socially supported respite is granted so that the primary mourners the members of the deceased's immediate family circle—may start the processes of replenishing their severely depleted emotional resources, reorganizing their lives, and often assuming new responsibilities. When funeral rituals, whether secular, religious, or humanistic, are acted out, they then serve to reinforce the reality of loss and help to dispel those forms of denial which, if not dealt with appropriately, may result in pathological grief. Dramatic testimony is presented that a death has taken place, that a loss has been sustained, that people are mourning that loss, and that these facts cannot be changed.

This period of acute grief permits the realities of loss to fall into a perspective that relates not only to what has been in the past but also to what will be in the future. As part of the sequence of post-mortem events, the funeral gives the bereaved a kind of "time out" as well as some "time off." In the hours and days of specified activity, temporarily divorced from day-to-day living and working, it relieves the grief stricken from accustomed routines. Orderly memorialization is encouraged, and a creative kind of grief can be fostered which at a later time transforms the energies of sorrow into potentially productive endeavors.

Each funeral serves each grieving individual in its own way; yet all funerals serve a common purpose in satisfying the common needs generated by sorrow. Whatever the circumstances surrounding the death—such as those associated with a long-term chronic illness when the bereaved have had a period of anticipatory grief or those encountered following death through accidental or natural trauma wherein no preparation for acceptance of the loss is available to the bereaved—adjustments to the changes within a family and within a community must be made. In every situation these changes occur: roles are altered for many people; valued and trusted professionals are replaced by other professionals; scenes of activity are shifted to other and often unfamiliar sites.

At the hospital, the home, the church, the funeral home, or the cemetery, each individual confronts a new status quo and a new environment and plays out his own role in accommodation to these. Before the death, the hospital or other institution had attempted to provide a secure and stable setting for moments of hope, perhaps for prayers for cure, and finally, the ultimate in care from physicians, nurses, social workers, clergymen, family members, and friends. Thanatological studies have shown that team effort can, indeed, be most effective in giving therapeutic support to the dying patient and his family. When death occurs, the survivors must seek out a different team; although this group may be from their own cultural, religious, social, or family milieu, it often cannot function as well or be as helpful as the one it replaces. Frequently, the transition is excruciatingly painful. At this time, the survivors must also engage the services of the funeral director who, by virtue of his education, his license, and his experiences, functions as a major member of a new care giving team. His entrance is rarely seen as the useful intermediary step it usually turns out to be; more than likely it is assessed initially as an unwanted, disagreeable intrusion which provokes extreme anxiety.

The funeral director responds to calls for his services at any hour of the day or night. He is with the bereaved at the most shocking moments of intense sorrow and decision making. Physicians, clergymen, and those in the allied health professions are trained to serve the needs of the dying and the living; funeral directors are trained to assist the bereaved with service and counsel, to give guidance during the period of acute grief. The funeral director's role is multifaceted: he is a technician, a coordinator, a counselor, an observer, a comforter, and very often a friend. During hours of turbulence and stress, he is a figure of substance and direction in the lives of the grief stricken. The performance of the ritual of the funeral extends far beyond the rigid enforcement of legalities; and if extraneous trauma can be avoided while realities are faced, the period of acute grief can signal the beginning of restitution for those who have been bereaved.

The process of recovering from bereavement is aggravated by internal conflicts that must be resolved. Harsh memories from the days of illness and suffering, feelings of guilt—classical symptoms which may be experienced during acute grief—should begin to yield to a strong sense of not unremitting loss, then eventually to the acceptance of that loss, and finally to an amelioration of emotional symptoms. What is to be hoped for is not the repression of emotions but their therapeutic expression. From this should develop resolution of both the emotional and practical problems caused by the fracture in the family structure, a constitution of the significant survivors' lives into new patterns, and the emergence of new relationships.

Usually, only those closest to the deceased suffer the crucial components of this experience or comprehend fully through self-involvement the magnitude, intensity, and total pervasiveness of acute grief and the disintegrating impact of the frequently ambivalent emotions which form the essence of the "acute grief syndrome." The balancing effects of objective thoughts from those who are removed from emotional involvement by either relationship or professional distance are important to the bereaved. With concern, knowledge, and all the material symbols and necessities he is capable of providing, the funeral director gives guidance, service, and comfort in a setting that can give meaning to a ceremony and allow for the emotional catharsis so needed in periods of heightened stress. He has elected to serve his community in a specific way; he has succeeded as a professional when his image of himself can be projected meaningfully into therapeutic care giving for those who have been bereaved.

When questions about death and dying, loss and grief, and recovery from bereavement are posed, physicians. psychologists, nurses, social workers, clergymen, funeral directors, philosophers, scholars, and students in many disciplines seem to provide the definitive answers. For almost a decade these workers have tried to stimulate productive thinking about topics which most people try to avoid. Investigating as pioneers in the field of thanatology, they have been able to break down certain of the barriers which have inhibited open discussion of death and aggravated the death-fears of many. They have exposed and opened for examination the ethical and moral issues that a highly sophisticated medical technology has forced families to confront when making decisions for the care of terminal or critically ill members. Terminal illness can strip a patient of every ounce of his dignity; bodily disfigurement can affect the patient, his family, and even hospital staff; the aftermath can bring a plague of additional suffering upon those survivors who are unable to cope with the decision making forced upon them and with the tragedy of bereavement.

Health science professionals seek to serve both honor and integrity, to recognize the rights of all human beings in sickness or health, and to make every effort to preserve the dignity of the person. The average citizen does not involve himself in clinical hypotheses, mainly because he is not oriented in that direction. He is concerned primarily with the realities that affect his own life and those of his intimates—the realities that can disrupt what he has established as the way of life. When he avoids talking and thinking about death and its consequences or avoids preparing for these in practical ways, he is displaying his phobias and surrounding himself with a shield of denial. All too often he refuses to talk about, contemplate, or even go to a funeral. At the time when he is forced to drop his defense mechanisms, he needs all the support that psychosocial insights, scientific information, medical care, and humane care giving can provide for him. In a state of shock, he finds it easier to conform to what is comfortable, comforting, and compatible with his emotional situation than to be a nonconformist. Mourners seek sanctuary in what has been traditional and safe or in those activities or thoughts which can be summoned up for or adapted to their emotional needs from moment to moment.

In conclusion, or by way of introduction, it seems crucial to recall the fundamental thesis that is the core of positive thinking about acute grief and the funeral: as the elements of acute grief are subjected to analysis, the series of events which we generalize as the funeral invariably emerge as central and important. Likewise, as the funeral is analyzed, this event cannot be conceptualized without perceiving that it can never of itself be more than a profoundly effective, but time-limited, event in the larger spectrum of acute grief. However seen or by whom, the funeral appears to symbolize the termination of human relationships while it reinforces the reality of individual and societal evolution.

Acute Grief and The Funeral

RAOUL L. PINETTE

As we begin to consider the complex problem of acute grief and the place or value of the funeral in its resolution, there are a few basic premises that must be acknowledged:

(1) Grief is the emotion experienced by man as a result of a loss or separation.

(2) It is impossible to determine just how much grief an individual has simply by looking at him.

(3) It is unwise and unfair to "specify" how much grief the bereaved should have.

(4) No two persons will suffer from the same intensity of grief or react in exactly the same manner to a loss.

(5) An individual acts and reacts within his own basic personal capabilities and limitations. He must not be expected to perform or display behavior that is outside of this spectrum.

(6) Grief is the strongest emotion suffered by human beings, especially in relation to the loss of a spouse.

(7) The funeral is not only an acknowledgment that a death has occurred, but also a societal proclamation that a life has been lived.

(8) The funeral can be a positive experience when it meet the needs of those who mourn.

(9) The funeral can be an occasion for personal growth.

EMOTIONS

Emotions are responses to stimulation and involve: (a) a mental attitude; (b) physiological stresses and changes; and (c) behavioral phenomena.

92

Emotions can be classified as positive or pleasant in contrast to negative (introverted) or unpleasant.

GRIEF

Grief as an emotion represents a disturbed psychological condition which can be described as disintegrative but which has the potential of acting as a stimulus to future integrations. Grief involves: (a) a disturbed relationship between the individual and the environment; (b) a diffused and hyperactive condition; (c) visceral responses (vasomotor, respiratory, gastrointestinal, glandular, and others); and (d) somatic behavior involving autonomic nervous mechanisms and centers.

To mitigate the effects of grief (emotion) on the bereaved, it would appear that the best response would be to take immediate action to accept the reality of its causative factors and seek emotional support (either social or therapeutic).

REACTIONS TO UNDESIRABLE EMOTIONS

Reactions to undesirable emotions include: (a) the individual tries to escape from the situation by avoiding it either physically or mentally; (b) the individual tries to overcome the situation; and (c) the individual attempts to derive pleasure from what is normally an unpleasant situation.

The last is usually considered to be abnormal by society if it is recognized as such. The second, if successful, obviously can help in adjusting to the situation. The first exists in many disguises and is a very common reaction.

ESCAPE MECHANISMS

Escape mechanisms include: (a) migration—the simplest mechanism of all, literally running away from the situation; (b) rationalization—searching for socially acceptable reasons to cover "loss of face" which might come from simple withdrawal; (c) projection—blaming others for misfortune; and (d) compensation—compensating for personal shortcomings in coping with emotional trauma by diligent application of energies in areas which can give success and gratification. (Such an individual is likely to label the things which he cannot do as not worth doing.)

DENIAL

We live in a youth-oriented society with strong desires to live; few of us wish to grow old or to die, and we do not want others to die either. It is normal to refuse to accept the fact of someone's death and to try to deny that the event has really happened. This denial can create a conflict between the mind and the emotions (with the mind acknowledging the fact and the emotions trying to deny it). The result of this ambivalence, if it is unresolved, can be serious mental or physical disorders or both.

COMPENSATION

There are those who have not resolved their personal anxieties as they relate to death, grief, bereavement, and the resultant funeral. By virtue of feelings of incompetence in this situation, they find it very easy to withdraw by the emotional means of denial and the physical activity of trying to get rid of death by disposing of the body as quickly as possible. Many may seek adjustment and compensation by becoming strong and verbal advocates of disposition without ceremonies or their own personal involvement.

Such approaches may produce relief as a form of response to the discomfort brought about by grief, but this relief for most individuals does not offer a satisfactory and lasting adjustment to grief itself. It often leaves the individual with the problems of adjustment to life without the person who has died, without an effective confrontation with the fact of mortality, or without acceptance of the fact that a significant death has occurred.

INTELLECTUALIZATION OR RATIONALIZATION

There are those who would like to resolve their grief by intellectualization or rationalization. We have already noted that rationalization is an escape and not a solution to the problem. If we approach the problem by intellectualization, we try to resolve it by separating it from its emotional ramifications. It is impossible for most people to achieve intellectual denial of the unpleasantness caused by the emotion, which is accompanied as well by physiological disturbances and aberrant behavioral responses.

Most who turn to intellectualization as a mechanism for resolving grief are simply at the wrong end of this spectrum. It might be possible for some to condition or insulate themselves from emotion before the fact, but once the emotion has been triggered, it must be expressed. For most people, it is too late to intellectualize it. Since our concern is acute grief, the emotion is a fact and the need for expressing it is also a fact. The problem to be concerned with is whether such expression will be constructive or destructive.

DEPTH OF EMOTIONS, EXPRESSION, AND REPRESSION

Depth of emotions, expression, and repression have serious implications for the individual suffering grief. The person with the most serious problem is the one with the capacity for deep emotions who finds it difficult to express them. Therefore, he may repress them until devastating emotional explosions result. If grief is not expressed at the time of the death, it will certainly be expressed later in a more regressive syndrome.

The bereaved need to express their grief, they need a platform to do it on, and they need a means of doing it. Dr. Paul Irion has said that the funeral offers a proper climate for the beginning of the work of mourning. Mourning is the pattern of behavior observable in an individual while he resolves the complex emotion of grief and the many other emotions that accompany it.

ATTITUDES TOWARD THE FUNERAL DIRECTOR

People approach the funeral director with various attitudes:

(a) There are those who have had experience with funerals and understand that they can fulfill the needs of the survivors. Many times they really know how the funeral can help them to express their emotions, to provide a setting for social support and direct confrontation with the fact that a death has occurred, and to assume sanitary disposition of the body. They have seen the funeral function as a first step in the resolution of grief. They approach the funeral director with respect and confidence.

(b) There are those who have not had experience with the funeral but who do have an open mind. They expect the funeral director to counsel with them. They expect him to give them the facts and the courses of action available to them so they can make their own decisions. They also approach the funeral director with respect and confidence.

(c) Dr. Jacques Choron, the late French philosopher, said that a philosophy of life cannot be mature unless it considers the prospect of eventual death of the individual and those around him. There are many people of all ages from every social and educational stratum who have not matured to the point of being willing to think of their own death and to contemplate that of others. When a death occurs, they withdraw into denial and try to ''get rid of it'' as quickly as possible. Many such persons seek all sorts of means of escape from confrontation with the truth. They try actively to rationalize their denial and withdrawal by deriding the funeral and the funeral director. Counseling is very difficult. The funeral director is viewed as the symbol of the death they are denying. They find him threatening and resent his person and presence.

(d) There are those who have not had experience with the funeral but have been exposed to a multitude of rationalizations, intellectualizations, pseudo-experts, and universal formulas, and who have taken a strong position against the funeral. They approach the funeral director as the symbol and merchant of death, expecting him to take advantage of them, distrusting what he says and does, and unwilling to accept his counsel.

(e) There are those who have had a bad experience with a previous death for one reason or another. Counseling these individuals may present problems.

NEGATIVE THOUGHTS

- Funerals are barbaric—most barbarians viewed their dead and cared for them with ceremony. Would it be an acceptable criterion of civilization to have less respect for the dead than pagan societies did or than primitive communities have today?
- Viewing is pagan—where is this thought expressed in the great books formulating religious doctrines or in the writings of those who have studied the psychological needs created by bereavement today?
- Funerals and everything to do with them are morbid—this is said very often by those who have never even been to a funeral. Regarding something as morbid can be a frame of mind, an attitude; ''morbid'' is never a synonym for ''sorrowful.''
- Funerals are too elaborate or too extravagant—who has the right to judge the actions of others? Those who need less elaborate funerals should have less elaborate funerals. Those whose needs call for the total funeral also have a right to have their needs fulfilled. It should be recognized that there are certain

basics in a funeral to meet certain individual emotional needs just as there are basics in consuming food to meet certain physical needs.

- Funerals are too expensive—some say categorically that funerals are too expensive. If one is not familiar with the positive values of a funeral, such a statement is easy to make, especially when "expensive" is not defined. If the funeral helps meet the needs of the survivors and it becomes an experience of value for them, how much is it really worth?

SOME POPULAR ESCAPE MECHANISMS

The Closed Casket

What better way is there to run away from death than to have a closed casket and not look at the dead person at all, unless one has seen the person die or viewed him in solitude? Regardless, the closed casket is a very convenient manner of withdrawing into denial. Whether the denial is conscious or subconscious is irrelevant. As long as it is allowed to persist, it could be unhealthy.

Dr. Erich Lindemann, when questioned after his many years of involvement in research on grief as to what was the most important moment for the survivors, said that it was the moment of truth when the survivors would stand in front of the open casket and look at the dead body. This visual confrontation by the survivors is the most effective manner of combating denial.

There are some who have an endless number of reasons why it is improper to look at the body. They say that it is pagan, that the embalmer makes the body look alive to conceal death. The only way of concealing death effectively is to make the person truly alive. The embalmer is obviously incapable of such a feat. The embalmer does not even try to make a body look alive, he simply tries to make it look lifelike in order to give the survivors a better image than the death mask by which to remember the deceased.

Many persons die of ravaging illness or from violence. At death their appearance is most disturbing for the survivors. First and final impressions are lasting, especially if the final one is traumatic. Unless something is done to present these survivors with a more acceptable or consoling image to remember the person by, they may be shocked by a haunting visual image. To believe that the survivors will be able to cast aside a traumatic confrontation in favor of a previous familiar image is in most instances naive.

No Visitations

There are some who feel that the period of visitations is a hardship for the survivors, an ordeal. Again, some use "no visitations" as an escape, a way to avoid the aftermath of death. But visitations give relatives and friends an opportunity to share their concern for the survivors and also to express their own grief. Appropriate conversation comes more easily there. It is axiomatic that joy shared is joy augmented, and grief shared is grief diminished. We must remember that there is nothing worse than going through a crisis alone.

There is a principle in psychology that says that for emotions to adjust properly to a nonrepetitive event, it must be accompanied by repetitive behavior. When the family stands next to an open casket and the visitors come, the conversation will center repeatedly around the deceased and the circum stances of the death. This constitutes repetitive behavior accompanying a nonrepetitive event, a death. These repetitive conversations also help to re lease pent-up emotions, a process known as catharsis.

Instead of visitations with the viewable body present, some recommend "no visitations" at a funeral home and that the family receive people at home. If the family separates itself from the body in this manner, relevant conversation becomes stultified. The visitors will not be prone to talk about the deceased, and the family may not get the necessary catharsis.

No service, either religious or nonreligious, should be a way of getting things over quickly. It could very well be that a short-term gain carries with it long-term negative consequences. Rites and ceremonies are like buffers against change. With the death of a loved person, the life of the closest survivor changes. It seems unwise to eliminate any buffer against such abrupt changes.

No Committal Service

There are people who do not want to go to the cemetery for the committal. They say the funeral should end at the funeral home or at the church. Committal prayers may or may not be made. There are many students of grief who believe that for those with a strong inclination toward denial, seeing the last station, the casket on the grave, may be helpful in dispelling this denial.

In the words of Paul Irion, "The committal service provides, as nothing else. does so graphically, a symbolic demonstration that the kind of relationship which has existed between the mourner and the deceased is now at existed between the mourner and the deceased is now at an end.

Limited Funerals

There are some who would limit the number of cars at the funeral. They say that a long funeral procession can be a traffic hazard. What greater hazard is there than a number of cars racing separately to the cemetery, trying to be there on time, with many drivers not knowing where the cemetery is and where the grave is within the cemetery. The safest way to get the people from the services to the cemetery is in a funeral procession.

Who really has the right to dictate how many people should or should not grieve and how many should be accorded the right to express their grief through the funeral? Much has been cited about constitutional rights of expression on television and radio, in the newspapers, and in the public square. Throughout history when people have done something important, they get together, proclaim its importance, and express themselves by means of a ceremonial parade. Funerals serve as such an avenue of expression and have been throughout history the most dignified and most solemn of all ceremonial processions. The number of marches on city halls, college presidents' offices, public monuments, or what have you these days exemplifies that the social need for parades is still here, even in our own culture.

It is interesting to see how some will object to a few cars at a funeral but will not object to the hundreds of cars entering and leaving a shopping center or the thousands of cars leaving a race track or a ball game.

PERSONAL REACTIONS

Five factors that will influence one's reaction to a death are: (a) personality; (b) depth of emotion; (c) ability for emotional expression or repression; (d) structure of values; and (e) importance of deceased to survivor.

SOCIAL NEEDS

Six social needs have been documented as being constant in all cultures when death occurs: (a) social support; (b) confrontation; (c)

99

rites and ceremonies; (d) procession; (e) sanitary disposition of the body; and (f) payment of some form.

WHAT IS A FUNERAL?

Dr. William Lamers, Jr., a psychiatrist, has defined a funeral as "an organized, purposeful, time-limited, flexible, group-centered response to death." With the studies that have been made recently we must add "with the body present" if the survivors are to derive all the benefits of the funeral.

WHAT DOES A FUNERAL DO?

A funeral must: (a) fulfill the needs of the survivors; (b) be a tribute to a life; (c) leave a recall image to assist the grief-resolution process.

We have already discussed the values of the recall image. The funeral must fulfill the particular needs of the family on this particular occasion. The funeral should be flexible. Since a person's reaction to death is influenced by a number of personal and social factors and the same person will not necessarily react in the same manner on different occasions of death, there should not be any universal formula for the funeral.

The funeral does not say, "John has died." You do not need a funeral to pronounce this as a fact. You just say it. However, the funeral does say, "John lived." It says that he lived a life so important that people have taken time out from their busy schedules, to acknowledge it and to pay tribute to it. The funeral is a tribute to a life.

ELEMENTS OF A FUNERAL

What does the funeral include? The funeral has five ritualistic elements: (a) visitations or wake; (b) viewing; (c) rites and ceremonies; (d) procession; and (e) committal.

THE FUNERAL DIRECTOR

From his studies and his experiences the funeral director knows: (a) that the funeral has evolved in response to human needs and the basic social and personal needs of the bereaved; (b) that the funeral is a time-tested vehicle for the expression, recognition, and resolution of grief; (c) that there are dangers of repression or denial and possible repercussions if shortcuts are taken; (d) that there is no eraser on the pencil of the funeral—there is no second chance; (e) that the funeral as a tribute to a life must be right the first time; (f) that the funeral can be made effective as a vehicle for the expression of grief for those who tend towards emotional repression; and (g) that the funeral can be a first step towards rebuilding a sense of security.

The funeral director wishes to help the bereaved by providing the expertise, facilities, and merchandise for a funeral. He wants to share his understanding and his experience with his clients. He knows that his sincere efforts shall be interpreted by some as exploitation, but he must have the courage of his convictions and counsel with the people. After the bereaved have been told of the choices available to them and of the consequences of certain requests, he must and will serve them according to their wishes.

ACTUAL EXPERIENCES WITH THE FUNERAL

A widow received great consolation form the large number of people who showed up for the visitations, the church services, and the committal services for her husband. She said that she knew how she had loved him and how wonderful he was, but had never imagined that so many other people loved him and appreciated him that much. Had she not had the traditional funeral for her husband she would never have found out.

A mother who found her baby dead in the crib did not want to remember the horrible sight of the dead, cyanotic infant. After the funeral she was grateful that her baby could be viewed as beautiful as she had been in life and could be remembered that way.

A doctor whose wife had died of brain cancer was afraid of what he might see in the casket. He received great consolation from seeing a peaceful expression restored to her face and the traces of her suffering removed.

A woman who died of cancer of the face had not been seen for several months without a veil covering half of her face. She had lost much weight, and the husband wanted the casket kept closed. The embalmer performed his services, and the husband and his two teenage daughters were called in to view the results. One daughter said, "Thanks, Dad, for having had this done. We had forgotten how pretty mother was."

WHEN THE FUNERAL IS OVER

Some of the needs of the survivors for catharsis, for expression—personal, social, religious, or nonreligious—have been served.

The family has been helped to return to productivity because there were things to do, there were decisions to be made, there were people to meet. These activities help prevent withdrawal and internalization, which can result in an extended period of severance from normal productivity.

The importance of the life of the person they loved has been proclaimed, and tribute paid to it through the funeral.

On occasion, the funeral has offered the survivors an opportunity to purge themselves of some negative emotions, such as guilt. The question of whether there should or should not be guilt at this time when nothing helpful can be done on behalf of the deceased, whether the bereaved is or is not guilty, is irrelevant. The point is that if the survivor is stuck with a guilt complex, and if he can resolve it through the funeral (as is often the case), then he will be healthier in the future. Since we serve the living through the funeral, these are the kinds of needs to which we must also address ourselves.

WHAT HAS BEEN ACCOMPLISHED BY THE FUNERAL?

The funeral director, in most instances in cooperation with the clergy, has led the survivors by the hand over the turbulent waters of a crisis, with the funeral as a bridge, back to the mainstream of life. He can serve well as a true "crisis intervenor."*

*This chapter is reprinted from *Grief and the Meaning of the Funeral*, O.S. Margolis et al (eds.). New York: MSS Information Corp., 1975.

The Funeral Service

ELIZABETH L. POST

No matter how much in advance a family knows of an impending death, and no matter how prepared they may think they are, the shock is, nevertheless, devastating when the event occurs. At this time etiquette performs a most valuable service by easing the tensions inherent in the necessary personal contacts and by assuring that all the details of the last rites will be carried out with the utmost dignity and beauty. By providing an established guide, etiquette relieves the bereaved family of the burden of a multitude of decisions.

IMMEDIATE STEPS

At the time of bereavement, when the family stands baffled and alone, it is of immeasurable help if a very close friend or a relative, who is not a member of the immediate family, is willing to take charge of the funeral arrangements. Those closest to the deceased are generally in a highly emotional state and may rush, or be pushed, into decisions which they regret later. If no such person is available, the responsibility usually falls on a son or a brother of the deceased. Because of the close relationship, this may be a cruel experience, and he must exercise tremendous self-control.

When the death occurs, those members of the immediate family who are not present should be notified. This is done by telephone, or, if the expense of many long-distance calls is too great, by telegram. One or two intimate friends may also be called in order to enlist their aid. If the illness has been a long one and a trained nurse is in attendance, she may be induced to turn her ministrations from the one she can no longer help to those who have a real need for her.

If a physician has been in attendance, he immediately fills out and signs a death certificate. In cases of sudden or accidental death, when no physician has been present, the county medical examiner or the coroner must be notified immediately. No other steps may be taken until the death certificate is properly signed.

If the family does not know which funeral home to call, the church or synagogue office will be able to help with the selection. The doctor in attendance will also provide such information. If the illness has been of some duration, this question will undoubtedly have been dealt with beforehand.

The funeral director arrives at the house as soon as possible after he is called. Whoever is in charge for the family should discuss all the arrangements with him, including how elaborate a funeral the family wishes or can afford and how each detail is to be handled. The family's clergyman must be consulted before the day and hour of the funeral service are set. He may also help in deciding whether the service should be held in the church, in the funeral home, or in the deceased's home. If the deceased has died at home, the funeral director will remove the body after this meeting.

The newspapers should be notified immediately, so that friends who are not called personally will know of the death and the funeral arrangements. If the family lives in the suburbs, the newspapers of the nearest large city, as well as the local papers, should carry the notice. There is a fee for items in the obituary column. The only exception is when the newspaper considers the deceased prominent enough to run an additional column as a news item.

The notice may be telephoned to the papers by the person in charge of funeral arrangements or by the funeral director. The following information should be included:

1. Name of deceased and date of death.
2. Names of immediate family.
3. Place and time of funeral.
4. Hours for visiting if family wishes to receive.
5. A request that donations be sent to a particular charity in lieu of sending flowers, if desired by the family.
6. Specific directions, such as "Funeral Private" or "Burial Private."

In the obituary notice, the name of the wife or husband always follows that of the deceased. If he or she was unmarried, the parents' names come first. Otherwise, they are not usually mentioned. The age of the deceased is not noted except occasionally, as in the case of a young child.

When the words "Funeral Private" appear in the paper, those friends who are welcome are notified of the details by telephone or by note. This duty is also the responsibility of the person in charge of the funeral arrangements, but he will, of course, consult the bereaved family as to whom they would like to have present.

These instructions are important, especially in the case of a well-known person whose family might otherwise be deluged with flowers they did not wish to receive or whose funeral, if not private, might become a spectacle for the idle or curious. It is a severe breach of etiquette to ignore the requests made in the obituary notice.

A typical notice might read:

FAIRBANKS, John Carl, on April 4th, 1989. Beloved husband of Mary Krebbs Fairbanks, devoted father of Ellen Fairbanks Jones, brother of William Fairbanks. Reposing at Carter Funeral Home, 7 Mill Lane, Oakdale, Wednesday and Thursday from 4 P.M. to 8 P.M. Funeral Friday at 11 A.M. In lieu of flowers, please send donations to Cancer Care, Inc.

At some time, an attorney, preferably the one who drew up the will of the deceased, should be notified. If he is not available, any reputable lawyer who is known to a friend or to a member of the family may be called.

THE CLOTHING FOR BURIAL

The selection of clothing for the deceased can be a heart-rending experience for a husband, wife, or parent. The closest relative should be consulted so that a favorite dress may be chosen, or a special color or style preference may be honored, but the physical act of taking out the clothes and delivering them to the funeral director should be done by someone less intimately connected with the deceased, perhaps the one in charge of arrangements.

Members of certain faiths, notably orthodox Jews and some conservative Jews, bury their dead, as they have for centuries, in shrouds. There are no set rules for others, but certain costumes are in better taste than others. Women's dresses should be in solid, subdued colors of a style that might be worn to church. Black is not appropriate. Young girls may be dressed in white, but their church clothes in soft colors are equally correct. Men are dressed in conservative suits such as those they might wear to church. Cutaways were used frequently in the past, but few men own one nowadays. Generally, only those in public life are buried in such dress.

A woman should wear no jewelry except her wedding ring.

EMBLEM OF MOURNING ON THE DOOR

When a family wishes flowers hung on the door as a symbol of mourning they either order them from their florist or request the funeral director to order them. White flowers are used for a young person, purple for an adult. If the expense of flowers is more than the family can afford, the funeral director may hang streamers on the door—white for a child, black and white for a young person, black for an older person. The flowers or streamers are removed by an employee of the funeral home before the family returns from the service.

HONORARY PALLBEARERS

Honorary pallbearers are chosen from among a man's closest friends, or if the circumstances warrant it, from his political or business associates. There are never fewer than four, and there may be as many as ten or twelve. A member of the family, or the person in charge after consultation with the family, calls or telegraphs those chosen. It is obligatory that they accept unless there is an extremely valid reason for refusal. Members of the immediate family are never chosen as pallbearers because the family should remain together as a single support unit through the service and interment.

Although Jews use pallbearers for both men and women, Christians use them only for men. Their duties are, as the name implies, mostly "honorary." In past times, pallbearers actually carried the casket. Today, this is done by trained men from the funeral parlor. If the casket is already in the front of the church when the funeral begins, the honorary pallbearers sit down in the front pews on the left of the aisle. If there is a procession, they precede the casket, walking two by two. After the service, they leave in the same way, directly in front of the casket if it is removed at that time. They generally accompany the family to the cemetery.

USHERS

Ushers may be chosen in addition to, or in place of, pallbearers. Although funeral directors will supply men to perform the task, it is infinitely better to select men from the family (not immediate) or close friends who will recognize those who come and seat them according to their closeness to the family. When there are no pallbearers, the ushers sit in the front pews on the left and precede the coffin at the end of the service as the pallbearers would. If there are pallbearers, the ushers remain at the back of the chapel.

106

FLOWERS FOR A FUNERAL

When the sender knows the family but was not personally acquainted with the deceased, he sends flowers to the home address of the individual he knows best or to the next of kin of the deceased. Otherwise, flowers are addressed "To the funeral of John Doe" and sent either to the church or funeral home. A calling card, or a plain card with the sender's name, is enclosed. On those sent to a member of the family, one writes "With deepest sympathy," "With love and sympathy," or whatever is most appropriate.

A member of the family of the deceased, or a close friend, should be appointed to take charge of the flowers, cards, and condolence messages. The simplest way to keep an accurate record is to write on the envelope a description of the flowers that come with the card. This is sometimes done by the florist. Without such a notation, the family has no way of knowing who has sent what. Such descriptions make possible a much more personal note of acknowledgment.

At a Protestant funeral, a close friend or a relative generally goes to the church an hour or so before the funeral to help the florist or a member of the church staff arrange the flowers. The wreaths and arrangements are placed at the direction of the family friend, who sees that those sent by relatives are given the most prominent positions. The sexton of the church usually collects the cards and notes the varieties of flowers, as mentioned above. He gives these to the friend of the family for delivery to the one in charge of all the flowers and cards.

Catholics usually prefer Mass cards as a "spiritual bouquet" for the Catholic family. Arrangements may be made through any priest, who will accept a donation for the church, for a Mass to be said for the deceased. A card is sent to the family, giving the hour and location of the Mass and the name of the donor. Flowers may be sent to the church or the funeral home. From there they are usually taken to the cemetery.

AT THE FUNERAL HOME

The body of the deceased usually remains at the funeral home until the day of the funeral. In many ways it is preferable that the family receive their friends there, rather than at home. It relieves them of any need to do extra "housekeeping," and the facilities for accommodating a number of people at once are available.

The hours during which someone will be there to receive visitors are included in the newspaper death notice. Those who are mere acquaintances, but would like to pay their respects, may stop by and sign the register provided by the funeral parlor. The family need not thank each caller by letter, but whenever a special effort has been made, they will undoubtedly wish to do so. Friends from out of town may call on the family after the service or visit with them briefly beforehand.

THE FUNERAL SERVICE

Some people find the thought of leaving the seclusion of their home to attend the funeral service more than they can bear, but others find that the ritual and dignity of a church service is a source of great comfort. Choir and organ music bring serenity to some, and the mere act of having to face outsiders helps others to maintain their composure. The widow, or person closest to the deceased, must decide whether these considerations are more important than the comfort and privacy of a funeral at home.

The front pew, or pews, on the right of the center aisle of the church are reserved for the family of the deceased. As the hour of the service approaches, the congregation arrives, seating themselves wherever they wish or, at a large funeral, being escorted in by the ushers. Closest friends generally take, or are led to, seats in the front near the family. At Jewish services, the coffin is closed. Protestants and Catholics may prefer to have the casket open. At Protestant funerals the casket is often covered by a blanket of flowers or several floral pieces. The coffin of a military man may be covered with the American flag. The field of stars is placed at the head and over the left shoulder of the deceased. The flag is removed before the casket is lowered into the grave. The processional is generally seen only at very large funerals or those of prominent people. Instead, the coffin is placed on a stand at the foot of the chancel a half hour or so before the service. The members of the family do not walk down the aisle but enter from the vestry or from the room where they have gathered just before the appointed hour.

Should the family decide on a processional, the order is as follows: the minister; visiting or assisting clergymen; the choir (if choral music is desired); honorary pallbearers, two by two; the coffin; the family. The chief mourners walk first with whichever other member of the family can be of the most comfort. Other members of the family walk two by two, with whomever they wish.

When the procession reaches the end of the aisle, the members go to their appointed places. The professional pallbearers, supplied by the funeral home, walk quietly to their stations on the side aisles.

After the service, the procession leaves in the same order in which it has entered, but the choir remains in its place.

When there is no processional or recessional, the rest of the family departs through the same door they came in and enter the cars waiting to take them to the cemetery. The casket is taken to the hearse by the professional pallbearers after the congregation leaves the church. If there are many flowers, they may be put into a limousine and taken to the cemetery to be placed around the grave before the hearse and the funeral party arrive.

Frequently, a male member of the family stands at the back of the church and thanks those who have attended the funeral. It is a difficult task which should be entrusted to someone of great composure.

THE HOME FUNERAL

A house service is easier in many ways than the church funeral. The family may remain secluded in an adjoining room with no need to mask their sorrow. The familiar surroundings are a source of comfort for many people.

If music is desired, excellent recordings of organ and choir music are available from the funeral director.

The coffin is placed in front of a mantel in the largest room. If there is no fireplace, it is placed in the center of one wall. The funeral parlor provides the stand and also the folding chairs.

Women wear hats, as they would at a church funeral, and keep their coats on. Men remove their overcoats and carry them on their arms and their hats in their hands.

THE SERVICE IN THE FUNERAL HOME

The service held in the funeral home falls between the formality of the church service and the intimacy of the home service. The chapels are often very dignified and provide a religious atmosphere that the home cannot. There are convenient reception rooms where the family may receive close friends, and often there is an alcove to one side of the chapel where the family can sit in privacy. One may ask for one's own clergyman, or the funeral director will assist in contacting one of the faith requested.

AT THE CEMETERY

Ordinarily only the immediate family and closest friends of the deceased attend the burial. If the deceased was a prominent person, a long line of cars filled with admirers or constituents sometimes follows the hearse to the cemetery, but, nowadays, at a private funeral, only those closest to the deceased are expected to witness the interment.

CREMATION

Cremation is often preferred by those whose religions sanction it. The service is the same as that preceding the burial, and the family may, if they wish, accompany the body to the crematorium. If so, a short service is held there, similar to that conducted at a gravesite.

The ashes may be disposed of according to the wishes of the deceased. Often the urn is buried in a special section of the churchyard or graveyard, or it may be buried in the family plot.

CHURCH FEES

The clergyman never asks for a fee for his services, but the family is expected to make a contribution to the church as a token of appreciation. The amount depends entirely on the size of the funeral and the financial circumstances of the family.

A bill is rendered by the sexton to cover other church expenses.

ACKNOWLEDGMENT OF SYMPATHY

If the deceased was a prominent person or was closely related to a person in public life, hundreds of messages of condolence may be received. In this case, engraved or printed cards of acknowledgment may be sent to those who are strangers:

The family of
Harrison L. Winthrop
wish to thank you for
your kind expression of sympathy

A handwritten word or two and a personal signature must be added when there is a personal acquaintance with the sender. In no circumstances may a printed card be used to thank those who have sent flowers or close friends who have written personal letters.

A handwritten message on notepaper is preferable to the most beautifully engraved card. It only takes a moment to write "Thank you for the beautiful spray of carnations... ... Thank you for your kind expression of sympathy," or "Thank you all for your kindness . . ." Nor does it take much longer to add "Your sweet letter meant so much" or "We were so strengthened by your wonderful letter."

If the list of people who must receive acknowledgments is unduly long, or if the person to whom the flowers and messages were addressed is too distraught to do the writing, one or more members of the family or a close friend may write for him:

"Mother (or Father, or Grandmother) asks me to thank you so much for the beautiful chrysanthemums. We all join her in our appreciation of your kind expression of sympathy."

No more than that is expected, but the message should be personal and written by hand.

MOURNING CLOTHES

No changes in etiquette have been more drastic over the last twenty-five years than those concerning the wearing of mourning attire. Years ago the regulations were prescribed exactly, according to the closeness of the mourner to the deceased. One was expected to wear a certain degree of mourning for a certain length of time assign of respect. This attitude has changed completely, and we have come to realize that wearing black clothing and displaying an air of tragedy and martyred resignation have little to do with our innermost feelings.

An increasing number of people today do not believe in going into mourning at all. There are some who believe, as do the religions of the East, that, instead of mourning an earthly loss selfishly, great love should be expressed by rejoicing in the rebirth of the loved one's spirit. Few not brought up in those religions can attain such an entirely selfless attitude. Most simply do their best to keep occupied, make their adjustments to living without the loved one, and avoid casting the shadow of sadness on those around them. The sooner the bereaved can turn his thoughts away from his pain and resume an active life, the better. Mourning is a continual reminder of loss;therefore, it can only delay the return to normal living.

A WIDOW'S MOURNING

There are still many wives, especially among the older generation, who do want to wear mourning attire for a time, either as a sign of respect for the deceased or as a protection against intrusion into their private grief. Six months is the maximum length of time a young widow should wear deep mourning. An older woman might continue to do so for a year, but this is very unusual. A more practical method is to buy black clothes appropriate for the season of the year and when the season changes return to regular clothing. This is reasonable because it avoids the expense of a second mourning wardrobe.

Even during first, or deep mourning, unrelieved black should not be worn to work. This evidence of innermost feelings has no place in the impersonal world of business. If the widow wishes to wear black or gray, it should be relieved with a touch of white or soft color. No matter what she wears at other times, she will never be criticized for wearing her ordinary wardrobe at work.

Deep mourning should also be set aside when the widow is indulging in any sport. For golf, tennis, swimming, or whatever she enjoys, she wears the appropriate costume of a conservative style and color.

When a widow is asked to be a bridesmaid, she wears the same clothes as the rest of the bridal party.

When a woman becomes interested in another man—and there is no reason that she should not—she leaves her mourning aside. Wearing mourning for other than a husband or wife has become so rare that it is hardly worth discussing. Suffice it to say that one season—two or three months—would be the maximum period of mourning for a sister, a brother, a parent, or a child.

MOURNING FOR MEN

Wearing a black armband, a black tie, and black socks with regular suits is so easy and so inexpensive that some men choose to do so when mourning the death of a wife. However, as in the case of a bereaved woman, it is entirely up to the individual. In any event, he restricts the length of time to a few months, although he may continue to wear a black tie for a year.

THE BEHAVIOR OF THE FAMILY AFTER THE FUNERAL

The sooner the life of the family returns to normal after the funeral, the better. The many things that must be attended to may seem like insurmountable burdens, but the necessity of taking prompt and proper care of them and of having to turn one's thoughts to others is a great help.

A letter of thanks must be written to the clergyman in appreciation of his services. The pallbearers and others who also performed some service must be thanked. The gifts of flowers or contributions in lieu of flowers must be acknowledged and each handwritten note of condolence answered.

The return of the family of the deceased to an active social life is, like the wearing of mourning, up to each individual. As soon as he (or she) feels up to it, a person who has lost a husband or wife may start to see friends and go to their homes, to attend movies, sports events, classes, and meetings. For a few weeks, he will prefer to stay away from dances and parties, and he will surely be criticized if he does not do so. He must, however, continue to pursue his career or fulfill his duties if he is in public life, no matter what sort of appearances it may entail.

A man or a woman may start to have dates when he or she feels like it, but for a few months they should be restricted to evenings at home or with friends, or movies, theaters, and other inconspicuous activities.

Young children are never put into mourning attire. They wear their church clothes to a funeral; otherwise they wear the clothes they would wear ordinarily. They should return to school, participate in their regular activities, and attend after-school entertainments after the day of the funeral.

Older children do not wear any sign of mourning but may choose to stay away from school for a few days. They should be able to take part in all school activities as soon as they return and should resume their ordinary amusements. For two or three weeks after the death of a parent, however, they might want to avoid dances, proms, and large parties.

MEMORIALS

Many bereaved families wish to make a material gesture to honor their dead. For the wealthy, this may take one of many forms, from the erection of a monument to the donation of a piece of equipment to the hospital that cared for the deceased. This type of memorial does not call for a great deal of discussion here because its very nature requires that it be considered carefully, and that time will be necessary for extensive planning before it can be done. The advice of other people will be involved, and that will put an automatic restraint on those who might otherwise go emotionally overboard.

Most of us, however, are not in a position to provide an enormously expensive memorial, and the gravestone we choose for our loved one is the only permanent memorial that will exist. The stone, therefore, and the inscription on it, should be chosen with great care. The worst mistake one can make is to rush into ordering an ornate stone with sentimental carvings and a flowery inscription which may later seem in poor taste or objectionable. For example, one might wish, in the emotion of the moment, to write something about the deceased being "the only love," or "the greatest love" of the spouse. This could conceivably cause considerable anguish to a future husband or wife.

The wisest course is to choose as handsome a stone as one can afford and to refrain from excessively ornate decoration. Almost invariably, the simplest constructions—be they monuments, buildings, or any work of art—are those which endure and continue to please forever. The inscription, too, should be simple. "Beloved husband of" expresses true devotion without excluding other members of a present or future family.

Whatever is chosen, one should remember that the feelings of the living must be considered. The memorial is something which will be seen and shared with others, and surely the one who has died would prefer a memorial that could be both an honor to him and a solace to those he leaves behind.

The Condolence Call

REGINA FLESCH

OUR CHANGING CUSTOMS

At no time are we so indifferent to the social world and all its code as when we stand baffled and alone at the brink of unfathomable darkness into which our loved one has gone. The last resource to which we would look for comfort at such a time is the seeming artificiality of etiquette. Yet it is in the hours of deepest sorrow that etiquette performs its most real service. All set rules of social procedure have for their object the smoothing of personal contacts,and in nothing is smoothness so necessary as in observing the solemn rites accorded to our dead.

These words of Emily Post show a profound understanding of custom worthy of an anthropologist. Every system of society has developed social procedures regarding the ceremonies of birth, marriage and death which bind the individual to the group, emphasizing that he is, indeed, a social being. In more rigidly structured societies, as in some primitive cultures, appropriate behavior for the bereaved and for other members of the group is prescribed by ritual. There is an article by Edmund Volkart and Stanley Michael about the Ifaluk people, who obey the custom of showing visible pain upon the death of a family member.[10] Their display of distress coincides with the funeral, and, also by custom, disappears as soon as the funeral is over. Various interpretations are offered by students of social life for this highly ritualized response to death. Whatever interpretation one accepts, the paths of both the bereaved and participants in the funeral seem to be made easier through these dictates for appropriate behavior.

Formerly, in our Western civilization, there were, among certain groups some approximations of highly ritualized behavior connected with mourning; some of these customs still are maintained in various forms. The traditional Irish wake and funeral required strict adherence to an established pattern, down to the actual words and wailing which followed the corpse to the grave.[2] Participants in this kind of funeral came back to the house for food and drink after the funeral. In this Irish society, a bereaved family must have felt a close tie to the group which provided so dignified an expression to their grief. The public display of grief by the bereaved, accepted as it was by the group, would diminish the need for withdrawal and concealment of emotion by the bereaved.

Orthodox Jews also follow rigidly described behavior for the bereaved after the funeral. According to orthodox Jewish custom,the bereaved family sits together for seven full days and nights (shiva), an open practice which makes virtually impossible the hiding of private grief. To these orthodox mourners, custom dictates not only what the bereaved should say and do, but also what greeting their callers should use when they come to express their sympathies to the bereaved. An English student of mourning, the anthropologist

Geoffrey Gorer, believes that these strict rituals are profoundly useful to bereaved families and sympathizers and that their disappearance from contemporary British and American society is a serious loss.[4]

The breakdown of custom concerning funerals and mourning is attested at almost any funeral today, where somber garments, for instance, frequently are replaced by clothing acceptable at any other social function. Books of etiquette have very little specific advice about appropriate behavior for either the bereaved or friends at this crucial time. There appears to be a general agreement that a condolence call is obligatory after a death in the family of a friend, but close reading of the text leaves a strong impression that the call should be made and terminated as quickly as possible.[9] Precisely what the caller should say or do on these occasions remains unspecified, as the bereaved family frequently appears to delegate to a friend the task of meeting callers. Close and sympathetic contact between the bereaved and their social group, as exemplified in the Irish wake and the orthodox Jewish shiva, is not fostered, to say the least, by our current customs.

This throws the mourner back upon his own resources, to find his own way, at a time when his resources are most depleted by his grief. What is needed, of course, is a period of time for a "formal withdrawal from society, a period of seclusion, and a formal re-entry into society."[4]

The absence of ritual obliges us to develop understanding, so that the complex feelings of bereavement and mourning may not create obstacles to comfort and consolation in the bereaved and sympathers. Gorer writes,

> Nowhere is the absence of an accepted social ritual more noticeable than in the first contacts between a mourner and his neighbors, acquaintances or work mates after a bereavement. Should they speak of the loss, or no? Will the mourner welcome expressions of sympathy or prefer they pretend that nothing has really happened? With mention of the dead provoke an outburst of weeping in the mourner, which might prove contagious?"

Elsewhere in his book, Gorer criticizes our society for "failing to provide . . . members with the support which most societies make available."

Hence, our discussion that follows will concern itself with feelings about condolence calls, both in the bereaved and in the callers.

FEELINGS OF THE MOURNER ABOUT THE CALL

Let us be clear at the outset that our discussion will deal only with condolence calls to the bereaved made by those who are not members of the family. Obviously we cannot discuss all complex responses in the bereaved, following a death in the family, nor is it our purpose to consider how the bereaved deal with these responses, and gradually resume social life. Grief, like any other pain, has very private aspects, which we cannot examine here. Our concern here is only with calls of condolence, and with some feelings that the bereaved family members often have about these calls and about those who call.

1. Our society not only provides few guides to proper behavior during mourning, but compounds this error by subtly frowning on displays of grief,[4] giving approval to those who successfully hide their grief. In the author's interviews with recently bereaved families, the single instance encountered of open copious weeping without apology on the part of the bereaved was that of a family newly come to this country, emigrants from the southern Mediterranean area. Not yet sufficiently acculturated to feel ashamed of any display of emotion, they frankly showed how they felt. To a person who mourns, suppression of feeling represents one more burden when he already has many to bear. Suffering from a latent fear of losing control, he may yet be constrained to accept condolence calls, however hesitantly, rather than to defy custom by withdrawal from outside contacts. Even individuals who, for whatever reason, do not grieve deeply for a lost relative, fear the display of inappropriate, socially unacceptable behavior, and thus tend to avoid such opportunities. In our society, our conventions imply that to show grief is undignified and undesirable and thus the mourner's natural tendency to concentrate on his sorrow and withdraw from human contacts must be controlled if be is to maintain his status in the environment of grief.

2. In a society in which it is not quite acceptable to how grief, how can there be intelligent practices regarding the duration of mourning? It is the essential nature of the sorrow of bereavement that the sufferer can hardly conceive of a time when the present acute pain may be eased. To hear a would-be comforter declare, "You'll feel better in a week or two" is a painful experience to the mourner, who often wants to cling to his suffering, for at least that is part of what he has lost. Bereaved families perceive and resent the subtle pressure extended by our culture in the direction of rapid termination of mourning.

As examples of this pressure, the author is reminded of our accepted tendency to wear our mourning clothing for ever shorter periods of time. Some experiences related by families in mourning strain one's belief. One twelve-year-old boy, whose teacher had observed him staring blindly out the window only four weeks after his father died an accidental death, was reprimanded in the classroom for failure to concentrate. "Four weeks is enough time to get over it," was the teacher's comment, which the fatherless child repeated to his mother. Her reaction is easy to imagine. In another example, a woman calling on a mother, visibly grieved over the death of a lovely, teenage daughter, reproached the mother for her continued grief. "If you do not stop, won't the other children think you don't care about *them*?" she asked. Clearly, it had not occurred to this caller that the other children, seeing their mother grieve, might think instead that they had a devoted mother who felt a profound and continuing attachment to her children.

In the writer's experience, wide individual variations in the duration and intensity of mourning may be related to many elements, such as the age of the deceased, the closeness of the relationship, the degree of interdependence in the relationship, and even the nature of the death. It is understandable that families in mourning should resent dicta from individual "sympathizers" about the length of mourning, since in this area there are no definite lines of behavior acknowledged by everyone. The prescribed custom of wearing mourning clothes, and the right of withdrawal from social activities for a year were, at least, a protection against unwelcome advice.*

3. John Donne's much quoted "No man is an island" and "Every man's death diminishes me" are perhaps the most familiar statements of the diminution of self-esteem which the bereaved person feels. When the death is that of a family member, how much more of a

----

*Some of the literature on funerals reveals what seems an unfortunate tendency to regard the funeral as therapy and to equate it with a therapeutic experience. One can accept that the funeral is a necessary social custom, with both desirable and undesirable aspects. However, to call a social rite "therapy" appears to the author to be a distortion of the concept of therapy, which means treatment of an ailment. A funeral service may be appropriate, beautiful, and comforting to the mourners, and still have no bearing on the duration and intensity of mourning or the healing of sorrow. The phase "therapy of the funeral" lends support to the notion that when things are done properly, grief should be dispelled rapidly. Such a misconception tends to foster withdrawal on the part of the mourner.

loss of self is involved! Even when aged parents die in the fullness of time, their children often feel the loss is irreparable, although they have long ceased to be dependent. The death of a spouse is felt commonly as a loss in self-worth and even of social status. Bereaved marital partners are extremely sensitive about their social acceptability and desirability after the spouse is gone. Similarly, the loss of a child may mean to the parent that he has less to give and receive from life, and that he is worth less as a person. These feelings may be recognized by the mourners as irrational; nevertheless they may persist. The loss of self-esteem, awareness of injury, and feeling of a loss of social status all contribute to the mourner's extreme sensitivity with regard to human contacts. As one bereaved mother put it, "You must learn to protect yourself from those who tear you down."

In the author's opinion, only through open recognition that such feelings are universal and natural can the stricken mourner accept his own hypersensitivity as a temporary phase which he must live through.

The nature of the unconscious is such that, not far beneath this hypersensitivity, lurks the unspoken, treacherous feeling that something one did or did not do, could have prevented the loss. Thus, one hears from one mourner after another, the pitiful questions, Why did this happen to me? What did I do that was wrong?—questions raised without any expectation of answers. The idea of being singled out for grief or punishment is, of course, a misreading of reality, which is induced by the mourner's strange, unfamiliar frame of mind. This frame of mind may some times unconsciously distort the mourner's perception of the actions or intentions of others.

The author recalls one family which had lost a dearly beloved adolescent daughter through accidental death. The heartbroken father related that one of the things that was hardest to bear was the indifference he encountered in the community. "No one came after she died." Inquiry revealed that the girl's classmates and teachers had attended her funeral and continued to visit the family. Neighbors, friends, relatives, and clergymen also stopped in to offer help and sympathy. The father's feelings of neglect represented an unconscious distortion, in accordance with his own sense of loss of worth and hope. Mourners cannot change their feelings, but they can be helped to acquire a broader intellectual orientation and the awareness that these feelings are universal, deceptive, and transitory.

4. A most important element in any grief, and perhaps the least discussed, is the rage that accompanies bereavement. In the author's interview experience, it is indeed rare to encounter grief not accompanied by rage. The rage may be directed almost any where, against the agent causing death, against medical science for ineptitude, even

against the Almighty for allowing the death. In contemporary psychology, this is seen as natural, the outcome of frustration. The loved one, the source of former satisfaction, no longer is present, as the object and minister in one's emotional life. The emotion centered on the lost person no longer has a target and must be frustrated; the anger of the frustrated mourner is as natural as gravity.[1]

Popular writing does not depict the bereaved as angry or prone to anger, and religious writings, to which many mourners turn, tend to emphasize the acceptance of death without question, with reliance on religious faith. Yet throughout the centuries, profoundly devout and religious persons have questioned "God's ways to man," even reproaching the Almighty as did St. Theresa of Avila, for "treating so badly the few friends He had." Jewish legend tells of a rabbi who lost all his many sons. A sympathizer remarked, "Whom the Lord loveth, He chastiseth." "I do not want His chastisement and I do not want His love," replied the grieving father. Perhaps it should be emphasized for the bereaved that profound religious faith may coexist with altercation with the Lord.

Mourners who know their own anger and tendency to become irritable with others, even with those who mean well, are in a better position to control their behavior. When custom fails, self-control and self-unclerstanding become essential. "Know Thyself," always a good precept, is a beneficial commandment when feelings are aroused that generally are taboo to the average person.

FEELINGS OF THE SYMPATHIZERS ABOUT THE CALL

The sympathizer, no less than the bereaved family, has complex feelings which create obstacles between himself and those with whom he has come to condole. These obstacles to communication also are in part the products of cultural omission and confusion. Here we shall review only problematic feelings of the caller relating to the call itself. Any attempt to explore possible personal responses to a death would be hypothetical and here, extraneous.

1. Just as the bereaved family has a wish to withdraw, so has the caller. Like the bereaved family, the caller has been partially indoctrinated against the display of feeling, with a consequent reluctance to become involved in an emotional crisis. To the would-be caller, it often seems best to believe that grieving individuals actually prefer to be left alone, rather than to share or to talk about their sorrow. This belief in a preference for solitude is facilitated by the caller's understandable wish to avoid the sight of another's pain. Only the

callous can be unaffected by another's suffering, and the callous usually do not set out to make condolence calls.

The caller who arrives at the door really ready to express his sympathy, not simply to leave a card (in accordance with the recommended procedures of some volumes on etiquette), first must conquer his hesitation, due to the mourner's anticipated unwillingness to see visitors. He must overcome the latent conviction that the individual prefers to be alone, that the expression of sorrowful feelings somehow is undesirable, and that be himself is in for a difficult interview, in which he rarely feels comfortable, not knowing what to say or do. The author has found that the best way to overcome these inner obstacles to calling upon a grieving family is to recognize that the family wishing to be left alone usually makes that wish clear. Furthermore, it is important for the caller to remember that pain suffered in solitude is heavier to bear than is pain shared. The privilege of entry into a house of sorrow can be earned only by the willingness to share the feelings in that house, without embarrassment, discomfort, or annoyance. If the wish to console and bring comfort is genuine, whatever the caller says will be received well. The sympathizers presence symbolizes the support of the living community, as much as the reality of the loss, and thus has a true therapeutic function.

2. Misconceptions about the duration of mourning and appropriate private behavior during mourning are likely to exist on the part of the caller no less than of the mourner. Procedures outlined in current books on etiquette encourage the brief call, as soon as possible after news of a death, without repetition of the visit. However, the time when supportive calls are most needed is after the funeral, and after obligatory condolence calls have been paid. Here, social custom provides no guidelines for the bereaved family or for their friends. Individuals who have talked with the author about their personal reluctance to continue contact with bereaved families attribute this reluctance to ignorance as to what to say and do, surprising in socially sophisticated adults who are at ease in almost any conceivable situation. Yet these knowledgeable people ask for precise instructions on behavior, just as would an adolescent going out for the first time into a new social situation. The caller instinctively recognizes the extreme sensitivity of the bereaved family at this time of crisis and needs to have elementary rules of behavior outlined, such as how long to stay, precisely what to say, whether to show his own feelings about the death, and at what times and how often such calls of comfort may be made.

Our cultural condensation of the period of mourning somehow implies that condolence calls have no place after the initial period of mourning. In this regard Gorer [4] writes of his bereaved sister-in-law: "At the period when she most needed help and comfort from society, she was left alone." Mourning that terminates early of course makes it impossible to condole with a person who no longer grieves. Cultural silence and confusion about the duration of mourning and what the condolence call can achieve positively for the family's readjustment increase the caller's hesitation and awkwardness in making these calls.

3. It is a truism that the sick patient envies a healthy caller his ability to carry out the daily requirements of living, unhampered by physical discomfort. On a fine day, the visitor to the hospital bed knows, although nothing is said, that the patient wishes he, too, could leave his hospital room, and go out to enjoy the sun. In the same way, the one who calls on a bereaved household is dimly aware of their latent feelings of diminished self-worth and self-esteem, and of their envy, of those who appear to be unhurt and whole.

When we hear, "Why did this happen to me?" what answer can we give? Were we allowed to yield to impulse, the only logical response would be, "Why should you expect to go through this world without sharing in its trouble?" By merely raising the question, the mourner implies that his should be a special fate.* In doing so, he puts the caller at an unfair disadvantage. Unless we ourselves die young, all of us have suffered, or will suffer, bereavement. The identity of the bereaved is merely the matter of a point in time. The question itself is that of a childish mind, overwhelmed by an experi-

---

*The poet, John Keats, raised this question of human trouble in his letters to his brother, George, and sister-in-law Georgiana Keats. According to the writer and critic, Lionel Trilling, Keats resolved the question "with sudden contempt for those who call the world a vale of tears. 'What a little circumscribed notion!' he says. 'Call the world if you please "The vale of Soul-makings!" I say Soul-making—Soul as distinguished from an intelligence—There may be intelligence or sparks of divinity in millions but they are not Souls till they acquire identities, till each one is personally itself.' " "There follows a remarkable flight into a sort of transcendental psychology in the effort to suggest how intelligences may become souls, and then: 'Do you not see how necessary a World of Pains and trouble is to school an Intelligence and make it a Soul? A place where the heart must feel and suffer in a thousand different ways.' And the heart is 'the teat from which the Mind or intelligence sucks its identity.' " [8]

ence beyond comprehension and control. If the caller himself is fearful of death or vulnerable to ill-disguised envy, be becomes uncomfortable. In this frame of mind, he cannot console or comfort others.

For the caller, the solution is to recognize the emotional regression behind the question, and to accept it as one accepts the reaction of an overwhelmed child. Barriers between the bereaved and the sympathizer are not created by the feelings themselves, but by the attempt to deny the feelings.

4. The greatest obstacle to communication between the mourner and the sympathizer lies in the sympathizer's unpreparedness for the mourner's anger. Although a common part of the mourning process, this anger is seldom, if ever, discussed openly. It is hardly to be expected that the average (or even the professional) caller upon a bereaved family is prepared to recognize or accept the rage he may see in the mourners. On the author's visits to bereaved families, the most frequent initial response she encountered was that of undisguised, open anger. Almost every interview was dominated in tone by expressions of resentment about the death. It is peculiarly painful to be confronted with such expressions of feeling because the caller can do nothing but listen. Until we realize that this is all we can do, we cannot even listen effectively. Through this outpouring and listening, mourner and caller together can express, accept, and understand the helpless anger that often follows in the wake of death.*

Perhaps an unconscious recognition of the mourner's rage and resentment contributes to the continuing difficulties of both parties in resuming normal social contacts after a death. If both mourner and sympathizer could accept that irrational hostility as a universal part of mourning itself, the roles of both would become easier. Both parties would be relieved of any implication that the bitterness expressed and observed is more than a "crisis characteristic" and need not be regarded as a permanent character trait.

WHAT THE CALL CAN CONTRIBUTE

The author believes that the purpose of the condolence call is simple. The call is paid to the mourning family to express sympathy

---

*We should make clear that these comments refer primarily to premature deaths, particularly from unnatural causes, not to anticipated death, "in the fullness of time," as the saying goes.

and to give assurance that they are not alone in their grief. Friends of the bereaved have a responsibility to lend what support they can, however awkwardly, in the direction of bringing the bereaved back into the mainstream of life. Their task is to help the bereaved relinquish the past, and to adjust to the present. Similarly, no matter how great the loss, it is the duty of the bereaved to go on living, to acquire the "identity" of which Keats wrote.

Most bereaved families know that despite their sorrow, they will resume the tasks of daily life because they must do so. They also have considerable awareness of the complexity and ambivalence of their feelings, in relation to daily tasks and to previous associations. By and large, their expectations from these associations are fairly simple. Many bereaved persons who consciously hope for sympathetic support are aware of the problems in themselves which preclude their reaching out for such support, and sometimes Understanding breaks down not so much in expectations on the part of either the bereaved or the caller, but because of inability to face underlying feelings such as those we have considered here. This article is a plea for understanding of the underlying feelings which build barriers, so that they may be broken down.

There is nothing unacceptable or shameful in the feelings themselves, only in the attempt to deny them. Feelings of ambivalence, hostility, guilt, and fear have received little attention to date in writings on bereavement, but this silence at last seems to be yielding to inquiry.* Whatever the feelings in response to loss, we believe they should be given opportunity for expression. Although our customs give little assistance to the bereaved or to those who wish to help, art has spoken, where custom is silent. Said Shakespeare,

> Give sorrow tongue;
> The grief that does not speak
> Whispers the o'er fraught heart and bids it break.

---

*Erich Lindemann discusses this aspect of acute grief, in his well-known paper, "Symptomatology and Management of Acute Grief," which first appeared in the American Journal of Psychiatry, in 1944, vol. 101, pp. 141–148. The loss of warmth and the furious hostility described by Lindemann appears on p. 145. Edmund Volkart and Stanley Michael also deal with anger as an aspect of bereavement, in "Bereavement and Mental Health," pp. 299–301. [10]

More recently, Dylan Thomas wrote: [7]

Do not go gentle into that good night,
Old age should bum and rage at close of day;
Rage, rage against the dying of the light.

ACKNOWLEDGMENTS

This work was partly supported by United States Public Health Service Grants MH #02203 and MH #02717, from the National Institute of Mental Health, National Institutes of Health. The work was partly supported also by Eastern Pennsylvania Psychiatric Institute.

REFERENCES

1   Bowlby, J. "Processes of mourning." *International Journal of Psycho-analysis*, 42: 317–340.
2   Colum, Mary. *Life and The Dream*. London: MacMillan, 1947.
3   Fenwick, Millicent. *Vogue's Book of Etiquette*. New York: Simon and Schuster, 1948.
4   Gorber, Geoffrey. *Death, Grief and Mourning*. New York: Doubleday, 1965.
5   Lindemann, E.: Symptomatology and management of acute grief. *Amer J. Psych*, 101:141–148.
6   Post, Emily. *Etiquette, The Blue Book of Social Usage*. New York and London: Funk, 1937.
7   Thomas, Dylan. *Collected Poems*. New York: New Directions, 1953.
8   Trilling, Lionel: *The Opposing Self—Nine Essays of Criticism*. New York: Viking, 1955.
9   Vanderbilt, Amy. *Amy Vanderbilt's Complete Book of Etiquette*. New York: Doubleday, 1958.
10 Volkart, E., and Michael, S.: "Bereavement and Mental Health." In Leighton, A. (Ed.). *Explorations in Social Psychiatry*, New York: Basic Books, 1957.

Children and Funerals

JOHN E. SCHOWALTER

Funerals are an accepted, institutionalized means for group mourning. They often work like group therapy, allowing the bereaved an opportunity to be supported while they express their grief. The consensual validation of the death provided by the funeral also acts to prevent the use of excessive denial. Because of the beneficial aspects of funerals for most people, they remain an important institution in our culture in spite of the financial and emotional exploitation which is often also present. While funerals seem to be useful outlets of grief for many adults, how helpful are they for children? This question, almost totally ignored in the medical literature, will be explored here, and some answers will be suggested.

To explore the question of children and funerals, an understanding of child development is crucial. Experience has shown that older children usually tolerate funerals quite well, while young children often suffer bad reactions (e.g., nightmares, anxiety reactions, phobias, etc.). The moot point then is at what age or, more exactly, at what stage of development can one assume that most children will be able to tolerate a funeral?

THE CHILD'S EVOLVING CONCEPT OF DEATH AND FUNERALS

Prior to the second half of his first year, the infant is not able to delineate himself as separate from his surroundings. He cannot distinguish his parents from other persons. Funerals will, of course, have no direct meaning at this age, and, if the parents wish, the infant can be taken to the funeral without the expectation that the experience will cause any special harm. This is not to say that the death of a parent or close relative has no emotional impact on the infant. The impact, however, is indirect and comes through the mourning survivors' inability to provide the infant with his usual care. Attending the funeral per se will probably neither add to nor detract from this impact.

During the second year, the infant becomes a toddler. According to both psychoanalytic and Piagetian theories, he develops a stable, internalized image of his parents and, later, of other important people in his life. From this age on, the death of a loved one becomes a real loss. The central question for this essay is whether or not attending the funeral will make that loss easier or less easy to bear.

My own belief is that children should not usually be taken to funerals before the age of seven or eight and should not ever be taken routinely if the child does not want to go.

Prior to about the age of seven, the child has great difficulty differentiating between the psychological and the physical. Cause and effect are commonly based on spatial or temporal rather than logical considerations. Animism, the bestowal of human characteristics on inanimate objects and natural phenomena, and egocentrism, the assumption that others think and feel the same as oneself, are commonly manifested in children up through the preoperational stage of cognitive development, which ends about age seven. Up to this age, death is often personified as something or someone who comes and takes the victim. In the mind of the child, a dead person often acquires this ability, and this is one reason why the corpse becomes so frightening. Of course, adults' fear of the returning dead has a long history too and probably was influential originally in the development of wakes and funerals. However, until the child can grasp intellectually the meaning of a funeral, attending the event will result in an additional emotional burden for him to bear.

Optimally, every child will have the death explained to him in a manner in which he can understand. The funeral should also be explained in those terms which describe how that family views it, and the child should be encouraged to ask questions. Around the age of six, seven, or eight, children may be asked if they wish to attend the funeral. If the child has no strong feelings or does not wish to go, my inclination is to not have him attend. If the child does want to attend, this wish should be given weight. Children who want to go but are not allowed sometimes exaggerate the mystery of the funeral or conjure up fantasies of skullduggery or murder. Even when the child decides to go, it should be with the understanding that he can change his mind at any time up to or during the service. This "escape clause" is important and is not infrequently used by a child who overestimated his own emotional strength or underestimated the strangeness of some funerals. Whether a child goes to the funeral or stays home, he should be accompanied by someone who is not so involved in the death that he cannot give undivided attention to the child.

A common question adults ask themselves in planning a funeral is whether or not to have an open casket. In some cultures an open casket is a tradition, although many younger adults believe it is more honored in the breach than the observance. My own experience is that although it is often helpful to allow a child to see a person who has just died, the prepared corpse is so artificially "real" that it seems unreal. Unlike what many morticians suggest, the image seen in an open casket is not what one would wish the child to carry with him. It is not life or death, but a confusing "fake life." The trip to the cemetery and the lowering of the coffin into the ground are also experiences which often overwhelm children and even young adolescents. Here again, however, at the older age the individual should have a voice in the decision whether or not to go. Periodic visits to the grave by the child with adults who are in control of their emotions can later help with mourning by stressing the permanence of death while also providing a permanent reminder of the deceased.

CHILD-ADULT INTERACTION

Probably the most important influence on how a young child acts around the time of a death is the response of his parents. When one parent dies, the child usually loses both, since the surviving parent's mourning often renders him unable to give of himself in a way consonant with adequate parenting. This occurs, of course, at just the time when the child desires and requires an increased quantity and quality of care. Even when it is a grandparent or other relative who has died, children are usually forgotten by grieving adults. When parents are unavailable emotionally to look after the children or prepare them for the funeral, an "outside" but familiar person should be appointed specifically to fulfill this task. A pediatrician, if he is close to the family, can be excellent in this role. An additional example of how children are forgotten at times of grief is the fact that adults seldom send children sympathy cards, even children to whom they regularly send holiday or birthday cards. This is unfortunate, because mail means much to a child, and the card remains as tangible evidence of the event and of its remembrance.

Around the time of the funeral and in addition to the shock of the death, it must be expected that the child will be bewildered by the presence of many strange adults acting strangely. Even those friends and relatives whom the child knows will probably be acting in ways he has never associated with them. For example, Christian children are often confused, especially if it is an older grand-parent who died, as to why the adults are crying if the dead person is now in heaven. In Sunday School they were taught that this is a joyous occasion. Unable to comprehend the permanence of death, young children may rate adults' behavior as excessive and tell them so. Contrariwise, the child's developmental inability to mourn like an adult often disturbs relatives and family friends. They find the child's frequent hyperactivity and lack of sadness as irritating signs of insensitivity or inhumane self-centeredness. If the child is reprimanded for not acting in a way he is not able to, his confusion will only be compounded, and his behavior will probably worsen.

How the child will react if he does attend the funeral will be a function of his past experiences and his present support. Children who have been active in arranging funerals for pets or who have discovered dead animals often seem better able to experience their passive role at the funeral. If the deceased is a distant friend or relative, children are usually and understandably better able to handle the funeral than if the death is of a parent, sibling, or someone else to whom the child is very close. How often the child has attended church or temple and how comfortable he is with the services are also important considerations. Again, if unfamiliar, the strangeness will tend only to compound his confusion and to increase the likelihood that the situation will be overwhelming.

Prior to the age of about seven years when the child becomes able to differentiate regularly between the psychological and the physical and to rely less on the primitive logic of animism and egocentrism, children are more often terrified than consoled by visiting funeral parlors or attending funerals. Even older children who wish to accompany the family to the funeral may be disturbed by an open casket or by being present when the coffin is lowered into the ground. Children over the age of eight or nine who want to attend the service should usually be allowed to do so. It is comforting, however, to allow an "escape clause" whereby they know they can leave at any time. Since children are usually forgotten by adults in their own grief, it is important that someone be appointed to be responsible for the children around the time of the funeral at the service and/or at home. Adults should also be aware that a young child's mourning often shows much less sadness than a grownup's and should not be misled into criticizing the youngster or into believing that his fear and anxiety are any less real than the adult's.

The Bramble Bush

SANDRA BESS

once upon a deathless spring
   life gave earth a gentle push
in God's green mantle blossoming
   a rose grew on the bramble bush

but oh the clouds when snowflakes fall
oh the shrouds of winter's pall

once upon a far ago
   she understood the dream of things
she didn't care—she didn't know
   what made the rain the scheme of things

but oh the distance of belief
oh the image drowned in grief

once upon a long away
   sunshine glistened on her brow
she listened to the lark at play
   and perched beside it on the bough

but oh the hot and burning plain
oh the weeping wailing pain

once upon a land of giants
   two plus two made many things
the lilliputian stood defiant
   and fell asleep on angels' wings

but oh the heavy weight in numbers
oh the heavy weight in slumbers

once upon a deathly spring
   earth gave life a gentle push
in God's green mantle withering
   a rose fell off the bramble bush

but oh the paper moon and sky
oh can paper roses....die

Part Three
THOUGHTS ABOUT DEATH

Judaism and the Experience of Death

RABBI IRWIN BLANK, D.D.

Early in the bible we are introduced to the subject of death. A considerable difference of opinion exists as to the context within which it is introduced. Does God intend death to be a punishment? Was it His initial intention that man would live forever? Has He introduced death into man's existence as a consequence of the disobedience of Adam and Eve? Or was death always a part of man's existence, a part of his existence of which he was unaware until the moment of moral awareness and responsibility came upon him through his eating the fruit of the tree of knowledge, of good and evil? Whatever the interpretation, it seems to be clear that the awareness of death, when it first comes upon us, is a painful experience. There are some who never overcome the experience of this pain. There are people who translate it into punishment or who regard death as the defeat of man; there are others who are able to integrate the awareness of death into their lives in a positive way by accepting it as a challenge. Aware of their finite nature, they accept their limitations as a challenge to respond to the ultimate as a creative, productive human being. There are still others who, because life is too much for them to bear, regard death as a lasting sleep, bringing with it the lasting peace for which they yearn. All of these responses to the phenomenon of death are to be found within the Bible. Ecclesiastes regards death as defeat for man, crushing his fondest hopes and frustrating his drive toward fulfillment. Deuteronomy equates death with evil and punishment. Job refuses the lasting sleep of death even though it will bring relief from his suffering. He refuses death as an answer because for him the spiritual struggle in which he is engaged must be resolved through a confrontation with God. Since Job lives in a time when there is no concept of immortality, death would be the end of his quest for meaning and understanding.

Belief in an afterlife, for some, dulls the pain resulting from the awareness of one's finite nature. It is, however, not till later in the history of the development of Jewish thought that a concept of the afterlife is developed. We do not find it in the Bible. Thus, for biblical man, death means the end of existence. For rabbinic man, death is the occasion on which he has opened to him the possibility for eternal life in the presence of his Creator. Even for rabbinic man, in

132

whom there is a concept of afterlife, there is no clearly defined concept of eternal punishment similar to that of the Christian hell and purgatory. After death, man is to be judged in God's judicial presence. He is either found worthy to dwell in the presence of the Almighty, or else consigned to a state of nonbeing. He either has a share in the world to come, or ceases to exist. The theological problem resulting from this state of nonbeing has to do primarily with the question of what then happens to the soul, since the world to come is based upon the concept of the eternal soul. It is the concept of an eternal soul inhabiting the physical body which makes belief in life after death possible.

Late in the rabbinic period, belief in the resurrection of the body became crystallized, a belief which Jews associated with the coming of the Messiah. One of the functions of the Messiah will be to resurrect those who are found worthy of eternal life and to gather these resurrected dead to the Promised Land. Ezekiel's chapter on the vision of the valley of dry bones is often interpreted in this messianic manner. Actually, Ezekiel was speaking in highly poetic terms of the restoration of the Kingdom of Judah, and it is highly improbable that he was speaking in messianic terms or in terms of the resurrection of the dead. The misinterpretation is understandable; for the language of Ezekiel throughout is poetic and charged with vibrant images.

All of these themes—death as the occasion for evaluating the meaning of life, the occasion for considering life after death, the occasion for becoming acutely aware of our infiniteness and the end toward which all of us are destined, and death as the path toward everlasting life and everlasting peace—all these elements find their way into the liturgy of the funeral service and the customs associated with mourning within the Jewish faith.

The funeral service consists of a selection of psalms encompassing these various motifs. Despite the existence of a generally accepted selection of psalms, however, the person who conducts the service is free to make his own selection, either of psalms or any other passages from Jewish or world literature which he feels appropriate, or which may be suggested to him by the family or friends of the deceased. The psalms from which the funeral service is most frequently selected are Psalms 49, 16, 90, 17, 91, 121, 23, 103.

Psalm 49 dwells on the theme of death as the great leveler claiming rich and poor, good and evil, alike. But, the psalmist assures us, the good shall be saved from wearing out their "forms" in the netherworld. God will redeem the souls of the righteous from the netherworld. Every man is accountable and:

133

No man can by any means redeem his brother,
Nor give to God a ransom for him
For too costly is the redemption of their soul,
And must be let alone for ever
That he should live away,
That he should not see the pit.
For he seeth that wise men die,
That fool and the brutish together perish,
And leave their wealth to others.

Wealth is perishable and does not descend into the pit with us. It is our relationship with God which is enduring.

Psalm 16 spells out that relationship with God which fills the individual with a sense of hope concerning his existence.

For Thou wilt not abandon my soul to the nether-world;
Neither wilt Thou suffer Thy godly one to see the pit.
Thou makest me to know the path of life;
In Thy presence is fullness of joy,
In Thy right hand bliss for ever'more.

Psalm 90 compares man's finiteness with God's eternal existence. Man's existence is as a shadow compared to God's. But man can triumph over his finite nature by acquiring a "heart of wisdom." Here we have the combination of qualities which truly defines human existence which redeems man from his finiteness: the ability to respond with heart and mind— "a heart of wisdom." Therefore, to be redeemed from the pit requires one to be a total human being. We are also redeemed through our work, through our contribution to the ongoing process of creation. "Establish Thou also upon us the work of our hand; Yea, the work of our hands establish Thou it."

Psalm 17 presents us with another motif, that of self-affirmation. The psalmist, somewhat like Job, feels certain that he has lived a righteous life.

I have kept me from the ways of the violent.
My steps have held fast to Thy paths,
My feet have not slipped.

This is not arrogance or boastful pride. It is a simple statement off act. Because he has led a righteous life, he does not draw back from petitioning God to "keep me as the apple of the eye, hide me in the shadow of Thy wings." This is quite different from a simple trust in God. It is a specific petition. It is not simply faith in the assertion that whatever God wills will be for the best. It is participating with God in a vital relationship, a relationship which gives one the right to ask of God that which one has the right to ask—His concern and His protection.

Psalm 91 contains an affirmation of the belief that God is a responsive God who satisfies the committed with deliverance. Psalm 121, in a nobler vein, portrays God as the watchman of man who protects from both the rigors of the day and the terror of the night. He is the eternal guardian who protects man from the vicissitudes of life.

> The Lord shall keep thee from all evil;
> He shall keep thy soul.
> The Lord shall guard thy going out and thy coming in
> From this time forth and for ever.

Psalm 23 portrays God as a shepherd who guides his flock safely through potential danger, whether that danger be the valley of the shadow of death or enemies lurking nearby. The trusting live with the certain faith that goodness and mercy will be with them all the days of their life and that they "shall dwell in the House of the Lord forever."

Psalm 103 emphasizes God's awareness of our frailties and His preparedness to accept them.

> He hath not dealt with us after our sins,
> Nor requited us according to our iniquities.
> Like as a father hath compassion upon his children,
> So hath the Lord compassion upon his children,
> So hath the Lord compassion upon them that fear Him.

Thus, the themes which emerge from the selection of Psalms from which the Jewish funeral service is developed have to do with those aspects of life which redeem man from the painful experience of death, bringing with it as it does the possibility of nonbeing and Divine retribution. But death also holds out the possibility of Divine compassion and protection, of graciousness beyond man's merit. The righteous, the Bible affirms, have a just claim upon God.

Righteousness is within the capacity of every human being. To achieve righteousness does not depend upon some special favor or special act of graciousness from God. To be human is to have the capacity for righteousness. To be truly human is to exercise that capacity and to redeem oneself from the anxiety which flows from the awareness of infiniteness. To respond to finiteness is to accept the challenge of life, to work within the framework of time to redeem one's life by joining with God in a creative partnership, by raising one's own level of existence through the development of the natural capacities of heart and mind, and by redeeming the human community from those forces which divide it.

The sadness which accompanies death is the sadness which accompanies the awareness of work unfinished, which one must now leave to others. Hopefully, the dead man has participated in the preparation of those who will continue the task, and thus the effects of his own labors will not be lost. Moses is perhaps the supreme example of this process, passing on the torch of leadership to Joshua, knowing that he himself will not complete the task of leading God's children into the Promised Land. His challenge is that of not succumbing to despair in the face of the certain knowledge that he will be unable to complete his mission. It may be that all of us to some extent cherish the hope that we will complete the task. The challenge is to live as if one could complete his work, and at the same time to open the way for those who will follow us, so that they, in turn, may accomplish it, knowing in our heart that our own labors have been a contribution to its fulfillment.

Perhaps, in the refusal of orthodox Judaism to permit flowers to adorn the coffin or the grave, and in observing the custom of having relatives or friends fill in the grave with earth, the purpose is served of requiring the participant to integrate into his life the experience of death so that the experience of death, source of grief that it is, will nevertheless urge us to use well the time we have.

The formal mourning period immediately following burial may last either one week or three days, depending upon the circumstances of the family of the deceased. Perhaps this may sound like a rather strange option. Yet, here too, the overriding concept is that the ultimate state of existence is to be totally engaged in the act of living. Tradition therefore reasons that if the observance of a formal mourning period should place the individual in a state of privation concerning his economic well being, it is best that he return to his normal duties by observing the shorter period of formal mourning known as *Shiva*.

Upon the death of a dear one we cannot delude ourselves into thinking that nothing has happened, so we do not immediately return to our normal pursuits. But neither do we flee from the challenges of life, even in our grief. The period of mourning is a period for reassessing our relationship with the deceased and integrating into our lives the profound sense of loss, reorienting ourselves so that we

136

can go forward true to the ideals which our dear one imparted to us, fulfilling his hope that those who survive him would carry on with his un finished work.

Thus, the sabbath which falls during the *Shiva* period is to be observed without any public display of mourning. The mourners are to pray in the midst of the congregation and to shed any signs of mourning in their dress. The process of return to the routine of life begins even during the period of most intense mourning. To be true to the memory of the dead is to continue the process of living.

The *Kaddish*, the prayer most closely associated with mourning, which is said at the gravesite and thereafter at each memorial com- memmororation (called the *Yahrzeit*), does not speak of death at all. It is, instead, a hymn to glorify, praise, and magnify God, the source of life and blessings. Thus, in time of grief, the mourner is called upon to reaffirm his faith that the Giver of Life intends life to be a blessing. Similarly, when the orthodox Jew has just learned of a death, he is called upon to affirm *Boruch dayan emes*, "Blessed be the righteous judge."

The rabbinic teaching is that one should not comfort the mourner while his dead is still before him, in other words, prior to burial. The understanding behind this is probably that grief is the natural expression of a significant relationship which has just been termi- nated; to comfort the mourners prematurely is to insult the signifi- cance of the relationship. Therefore, at least before burial, the mourners should not be comforted. Some members of the Jewish community interpret this to mean there should be no visiting of the mourners prior to the funeral, in a funeral home or elsewhere, that the mourners should be permitted an unobstructed period of time with their dead without the presence of friends. There is much wis- dom in this point of view, for all too frequently does one hear well- meaning friends attempt inadequate interpretations concerning a death; or, in an effort to offer consolation, they may recall memories which run counter to the painful fact of death and which, in fact, may confuse the emotions of the mourners, who may not know whether to smile or cry. There is a time for weeping, and this period is not the time for consolation.

For those not directly related to the deceased, there are two religious obligations: one is to comfort the mourners; the other is to accompany the dead to his burial place. (The Hebrew word for fu- neral is *livayah*, which literally means "to accompany.") Accompa- nying the dead to his last resting place is a sign of respect and also of concern that the burial be proper. Today, many who attend the funeral service do not necessarily go to the cemetery.

Following burial, there is generally a mourners' meal, which is held at the place where *Shiva* will be observed. This is considered to be the first act of consolation. Many have misunderstood this mourners' meal and have criticized it as being too much in the spirit of a festivity. To be sure, the mourners' meal should not be conducted as a celebration. It is, however, one of the first steps in bringing the mourner to accept the fact that his own life and relationships must be resumed, for to permit his grief to embitter him would not be a suitable tribute to the deceased. He is urged, therefore, by those who would console him, to partake of the food which they, out of their concern for him, have prepared.

Lately, there seems to be more discussion and writings concerning the appropriateness of autopsy. There are no specific injunctions against autopsy in Jewish law. It is a permissible practice. Traditional concerns have to do with preventing undue delay of burial as being disrespectful to the dead and cruel to the mourners, and the assurance that autopsy will be carried out under the most dignified and scientific circumstances. justification of autopsy lies in the knowledge gained from such a procedure, which may well help to save the lives of many who will follow. As a general rule, rabbis will not press the mourners to grant permission, although they may instruct them that autopsies are permissible and can yield useful information for the saving of human life. They will not urge autopsy upon the mourners, however, out of their recognition of the deep feelings of the mourners toward the dead.

Perhaps it may be unsatisfactory to some to discover that Judaism does not suggest that it has any answers to those situations in which death seems "unreasonable." But here we are confronted with the basic meaning of "faith." Judaism's principal test of faith is that life is purposeful, no matter how untimely the death. Thus, the response to "untimely" death is to maintain that faith. To offer explanations is to divest one's faith of that element which is at the heart of it, uncertainty. Herein lies the paradox. To offer pat answers is to offer the wrong kind of certainty; not to offer answers is to establish the climate in which faith can be operative. To have faith is to believe in an ultimate certainty beyond our comprehension.

In Judaism, the experience of death offers the mourner the opportunity to reaffirm his humanity and thus to establish a more significant relationship with God.

Christianity and the Experience of Death

REV. WALTER DEBOLD

It is on a rocky promontory of the Palisades overlooking the Hudson River that these reflections on death are beginning. The cliffs, majestic in their beauty, are comfortable in a cloak of summer green. But summer is over. Soon the leaves will fall and the green will be gone. The trees will be bare and the stone walls cold and lifeless. A look of death will come over the land.

There is some consolation. For two weeks in October, before the winds have stripped the trees, the leaves will burst out in a glorious explosion of color. Maples and birches and oaks will spend their final energies in a blaze of red, yellow, and russet. The late afternoon sun will collaborate to paint these cliffs with beauty for the brief season that is autumn's graceful last gasp.

But there will be one other consolation as we face into chilling winds. Winter is not forever. We can look forward with hope to another spring and another summer.

In this contemplation of nature we have the possibility of some analogy with our human experiences with death. That final separation from someone dear to us is like an entry into a winter of the soul. But here, too, there is some comfort in both *memory* and *anticipation*. We can look back gratefully to happy days. In faith, we can look forward to reunion.

The remembrance of happy days is good. But what of the inexpressible sadness in knowing that they are past, over and done with, gone never to return? Surely no one will pretend that this is a joy. Can one describe a memory as being at once sweet and bitter? Can pain ever be beautiful? As sorrow presses down heavily on the heart, it seems to force up the impulsive question, "Why?" "Why?" From the depths of one's being, this word leaps to the lips.

Even the Book of Job, for all its verbal wrestling, does not answer that anguished "Why?" Job may teach resignation, acceptance; but, in the final analysis, one is left with the pain. Is it not meaningless? If God gave me a taste for justice, how can He justify His behavior? If He is the source of all that is good and true, how can He pretend that He is consistent? Does He suspend the rules of reason on mere whim? Did He create me for a plaything? How could He expect my reverence?

If only I could learn from Job how to accept misfortune and to persevere. But the temptation to disbelief is so forceful. Better than psychologists do, I know that pain affects faith. If it is with faith that I am to face tomorrow, then I need a token. If I am to persevere inexpectation of some future reunion, on what can I base this hope?

How am I to adjust now to the present? The very word, "adjust,"seems a cruel euphemism. Am I to be "philosophical"? The Creator has placed us on this planet and faced us toward the future. Located in history, the human person must look to horizons, to goals. But more, he must pursue these goals; to fulfill his humanity, he must advance toward the horizon. With the companionship of loved ones, this is possible. Deprived of that companionship, the journey seems endless and pointless.

Now the prize appears in its true light: it is fool's gold. What reason do I have for taking my work seriously in the here and now? How can I bring enthusiasm to my duties? If ever I had ambition, it was not for myself alone. Of what use are life's little successes if the satisfaction is not a shared one? Will you say that the drive I once had should now be devoted in some altruistic way to "the good of society"? No, that is not enough. A man cannot live so impersonally. "The common good" has a fine sound to it, indeed. But can the heart of man live on this bread alone?

At the gravesite, family and friends recite what is sometimes called a New Testament psalm, which begins,"Blessed be the Lord, the God of Israel, for he has visited his people. . . ."[1] It is customarily referred to as the "Benedictus," from its first word in the Latin version. Saint Luke reports it as first uttered by Zechariah, the father of John the Baptist. That first utterance was on the occasion of the circumcision of his son. The prayer contains the elements of praise, remembrance, and thanksgiving that are characteristic of the Judaic tradition. It has many applications in the Christian ritual, but it is invariably a prayer of "beginnings." Therefore its usage in the burial rite is significant: it implies that this death is not so much an end as a begining. One verse is an echo of Isaiah 9: 1. It speaks of "our God who from on high will bring the rising Sun to visit us, to give light to those who live in darkness and the shadow of death, and to guide our feet into the way of peace."[2]

There are countless other passages in the Christian scriptures that are calculated to console one in the face of death. Some hint at, and others plainly promise a deathless life to come. Paul, for instance, in writing to the community at Colossae, feels able to promise immortality to all who are faithful to the commitment made in their initiation. At the time of their baptism, hopefully, they died to all that is ungodly and undertook a new life on a mystical plane, a "hidden" life, as Paul puts it:

> Since you have been brought back to true life with Christ, you must look for the things that are in heaven, where Christ is, sitting at God's right hand. Let your thoughts be on heavenly things, not on the things that are on the earth, because you have died, and now the life you have is hidden with Christ in God. But when Christ is revealed—and He is your life—you too will be revealed in all your glory with Him.[3]

But what is the nature of this life-after-death? Does the Christian gospel throw any light on that? Does it respond to the doubts of Hamlet, the uncertainty of Socrates, the curiosity of Everyman?

Jesus, when pressed on the point, gave answers that were rather those of the poet or mystic than of the philosopher. One time he said, in a way that was warm but laconic: ". . . there are many rooms in my Father's house."[4] He seems to imply that there are not many things in human experience that can help to comprehend the infinite Truth, Goodness, and Beauty awaiting us in the Land of Promise. In fact, it is expressly said by Paul: ". . . no eye has seen and no ear has heard, things beyond the mind of man, all that God has prepared for those who love him."[5] For Catholics there are several texts that are capable of instructing and, simultaneously, consoling those who mourn. The mass on the day of burial incorporates two readings. One is from Paul's first letter to the Thessalonians, in which he offers comfort by the promise of resurrection:

> We want you to be quite certain, brothers, about those who have died, to make sure that you do not grieve about them, like the other people who have no hope. We believe that Jesus died and rose again, and that it will be the same for those who have died in Jesus: God will bring them with him. We can tell you this from the Lord's own teaching, that any of us who are left alive until the Lord's coming will not have any advantage over those who have died. At the trumpet of God, the voice of the archangel will call out the command and the Lord himself will come down from heaven; those who have died in Christ will be the first to rise, and then those of us who are still alive will be taken up, in the clouds, together with them, to meet the Lord in the air. So we shall stay with the Lord forever. With such thoughts as these you should comfort one another.[6]

The second reading in the funeral mass is from the Gospel according to John. It offers comfort by recounting the dialogue between Jesus and the bereaved sister of the dead Lazarus. Christ presents himself as the one on whom the Christian hope for eternal life is based: he uses a mystery-filled expression, "I am the resurrection."

Martha said to Jesus,"If you had been here, my brother would not have died, but I know that, even now, whatever you ask of God, he will grant you." "Your brother," said Jesus to her, "will rise again." Martha said, "I know he will rise again at the resurrection on the last day." Jesus said,"I am the resurrection. If anyone believes in me, even though he dies he will live, and whoever lives and believes in me will never die. Do you believe this?" "Yes, Lord," she said,"I believe that you are the Christ, the Son of God, the one who was to come into this world."[7]

There are other masses for the deceased, employing a variety of scriptural passages to console those who mourn. Brief selections from them may reflect the motif:

When this perishable nature has put on imperishability, and when this mortal nature has put on immortality, then the words of scripture will come true:"Death is swallowed up in victory. Death, where is your victory? Death, where is your sting?"[8]

I tell you most solemnly, the hour will come—in fact it is here already—when the dead will hear the voice of the Son of God, and all who hear it will live. For the Father, who is the source of life, has made the Son the source of life ....[9]

Happy are those who die in the Lord Happy indeed, the Spirit says; now they can rest for ever after their work, since their good deeds go with them.[10]

I am the living bread which has come down from heaven. Anyone who eats this bread will live forever ...."[11]

One of the parables of Christ always favored by his followers is the one in which he likens the kingdom of heaven to a marriage feast. Interpreters can draw the lesson that the love between God and his people is as the union between bridegroom and bride. "From her the Bridegroom has no secrets; she shares with him the closest intimacy in the tenderest love; no union is more perfect than hers. The union between husband and wife far surpasses that between parents and children. 'A man,' our Lord tells us, 'should forsake father and mother and cleave to his wife.' No union exceeds this for intimacy, tenderness and fruitfulness.'' [12]

The Song of Songs is another segment of the scriptures that describes the mutual longing of lovers. It, too, can be read as a promise that earthly love will prove to have been a foretaste of the eternal.

One hears the bridegroom saying:

I charge you, daughters of Jerusalem, not to stir my love, nor rouse it, until it please to awake.[13]

Another translation can read, "Do not stir up love before its own time." There are, admittedly, many layers of meaning in this poetry but, from this verse, may one not infer that the "time" of love in its fullest realization is the Day of the Lord? If so, then what we experience here in even the noblest affection is only a foretaste which is somewhat alloyed: we bring to it hearts that are not yet fully purified of the dross of egoism.

THOUGHTS FROM THEOLOGY

One does not ordinarily attempt to console with the language of the theologian or of the philosopher. Nevertheless, the perceptions of these scholars, their distinctions and methodical formulations, can prepare us ahead of time for the tragic events of our lives. And, for some, they may be a means of sustaining hope after suffering what Teilhard de Chardin calls "diminishments."

The Christian theologian acknowledges the tragic element in death. He sees it in this light as a "death of Adam." But, in the light of his faith, he recognizes it as something that is capable of being transfigured: it can be a "death in Christ."

Death as merely "human," as the end of existence for one individual member of sinful mankind, symbolizes man's alienation from God. But, since a Redeemer has come, even this aspect of man's experience is redeemed. The believer whose life has been oriented toward the Divine Will is a person whose death is Christlike in its intention: his will is to surrender himself into the hands of God. He would find life by losing it: "Father, into your hands I commit my spirit."[14]

This final abandonment to the Father in and with Christ is made feasible by God's grace in the first place, of course, and by a temporal existence in which this harmony is initiated. The believer aspires during his lifetime to make his own the attitude of Jesus who prayed to the Father: ". . . Your will be done on earth as in heaven." [15]

Indeed, then, death is the end of an earthly pilgrimage. But its mystery is even more profound. For, since the Savior experienced all of man's humanness, even undergoing death, He altered the meaning of our existence—even of its termination in time. No longer is dying merely a symbol of alienation from the Father, nor merely a necessary evil which demonstrates our oneness with Adam in the community of sin. Now it is sacramentalized. It is a holy thing. Dying "in Christ" is a means of union with the "new Adam." It is a way of participating in his new life; it is the fulfillment of existence; it is an unfolding to full maturity. Now, everything which impeded the genuinely personal encounter with the Other falls away. Purified of egoism, the fully developed person, with freedom unrestrained, is able to be face to face with him who is able to say,"Let there be light. . ."[16]

The thief who died beside Jesus, pleading". remember me when you come into your kingdom,"[17] is one who had faith in Christ as leading the way. Perhaps as life ebbed he was experiencing that purification of self which is necessary to love perfectly. This man's hope was supported by the Lord's promise: ". . . today you will be with me in paradise."[18] Each Christian has the same longing. This is clear from the repetition of prayers for the departed that they may enjoy "a place of refreshment, light and peace."

Jesus' act of dying, says Father Karl Rahner, was the free transference of his created existence to the Father; it was the contradiction of sin and a manifestation of his "yes" to the Father's will.[19] "When the vessel of his body was shattered in death, Christ was poured out over all the cosmos; he became actually, in his very humanity, what he had always been by his dignity, the heart of the universe, the innermost center of creation."[20]

The mystery that is the life-death-resurrection of Jesus is that central reality in which the whole life of the Christian is caught up. One's existence is grounded in Christ in Baptism: "You have been buried with him when you were baptized; and by baptism, too, you have been raised up with him through your belief in the power of God who raised him from the dead."[21] This initiation into the mystery was completed—and is continually renewed throughout life—by the celebration of the Eucharist. This colors life with joyful expectancy: from the earliest days a most characteristic Christian prayer, *Maranatha* [22] reflects this eager anticipation. That Aramaic word has been translated as either, "the Lord is coming," or, "Lord, come!"

". . . anyone who loses his life for my sake will find it. . . . . ." [23]
Ideally, every Christian should be able to say with Paul,"Life to me, of course, is Christ, but then death would bring me something more. . . ."[24] What more? Job gives an answer to that:

This I know: that my Avenger lives, and he, the Last,will take his stand on earth. After my awaking, he will set me close to him, and from my flesh I shall look to God.[25]

REFERENCES

1   Luke 1:67.
2   Luke 1:79.
3   Col. 3:1–4.
4   John 14:2.
5   1 Cor. 2:9.
6   Thess. 4:13–18.
7   John 11:21–27.
8   1 Cor. 15:54-55.
9   John 5:25–26.
10 Apoc. 14:13.
11 John 6:51.
12 Dietrich von Hildebrand, *In Defense of Purity* (New York, Sheed & Ward 1935), p. 147.
13 The Song of Songs, 8:4.
14 Luke 23:46. Cf. also, Ps. 31:5.
15 Matt. 6:10.
16 Gen. 1:14.
17 Luke 23:42.
18 Luke 23:48.
19 Karl Rahner, *On the Theology of Death* (New York: Herder & Herder, 1965), p. 62.
20 *Ibid.*, p. 66.
21 Col. 2:12.
22 1 Cor. 16:22.
23 Matt. 10:38.
24 Phil. 1:21.
25 Job 19:25–26.

The Scripture citations are from the Jerusalem Bible (New York, Doubleday and Company, 1966).

145

Superstructure at High Tide

SANDRA BESS

it is late afternoon
I do not have more
than an eternity to walk
to the edge of my kingdom
by the sea
the gull's talk
is in tune
with the ocean's roar
at my feet
there is another
kingdom in the sand
how strange that
each will meet
the other and
merge as one
I sit down beside it
and watch the sun
resolve
I watch the sea
reclaim her land
wave by wave
inch by inch
moment by moment
the parapets and fortresses
dissolve
and now they are gone
poor little
castle in the sand
built by tiny hands
you were very real
a wave ago
the child was real
an inch ago
the dream was real
a moment ago
now there is nothing
left of it
only the memory
and that too washes away
bit by bit

as I turn on my axis
trying to keep up
with the world
arise
fair Venus
arise again
from your ancient home
fill my eyes
with your embryonic foam
let my tears fall
so I can taste the salt
of your breath
the salt of my own being
salt of all love
of all death
when the tide
is unfurled
one tomorrow
when the tide is low
I shall return and keep
this spot where
I now stand
I shall throw
my sorrow
all sorrow
into the deep
and seek the the sand
wave by wave
inch by inch
moment by moment
the tide shall claim me
with the setting sun
blinding my senses
I too
shall wash away
one day
with all my defenses
into the sea
and merge as one

Part Four
THE RECOVERY

Grief: The Road to Recovery

REV. ARNALDO PANGRAZZI

"My husband was never sick a day in his life. Then in the turn of five months, he was gone. Since he died, I've spent my nights crying for him. But my tears won't bring him back. I am just lost in the world without him." The woman was crying. Someone in the group put an arm around her shoulder and gave her a handkerchief.

"I know how you feel," commented a voice from another corner of the room. "It gets so lonely at times, you want to die, too. I find myself asking, "What is the purpose of life, day after day?' It seems I just go through the motions of waking up, dressing, going to work, coming home . . . but there's no life or meaning to it."

"The hardest part for me," said a young mother,"was the lack of having someone around telling me, 'You are worth something!' All I really need is just to have someone to talk with . . . to remember. My friends seem to avoid bringing up my husband's name. Maybe they are afraid I will break down or start to cry. What do they expect me to do . . . forget him?"

The sharing was intermingled with silence, tears, and laughter. "I'd like to know if other people who have young children are being asked the type of questions my four-year-old son asked me the other day," said a young man."Whenever a woman comes to the house, he thinks she's going to stay. Yesterday he said, 'Dad, I need a new mom because I want brothers and sisters.' I told him, 'Randy, you've got grandma.' He replied, 'She's not enough.' I sobbed, 'I'll get you a new mom when I find someone like your mother. I guess he thought I would buy a new mom at the store for a dime." There was a mixture of sadness and affection in the laughter that followed.

These comments came from people participating in a support group for the bereaved, which meets bimonthly under the sponsorship of St. Joseph's Hospital in Milwaukee. The purpose of the group is to create an environment where people who have been hurt by the loss of a loved one can come together to share and support each other. There is a sense of kinship and credibility that people feel for each other when they hurt together.

The death of a loved one is a major disruption that requires adjustment in our way of looking at the world and our plans for living in it. The reaction to this loss at the physical, emotional, spiritual, and social levels varies from person to person, and depends on the

150

circumstances surrounding the death—the type of relationship that existed between the deceased and the bereaved, the strengths one has, and the quality of one's support system. Certainly a person who can count on a positive self-image, an ability to relate easily, a faith to lean on, and the willingness to take initiative will do much better than a person who has an unclear self-identity, tends to withdraw rather than to engage, has difficulty learning from pain, and is afraid to take risks.

It has been suggested that the pain of grief is the price we have to pay for love. In a very real way, whenever we choose to love someone we are also choosing to be hurt. The time comes when we have to say good-bye, to let go. That is when grief begins.

As it takes time to love, so it also takes time to let go. People say, "Time heals." But time by itself does not heal. If a grieving person sits in a corner waiting for time to take care of bitter sorrow, time won't do anything. It is what we do with time that can heal. The purpose of this chapter is to offer some practical suggestions about what to do with time so that it may become a source of healing.

The biblical image of the exodus can offer us a good point of reference for understanding our grief. The Israelites, like us, experienced the grief of letting go. They had to let go of a place that was familiar. They were confronted with the uncertainty of the future, with the adjustment to a new life-style, with the experience of the desert. They wandered in the desert for 30 years, complaining, struggling, hurting, and hoping. During their desert experience, God gave them the Ten Commandments to guide them in their journey toward the future.

Bereaved people have a taste of that desert experience in their own lives. There is a danger of being stuck in the desert, in their grief. I offer ten "commandments"—guidelines that can help the bereaved who take time to practice them to find their way to hope, freedom, and healing.

1. Take Time to Accept Death

"My turning point was when I realized and accepted that my husband wasn't going to be there to open my door, and I wasn't going to find him in bed." Acceptance of death remains a condition for living. The pain will never get better until we face it. Often it is hard to realize that what happened has really happened, that life has changed.

Fantasy acts as an anesthetic to soften the pain. We hope it was all a bad dream, that we are going to wake up in the morning and

151

everything will be all right. We hope that our loved one will call us from work, or that we will hear that cherished voice when we step into the house. As the reality of death gradually sinks in we ask why it happened. It's really not important that we find an answer to that question because the answer is rational and our hurt is emotional. What's important is to realize that it did happen. The only way to deal with death is to accept it. We cannot fight death; we can only embrace it, no matter how painful that might be. Death confronts us with our mortality and vulnerability. We have a firsthand experience of what it means to be helpless, naked, lonely, and hurt . . . of what it means to be truly human. Yes, our loved one has died. But that doesn't mean we have to die too. We have to pick up the pieces and go on from there.

2. Take Time to Let Go

One of the most difficult human experiences is letting go and yet, from birth to death, life is a series of such actions, some temporary, some permanent. Letting go reminds us that we are not in control of life, and that we need to accept what we cannot control. So often we try to play God because it can be so painful to be human, especially in the face of death.

Letting go means adjusting to a new reality in which the deceased is no longer present. And yet, many bereaved people live in an atmosphere that means their loved one has not really died, that life has not really changed. Everything in the house is left as it used to be. They seem to live for the deceased, not for themselves.

Letting go takes place when the "we" becomes "I," when we are able to substitute the physical presence of the deceased with the memories they have left us, when we are able to change the patterns in our lives and in our environments. I remember a widow who used to wake up at night in the gesture of reaching out to her husband, only to discover that he wasn't there. That filled her with grief and kept her awake. She was able to make a significant change by deciding to sleep on his side of the bed. Physical change facilitated her psychological adjustment.

Letting go occurs when we are able to endure and accept the anger, guilt, fear, sadness, depression, or whatever feelings accompany the death. Letting go occurs when we are able to tolerate our helplessness and insecurity, when we are willing to face our fears, to wait, to trust, and to hope again. St. Paul assures us that "We are afflicted, but not crushed; perplexed, but not driven to despair" (1 Cor. 4:8-10).

152

3. Take Time to Make Decisions

"I am angry at myself for allowing myself to be spoiled. I never took care of the checking account. I never had to make decisions. He did all those things. Now I don't know what to do. . . I feel so helpless." The sense of dependency is echoed in the words of a man who said, "Whenever we went out with friends, my wife used to do all the talking. I just sat back and listened. It's so hard now. People look at me and I just don't know what to say or what topic of conversation to get into." People who have been very dependent on the deceased find themselves lost in the world. They are afraid to give themselves direction, afraid of making mistakes, afraid to ask, afraid to try.

Making mistakes is the way we learn and develop trust in ourselves, especially in unfamiliar areas. It's important that the bereaved be patient with themselves, and gradually learn to make decisions as a way of sustaining their sense of self-worth. It is wise to postpone major decisions. Small decisions are the most important ones to make, from writing out a schedule for the day to setting up tasks to be done.

Planning the day has to do with looking forward to something, whether it is the visit of a friend or a vacation. Looking forward balances that attitude of "I don't want to do anything." or "There is nothing that makes me happy" that often depresses and paralyzes people. Making decisions about our lives helps us gain some control over them and increases our self-confidence.

4. Take Time to Share

"No one, friends or family, cares to remember or cry with us anymore. It's like you want to shout it out to the ceiling: 'Talk to me, talk to me!'" The speaker was one of 25 parents who had gathered together to remember their children and share their grief. When we lose a child, we grieve over the loss of our future. When we lose a spouse, we grieve over the loss of our present. When we lose a parent, we grieve over the loss of our past. The greatest need of those who are bereaved is to have someone to share their pain, memories, and sadness. In life, we can only accept what we can share. Bereaved people need others who will give them time and space to grieve. At times, the comments of well- meaning friends can be insensitive and hurtful:

"Come on, it has been six months. You should be over it by now."

"He's gone; forget it!"

"The past is a closed book now."

When we are strangers to grief, it is easy to place our expectations on the bereaved when it becomes too uncomfortable for us to walk with them at their pace. I like the words of a widower who learned to make his wishes known to his friends:"I like to talk about Dorothy. I miss her touch, her presence. But talking about her helps me. It makes me happy to remember her."

Our children are not necessarily the people with whom to share grief. Children tend to look forward, not backward. Particularly during the early stages of grieving, we might need someone who looks backward, because the past, not the future, remains the greatest source of comfort at that time. Trusted friends can be the people who accept us as we are and to whom we can open our hearts.

Sharing memories and feelings with people who are grieving themselves is especially helpful and therapeutic. We learn to understand that our experience is normal, we become aware of different ways of coping, and we realize that the answers to our pain and our lives lie within us as we become free to give and receive in an open, caring way.

5. Take Time to Believe

To survive is to find meaning in suffering. Suffering that has meaning is endurable. However, meaning does not just happen. It takes time, openness, and faith to find positive and redeeming values in our suffering. It's important to realize that God is in the midst of our suffering. "We know that in everything God works for good with those who love Him" (Rom. 8:28).

It is also important to discover the ministry of suffering as a binding power with others who suffer. That's when suffering gives birth to new opportunity through the spirituality of wounded healers. This spirituality is well expressed in a prayer used in the memorial services offered periodically at St. Joseph's Hospital in Milwaukee:

"Our sorrow reminds us that life is not meant to avoid pain and that to love is to accept the risk of hurting. Help us, 0 Lord, to gain wisdom through our sufferings and give us patience and time to work through our feelings. Help us trust your presence in the events we do not understand. Put us in touch with the inner resources hidden in us and guide us through the future by gently transforming our grief into compassion, our hurts into new hope for others.''

At times, our grief can shake our faith. We wonder what God is up to, whether He has forgotten us. We may even be angry at Him for what we perceive that He has done to us. Often it becomes difficult to go to church, to pray, to go on living. The only way out of the desert is to go through it, trusting that God is there with us. For many people, religion, with its rituals, the promise of an afterlife, and its community of support, offers a comforting and strengthening base in the lonely encounter with helplessness and hopelessness. Our faith does not take away our grief, but it helps us live with it.

6. Take Time to Forgive

The feeling of guilt and the need for forgiveness accompany many of our experiences, especially those that remain unfinished. We feel guilty about what we did or didn't do, the clues we missed, the things we said or failed to say. In reviewing one's life and one's relationship with the deceased, there will always be things that seem to have been less than ideal. We need to accept our imperfections and make peace with ourselves. We cannot judge our yesterday with the knowledge of today. Torturing ourselves for things we did and wish we hadn't done, or dwelling on the things we didn't do doesn't change anything. It only makes us miserable.

We need to put our lives into perspective and accept what has been. Our love for the deceased wasn't perfect; it included our weaknesses as well as our strengths, and those of the deceased. Our loved ones have not become holy because they have died. We don't need to idealize them. It's healthy to remember them as they were.

The need for forgiveness emerges when we are angry. Here are the words of one mother:"I feel like I have a big sign on me: 'My son committed suicide.' I am angry at him and will never forgive him for what he did to our family.''

We might be angry at our in-laws because they disappeared after the funeral. We might be angry at people because of their insensitivity, or avoidance of us. We certainly need to own and express our anger. However, there must also be a time for forgiveness, or the anger can become destructive and alienating. The last thing that Jesus did on the cross was to forgive His enemies, ''for they do not know what they are doing." We need to find strength, through time, to forgive ourselves and others, to forgive life for hurting us, to forgive death for taking our loved one.

7. Take Time to Feel Good about Yourself

Bereaved people are not sentenced to unhappiness. We are not born happy or unhappy. We learn to be happy by the ways we adjust to life crises and use the opportunities life gives us.

At first, grief confronts us with a number of unpleasant discoveries. All of a sudden, many things seem to go wrong, from the refrigerator that doesn't work to the faucet that leaks, from the meal that doesn't taste right to the laundry that doesn't look clean. We need to be patient and to give ourselves time to learn, time to make mistakes. Especially, we need to affirm ourselves, patting ourselves on the back for every small thing we learn to do, whether it is replacing a light bulb or installing the storm windows. Every time we do something new, we expand ourselves. We grow beyond where we were and develop more confidence in the person we are becoming. I remember the excitement of a young widow who said:"I went to the library and borrowed this book on how to do things around the house. I decided to wallpaper my kitchen. You should see it! It really turned out pretty good. I was so proud of myself."

The death of a loved one affects our life-style and changes our self-image. Grief can rapidly shape us and help us discover a new independence and outlook. This is reflected in the words of a mother: "I am no longer the person I used to be. I've changed. I believe that my child now has a better mother because I am more tolerant and accepting. Before, everything had to be just right."

The process of building self-confidence is often sustained by being able to hold a job or keeping busy. It is also enhanced by other equally important factors, such as exploring new interests (reading, writing, or taking academic courses), developing new hobbies (swimming, dancing, yoga. or gardening), and taking advantage of new opportunities (traveling or doing volunteer work). All these activities can help the bereaved reinvest their energies in new endeavors that provide a feeling of newness, satisfaction, and pleasure.

8. Take Time to Meet New Friends

"I had 570 people at the funeral home. They all offered to help. Where are they now, six months down the pike?" The comment of this person reflects the feelings of many bereaved people who feel let down or uncared for by their friends. The loneliness that is present in grief may be nature's way of mending our broken hearts. Loneliness can also be transformed into solitude. That happens when we are not oppressed by our loneliness, but learn to live creatively with it by expanding our self-understanding and inner resources.

We need to reach out. We cannot avoid social contacts because of the imperfections of those we meet. We cannot devalue all relationships except the one that has been lost. Healing occurs when those who are grieving make the first step out of their safe boundaries and invest in others. Old friends may offer security and comfort; new friends will offer opportunities. We can meet new friends through support groups, card clubs, classes. and other activities. A widower who had just attended a support group for the bereaved expressed his feelings: "This group did wonders for me. At first, I was apprehensive. I felt I was entering a room full of strangers. I left with the feeling I was in a room full of friends. Some of these people have become my best friends."

Widows and widowers often feel that they have lost their sense of belonging, that they no longer fit into our couple-oriented society. Thus, they need to find a new sense of belonging. Dating remains helpful in the recovery process because it reminds the bereaved they are liked and appreciated. However, it might be dangerous to try to stop the pain or the hurting by compulsive involvements or remarriage. On the road to recovery, we need friends, not partners. The best way to find a friend is to be one. Like a smile, it returns to you.

9. Take Time to Laugh

"I used to resent people who were happy and laughed. I wanted to scream, 'Why do you laugh? Don't you know I am here? Don't you know what happened?' I felt that way until a friend of mine told me, 'Remember you were laughing too, when someone else around might have felt miserable.'" In life there are as many reasons to laugh as there are to cry. In grief, a time comes when our tears come with less frequency and intensity, and we learn to remember without crying. Laughter, on the other hand, helps us survive and to re-enter life. For someone who has been sad and depressed there is no better medicine than the ability to smile again. We can smile at memories that come to us. We can laugh at mistakes we've made, things we have said, thoughts we have entertained. There is a lot of comedy in our tragedies. Without laughter and humor, life would indeed become a sad journey.

Laughter is truly one of God's greatest blessings. It helps us accept our limitations, and it develops hope in the present. Laughter defines our movement from helplessness to hopelessness. It is somewhat reflected in the contrasting attitudes of one who wakes up saying, "Oh, God, it's morning" and another who is optimistic and says, "Good morning, God."

Laughter frees us from tension and helps us conserve energy. It takes only 14 muscles to smile and 72 to frown. So it's important that we give ourselves the benefit of relaxing and laughing, when we can without feeling guilty. Indeed, when we find ourselves laughing, we are on our way to healing. Then there is hope for us.

10. Take Time to Give

The best way to overcome loneliness and pain is to be concerned about the loneliness and pain of others. People turn away from grief when they feel wanted and needed by the living. Being able to help someone gives us meaning, makes us feel good. It makes us realize that our experience can be placed at the service of others. If you find someone who needs you, that will be your opportunity for healing. Here's how one person phrased it: "This time of grief in my life has probably been the time when I've given more of myself than at any other time. I don't think I'll be able to give as much again."

Being involved with others gives us the feeling that life goes on, and it takes us away from self-pity. Listening to someone, empathizing and sharing over the telephone, providing information, going out for lunch together, are all ways to give of ourselves. We accumulate tremendous wisdom through our encounters with grief, and it needs to be shared.

Healing takes place when we turn our pain into a positive experience. and when we realize that helping others is the key to helping ourselves. When that happens, our problems don't look so big. We expand our newly found strengths and discover that although one door has closed, many others have opened. Recovery from grief requires that we take time to do those things that will enable us to give a renewed meaning to our lives. That's when our journey through grief becomes a journey of discovering ourselves. our potentials, and our resources in the encounter with life. That's when we become better people rather than bitter people. In grief, no one can take away our pain because no one can take away our love. The call of life is to learn to love again.

158

Avoiding the Mistakes in Bereavement

JAMES P. CATTEL, M.D.

The bereaved, confronted as he is by a definitive disruption of his daily life and landmarks, may be tempted to pursue unrewarding activities. These can be classified in two major categories: (1) those activities that lead nowhere or are essentially destructive, and (2) failure to undertake those activities that are potentially involved with personality growth and constructiveness.

The quicksands to be avoided can be listed, for convenience, under two heads:

1. Bitterness and withdrawal: the flight into loneliness; and the temptation for self-destruction by self-medication with alcohol, sedatives and other drugs.
2. Pseudo-involvement: a flight into activity marked by social and sexual promiscuity; forced and self-seeking entanglements with family; superficial engagement in various areas; absorption in religion or politics, or devotion to the health-illness axis.

The more definitive paths that can be pursued, but that one is tempted to avoid, provide two other routes that can be followed more or less simultaneously:

1. Active participation in meaningful and realistic personal activities.
2. Seeking psychiatric consultation to determine the possible need for psychotherapeutic and pharmacological treatment.

BITTERNESS AND WITHDRAWAL

The plight of the recent widow or widower can be desperate. This is particularly true if the bereaved is relatively young and not completely engaged in meaningful work. He or she can isolate himself from the environment, withdraw into his room, and dwell bitterly on his sad and abandoned state.

What then can one do to find relief? "A glass of wine," the bereaved thinks, "can perhaps facilitate relaxation and sleep. But only one." Problems arise, however, when the bedtime drink gradually becomes wedded to the cocktail hour. When the cocktail hour begins increasingly early and finally merges with luncheon, drinking becomes a problem of major seriousness.

There is also refuge to be found in the medicine cabinet. The bereaved feels that sedatives and hypnotics which may have been prescribed for the deceased or for himself must be safe or the physician would not have ordered them. Those capsules that were given to relieve pain often provide some relief of anguish and thus promote sleep. "Why not try some of these, individually or in combination or even with a drink as a chaser?"

Such efforts at self-medication, using either alcoholic beverages or prescription drugs, are destructive and potentially dangerous. This approach may alleviate an anguished hour or a dreadful night, but it can become a way of life. This approach can lead to the ingestion of such a quantity and variety of chemicals that one becomes comatose. Some victims awaken the next day in the emergency room of a hospital, or as inpatients. Their emergency room tags read: OVERDOSE. Others who were not discovered in time are "innocent suicides." They had not wanted to kill themselves, but the death, however accidental, is irreversible.

PSEUDO-INVOLVEMENT: FLIGHT INTO ACTIVITY

One such approach is the active avoidance of being alone, a desperate search for social distraction at any cost. This can include successive telephone conversations of endless length, a continuous round of breakfast, luncheon, cocktail, or dinner meetings, or all-day or all-night bridge or poker games.

The bereaved may frequent cocktail lounges in search of companionship, recognition, and, ultimately, love. Inasmuch as realistic love objects are not to be found in such places, the result is often physical involvement with another lost person. There is an ephemeral release of tension or at the least an abortive effort, in the guise of making love, and a hollow aftermath of self-dislike that has solved nothing.

Some come to realize that this is a dangerous game. Others, always optimistic, continue to search for the really "true love" and may spend months in pursuit of repetitive disillusionment. Eventually, some attempt suicide; some seek psychiatric hospitalization; and some become hard, crass, brittle cynics, who continue to walk about but are spiritually dead.

One can always turn to the family for understanding, sympathy, and emotional shelter. One can move in with a married brother or sister and quickly perceive the faults of the in-law. But his critical observations and advice are soon rejected. These ploys can lead to family dissension and the bereaved may become the unsuspecting and expatriated victim, necessitating a return to the posture of bitterness and withdrawal.

The older bereaved person may feel that a married son or daughter and grandchildren need mature guidance, baby-sitting services, and a referee for marital quarrels. Who is better prepared to offer such assistance than the bereaved, particularly if he offers or promises some financial support?

Such a program really offers nothing to anyone. The family unit that the bereaved is trying to invade would welcome him as guest and grandparent, but will fight to keep its independence and will rebel against imperiousness. The result can be alienation, a new quality of aloneness, and the loss of a potentially solid area of support.

The flight into activity may take the form of conversion to a new religion, of fanatic dedication to some political movement or total acceptance of a dietary fad. Appropriate religious devotion, political dedication, or reasonable dietary habits are constructive and do not constitute a "flight." However, if the bereaved finds himself making a radical shift in any of these areas in search of salvation or meaningfulness in life, he is likely to find early disenchantment.

The bereaved can unfortunately misinterpret the various transitory symptoms of bereavement as evidences of serious illness and go from physician to surgeon to dentist, demanding that a diagnosis be made and that corrective medication be prescribed or surgery performed. The less fortunate prevail upon their doctors to take action when no disease exists. Then they haunt medical and dental offices for relief of the symptoms that the treatment did not rectify, or for relief of the symptoms that the treatment initiated. Some are so insistent that they eventually have a variety of major procedures.

As communication improves between psychiatrists and specialists in the various fields of medicine, an increasing number of such patients are wisely referred for psychiatric consultation before any treatment regimen is initiated.

ACTIVE PARTICIPATION IN REALISTIC
PERSONAL ACTIVITIES: A POSITIVE APPROACH

Set forth below are a number of brief statements about constructive activities which will prove helpful for the bereaved.

One should arise at a reasonable work-a-day hour, dress properly, and get out of the house, if only for a half-hour walk. One should revel in the day and plan how it can be most rewarding. One should plan days and weeks so that there will be time with relatives and friends, and a time to be alone, or, in company, enjoying outside activities: concerts, galleries, theater and so forth, and minimal time at home. One should arrange to be out one or two evenings a week to fill the long hours between sundown and sunrise. The best way to have a good night is to have a good day—a program superior to any sedative.

When one is ready, activities should be expanded to include some scheduled service or academic pursuit or both. Though once rich, the bereaved person has now been deprived but by giving of himself to the disadvantaged, he can regain some of that richness. He has been stimulated intellectually in the past; now he can find a structured situation for such stimulation and, at the same time, find others who share his interests.

PSYCHIATRIC CONSULTATION: ANOTHER POSITIVE APPROACH WHEN NECESSARY

One should think of psychiatric consultation as he would think of seeking medical help of any kind. If he has a cough that persists or ankle pain that recurs, he sees a physician. If he finds himself falling into some of the quicksands of bereavement, he should see his physician and discuss referral for psychiatric consultation. Often the personal physician will be able to be of great help, as an objective confidant and as an expert who can dispense medication, if indicated. If psychiatric referral is broached, one should accept it as he would accept a referral to any other specialist.

In conversations with a psychiatrist, one can obtain a more realistic perspective on his problems and the extent to which his efforts to solve them have miscarried. If he has unwittingly pursued some unhealthy bereavement patterns, this can be recognized. Then the opportunities for more positive and rewarding action, to which much of this volume is devoted, can be enunciated and undertaken.

Talking Out, Feeling Out, Acting Out

EDGAR N. JACKSON

It is usually assumed that grief is a universal emotion. This is not necessarily the case. Only those who are capable of love experience grief. The sociopath with his inadequate inner being seems to be unable to feel the deep emotion equated with grief. Grief is the other side of the coin of love. Those who love deeply accept a special type of vulnerability and become those for whom a special need exists as far as the wise management of their deep emotions is concerned. It is important, then, to make some verbal distinctions. In the context of our thinking, death or bereavement is the event in one's personal history that precipitates the emotion of grief. Mourning is the process that works through the emotion to retrieve the emotional capital invested in the life and love of the one who has died. The mourning process, then, is a way of managing grief that restores the vulnerable person to wholeness.

THE VULNERABLE PERSON

People in acute grief may be highly vulnerable. I say "acute grief" for there are other types. The patterns in which we experience death may modify the nature of our grief. At the turn of our century, more than half the deaths were among children. Now, the figure is less than 7 percent. At the turn of the century, average life expectancy was under 47 years. Now, almost a generation of life expectancy has been added. That means that in less than 100 years, we have moved from a culture where death was usually tragic and untimely to a culture where the majority of people live to the end of a normal life span, three score years and ten. When death can be foreseen and approached gradually, the defensive stance makes it possible to do anticipatory grief work, and so the acute response is reduced. However, our experience with acute deprivation is also reduced, and so people can be more vulnerable when tragic and untimely death occurs. These are the people who need special help.

Recent researches indicate how vulnerable the person in acute grief may be. One study shows that the death rate among widows the first year after the death of a husband is 700 percent higher than among other women in comparable age groups. A hospital study shows that admissions to a general hospital are 600 percent higher among those in acute grief than in the general population. A study of parents of leukemia victims shows that 50 percent of them were in psychotherapy before a year was over. So it is obvious that these persons are in a highly vulnerable state as far as their own death, illness, and emotional stress are concerned.

THE ROOTS OF VULNERABILITY

To understand the needs of these vulnerable people, it is also important for us to realize that the capacity for grief is a great achievement as well as a great burden. This helps us to perceive the resources we can use in grief management and to understand the deep distress that characterizes these powerful emotions.

It took millions of years of long, slow development to come to the place where social or other consciousness was refined enough to produce the heightened sensitivity for another that we call love. The writings of Pierre Teilhard de Chardin, Eilhard VonDomaris, and Erik Erikson stress this process and the meaning of the identity relationship that can become the identity problem or the identity crisis.

It is obvious that when you love someone you identify with him and so become vulnerable. When something good happens to him, you feel pleased, but when something devastating happens to him, you can feel devastated. It is this devastation that we are concerned about in acute grief.

There is also an anatomical or physiological dimension to this acute emotion. Deep in the nervous system and mental structure of each individual are the mechanisms that can be employed to protect the self against the intense stress of life or its intolerable pains. With the severe suffering of intense deprivation, the subthalamic regions of the brain may be activated, causing the spontaneous and irrational behavior that is related to the mechanisms of self-defense and self-preservation. The ancient equipment of the nervous system that was apparently employed originally to preserve life may now be used to react to acute psychic pain in a similar manner. This not only increases the need for understanding, but also in a highly organized cultural setting, may increase the vulnerability of the individual who feels constrained to modify his feelings to fit his environment.

When we add to that condition the atmosphere of a death-denying, death-defying society, we begin to see how heightened vulnerability is so significant a factor in contemporary grief management. If it is difficult or impossible to move from the pain of grief to the health-restoring process of mourning, the grief stricken individual is thrust into a chronic state of emotional stress with all the physical and psychological effects related to this prolonged disturbance.

THE NATURE OF VULNERABILITY

When emotions cannot be dealt with as emotions, they may find other and perhaps more damaging means of expression. Dr. James Knight, Professor of Psychiatry at Tulane Medical School, says that the major area of psychosomatic research now is in the side effects of unwisely managed emotional crises. When a person is unable to pour out his feelings wisely, they may become impacted and show up in physical symptoms that can be life-destroying. E. Lindemann alerted us to this possibility years ago with his pioneer study of ulcerative cofitis (1944).

LeShan (1961) has dramatized this process by his study of emotional factors related to the onset of neoplastic tissue growth and the mechanisms of spontaneous regressions. In papers on treatment of cancer by psychotherapy (1958,1961), he points out that almost invariably the onset of the disease was related to an emotional crisis that became chronic and produced a long-term modification of body chemistry and that the spontaneous regression, so called, began when the emotional crisis was dealt with in a psychotherapeutic process. This study brings into focus some of the cause-and-effect factors related to the vulnerability we have been mentioning.

Recent studies, then, verify the physical and psychological hazards faced by those in acute emotional crisis and, further, they indicate some of the cause-and-effect elements at work that compound the vulnerability of the crisis victim. Is there any comparable research that could help us to understand how we might cope with the human problems that are related to these crises in our work with people?

Yes, there is some rather significant work that has been done in the last couple of decades, and in the rest of my presentation these will be spelled out. I shall explore these researches under three headings: talking out, feeling out, and acting out.

TALKING OUT

No one has to be convinced of the therapeutic value of talking out. It has become basic to the perception we have of dynamic healing processes emotionally. In coping with the anticipatory grief that a person feels in facing his own death, the work of Cicely Saunders has been imaginative and important. She has found that the free expression of feelings verbally has been physically as well as psychologically useful. In her treatment centers in London, she has encouraged free communication as a way of life. She has found that this process relieves the anxiety that causes muscular spasticity and stress on lesions so that the result is reduced pain. Also, the ability to talk freely about anything that may be troubling the patient brings things into focus and tends to reduce the threat of the material that would otherwise be repressed or magnified out of proportion. In response to my request, Dr. Saunders gave me permission to interview 20 patients at random. The common expression of these patients was that it was wonderful to be in a place where everyone was honest and one could talk about any thing at any time. Repeatedly, there were contrasts with treatment centers where they had been previously and had experienced quite a different atmosphere regarding communication.

One of the dangerous trends I see in the management of acute grief is the retreat from therapeutic communication. The use of private or limited types of funeral services diminishes the opportunity to talk about what has happened and thus curtails sharply the whole purpose of the funeral process. The user of private or limited processes seems to be unaware of the purpose of the funeral. Basically, the funeral is a time to relate the grieving individual to the multiple resources of a larger community which can serve as a resonant sounding board for talking out deep feelings at a time and place that are appropriate and meaningful. The private process limits the opportunity for talking out and so proportionally reduces the healing benefits of the process.

Where the atmosphere necessary for socially centered talking out may not be possible for any number of reasons, the specialized forms of counseling maybe employed to take its place. But here it is often found that the counseling is delayed until a person has experienced excessive and unnecessary psychic pain. If the talking-out process can take place as quickly as possible in an accepting setting, the additional and needless suffering may be avoided and a healthier direction for the mourning activity may be provided earlier in the time sequence.

FEELING OUT

Feeling out adds another dimension to talking out. We have some unfortunate attitudes toward feelings in our culture. If, as we believe, grief is essentially a feeling, these unfortunate attitudes can do people real damage.

For instance, some people feel that emotions are a sign of weakness and should be repressed or denied. We assume that if we can build a better world through chemistry, there should be some ingestible chemical to take away the pains that come with our personal crises. The use of sedation and tranquilizers to suppress the discomforts of acute grief appears to be therapeutically unsound except for certain special medical problems.

Certainly, all the strong feelings incident to acute grief cannot be expressed at once, but the creating of an atmosphere where valid feelings can be expressed with confidence and accepting reassurance may be an important starting point in the wiser management of the strong emotions equated with grief.

The type of highly intellectualized behavior that tends to deny the validity of feelings may be prevalent, but it is not necessarily sound. Some disciplined activity only creates detours for feelings. Air Force physicians tell me that military jet pilots are among the most highly disciplined athletes, mentally, physically and emotionally. They are carefully selected for these qualities. But these same physicians say that stomach trouble is an almost universal symptom among these pilots. No matter how firm the external controls may be, there is an inner core of emotional response that asserts itself in its own way. With those who are less highly disciplined, it may be even more important to pay closer attention to the need for wise management of the emotions of acute grief.

We do not choose whether or not we will have feelings. The only choice we have concerns how we will manage them. If the grief-stricken person is encouraged to deny his feelings, he is apt to marshal his strength to repress this important part of himself. However, these feelings will continue to exist and they will be apt to express themselves in personality changes, psychogenic ailments, and social disorientation. This is a high price to pay for the unnecessary mismanagement of strong emotional responses to life crises.

Often, the more intellectually oriented members of the community try to prescribe, in the absence of acute feelings of their own, what they consider to be proper behavior for those who are experiencing acute grief. This explains why some of the more unfortunate guidance given in grief situations comes from educators, clergymen, physicians, and funeral directors—all of whom should know better. Their efforts to intellectualize, spiritualize, anesthetize, or generalize about death and grief may serve as protective devices for the professionals, but they are not usually valid guidance for the persons suffering the acute forms of grief. It may well be that those who have known grief and are resonant to the feelings may most easily understand and help the bereaved. These are the persons who can be made accessible through such processes as wakes and visitations, where the atmosphere is valid for meaningful communication and an honest expression of deep feelings.

ACTING OUT

Acting out of feelings is an ancient resource in managing crises. According to Geoffrey Gorer (1965), it may still be the most valid and useful resource for helping the grieving person to manage his feelings constructively.

Every culture has provided a cluster of rites, rituals, and ceremonials around the crisis events of life. These rites of change are usually centered about events like childbirth, the onset of adolescence, marriage, and political, historical, educational, and religious events. The ceremonial acting out related to death is also a significant resource for managing life's changes wrought by death.

These ceremonial events provide a time and place for the expression of feelings, the creation of both intellectual focus and large-muscle activity. Most ceremonials incorporate a parade, an emotional climate, and a meaningful expression of traditional ideas. Ceremonials use a variety of art forms to increase communication. They do not need to be explained, for everyone understands what is going on and why. They communicate in depth to the person who is feeling in depth. And, usually, they use a large, knowing, and supporting segment of the community.

Gorer says that the more ceremonial acting out there is at the time of death, the more readily the acutely bereaved seem to manage their grief. When the ceremonial acting out is curtailed either by choice or accident, the grieving persons tend to become withdrawn and maladaptive in their behavior and develop neurotic patterns of action. With more and varied ways for acting out, Gorer indicates, people more quickly work through their grief and are more readily restored to what might be called normal behavior.

Alvin Toffler (1970) says that one of the hazards of rapid change is the possible loss of the meaningful ceremonials that tend to cushion the impact of rapid or painful change. It may be that each age, especially an age of rapid change, has to examine and rebuild the ceremonial forms that help the person to adapt and adjust to the traumatic events of his life. This process would require an understanding of the needs, the values, and the methods that would be central to therapeutic acting out.

In relation to grief and death, some form of funeral practice has always been available to provide a climate for expressing feelings, talking out ideas, and finding supportive group action that verifies reality and accepts appropriate feelings. When times change rapidly so that old ways of doing things may have lost their value, it is important to discover new and meaningful forms of group action to accomplish the purposes fulfilled by the acting-out techniques of the past. Jettisoning old forms without replacing them with adequate substitutes may well leave vulnerable people doubly exposed to the impact of their grief. It appears that people in our age may need the values of sound funeral processes more than ever before to compensate for deficiencies that have developed socially and psychologically. It would be unfortunate if they came asking for bread and we gave them stones.

What have I been trying to say? I have been trying to bring into focus the research in the personality sciences that bears on our understanding of grief and its wise management. I have been pointing out the vulnerability of the bereft in our culture. I have been trying to indicate some of the reasons for this vulnerability as well as some of the resources we can use in more helpfully managing our approach to these acute needs. And, in conclusion, I have tried to assess our ways of doing things so that we can learn to act more wisely. As we look at the funeral as a form of acting out of deep feelings, we can see that we have been encouraging some unwise and psychologically unsound practices. But we can also see that the funeral or its emotional equivalent remains the most easily accessible and the most valid resource for meeting the whole range of emotional problems that modern man experiences as he encounters the acute loss that death imposes. Any useful changes in funeral practice must start from an awareness of the needs and move toward the most adequate social, psychological, and spiritual resources available. To these tasks we set ourselves during these days we spend together.

REFERENCES

Gorer, G. *Death, Grief and Mourning.* New York: Doubleday, 1965.
LeShan, L. L."A basic psychological orientation apparently associated with malignant disease." *Psychiatric Quarterly* 35:314.
LeShan, L., and M. Gassman. "Some observations on psychotherapy with patients suffering from neoplastic disease." *American Journal of Psychotherapy* 12:723.
LeShan, L., and E. LeShan. "Psychotherapy and the patient with a limited life span." *Psychiatry* 24:318.
Lindemann, E. "Symptomatology and management of acute grief." *American Journal of Psychiatry* 101:141.
Toffler, A. *Future Shock.* New York: Random House, 1970.

How We Should Mourn

RABBI JACK STERN, JR.

It has been said that there are three ways to mourn. The first is *to weep*; and we have done our share of weeping. In oriental countries, we are told, one can still find delicate tear vases used by mourners. The tears shed into the little vases are considered sacred. The tear bottles are kept and often buried with the person mourned. Even if our tears are for ourselves, for our ache of loneliness, for our pain of loss, they are still sacred, for they are the tears of our love.

A man who lost his son was weeping, and his friend said, "Why do you weep? Your sorrow will not bring your son back." And the father answered: "For that reason do I weep." But we may weep only if we do not weep too long, only if the spark of our own spirit is not quenched by a grief too drawn out, only if we do not indulge ourselves in the luxury of grief until it deprives us of courage and even the wish for recovery.

The second way to mourn is *to be silent*: to behold the mystery of love, to recall a shared moment, to remember a word or a glance, or simply, at some unexpected moment, to miss someone very much and wish that he or she could be here. The twinge lasts but a moment and passes in perfect silence. To weep. To be silent.

The third way to mourn is *to sing*: to sing a hymn to life, a life that still abounds in sights and sounds and vivid colors; to sing the song our beloved no longer has the chance to sing. We sing the songs of our beloved; we aspire to their qualities of spirit; we take up their tasks as they would have shouldered them.

As we turn backward in the Book of Life, we see emblazoned on each page a name, a date of birth, and the story of a life—and the date of a death.

Some pages are too brief—a story ended before it could blossom into full telling. The day of death arrived too soon, and the ink is blurred with the tears of our farewell. Some pages are ripely full—a harvest gleaned of years of love. But on these pages, too, the day of death is blurred with our tears. Whether the angel of death comes sooner or later, it is always too soon. There is always a task still unfinished one more song to be sung.

And we turn yet to another book, the Book Beyond Life. From cover to cover but one word is written: the name of Him Who gave us life, and Who takes it back unto Himself, our trusted Guide on the

170

homeward journey. The Lord hath given, the Lord hath taken away. Blessed be the name of the Lord. Amen.

The Magic of Time

AUSTIN H. KUTSCHER

When one suffers a grievous loss, well-intentioned relatives and friends make attempts at consolation which all too often fail to comfort. Almost invariably, only one pearl of wisdom emerges: "Time will heal the wound."

Countless books concerned with the facets of time (physical, psychological, physiological, theological, philosophical, and so forth) have been written. These brief words are not intended as competition for such treatises, but rather to spell out several concepts unique in the way that they relate the subject specifically to bereavement.

It is axiomatic that time is the great healer; but for the bereaved, time is a commodity which cannot be bought; it is, at best, a glimmer of hope in the far distant future. Good friends can help; but not always are they so constituted themselves nor have they been so conditioned by personal experience with tragedy that they are able to offer effective consolation for the moments of early grief. Indeed, even the best of friends are not always prepared to find the time it self required for a profound sharing of sorrow.

However, it is unrealistic to do nothing but wait for time and the passage of time to heal the wound. There are always things which it would be better to do and things which it would be better not to do. It is what one does and accomplishes with and in this time which determines how long the wound remains open and how well it finally heals.

Healing will come, in fact, first from the reshuffling of old thoughts, then from the introduction of new thoughts and plans, then from embarking on new trails, from weaving the old threads of life with new ones—friends, activities, interests, affections, responsibilities and finally, from finding new objects and persons to care for, be concerned about, and, yes, to love.

And when these purposefully active, as opposed to passive, efforts have been accomplished within the framework of a suitable period of time, innumerable new mental images and ramifications of these conscious and unconscious thoughts will be interposed within the mind, not to the negative effect of loss of memory recall, but to the positive effect that hope, and with it life, can be rekindled by that magic which is all too often referred to as just time alone.

Expression of Grief

JOSEPH BESS D.O.

All normal patterns of grief are closely related in terms of their final transcendence of grief. Creative grief represents at least one path in the direction of such recovery. Creative grief might be considered both as a reflection of an abiding love for the deceased as well as the response of a bereaved person who does not content himself with only the usual "work of mourning." It encompasses a certain purpose or goal to be sought and finally attained.

It is a realistic hypothesis that everyone has within himself a seed of creativity. The bereaved, in addition, experiences a catastrophic event that causes such seeds to germinate and hence flower into a truly beneficent response to his bereavement. Creative grief may be expressed, among other ways, by bequeathing a memorial monument, a hospital bed, a personally assembled art collection or a museum exhibit, a library; by organizing a permanent group or society or foundation; by undertaking or sponsoring a research program befitting the circumstances, and so forth. In still another context, grief might take the form of an artistic creation such as a symphony, a song, a book, or a poem inspired by the loved one's memory.

However, it is pertinent to question whether tangible productive works, monuments, or grief-inspired gifts to mankind are the *sine qua non* of creative grief. What of him who lacks artistic talents, material wealth, and intellectual interests? What of him who nonetheless experiences to the depths and core of his being genuine grief?

In answer it should be stated categorically that an adequate description of creative grief extends beyond the tangible. We must also consider acts of the human personality as expressions of creative grief, acts which result in the enrichment of the human spirit, heart or soul—those acts which have a real and enduring inspirational influence on the lives of all who are touched by them. The above should suffice to define creative grief. Meanwhile, the individual who expresses grief in this fashion, while resolving his own grief, resolves the continuation of the joy and sorrow of the past. He transcends his own individual grief and transforms it into a universal good.

Transitions for the Bereaved: The Future

C. MURRAY PARKES, M.D.

What does the future hold for the bereaved? Research studies on the adjustment of bereaved people have revealed many answers to this question. Some of the subjects have made healthy adjustments and talk realistically about plans, jobs, children, home; about playing apart in the life of the community and the family—about redecorating the house, caring for the children, about all the possibilities which are open to a mature person in this exciting world. But I have also come across other attitudes—feelings of aimlessness, bitterness, despair, or a blank refusal to think of the future at all.

One never ceases to be impressed by the human being's capacity to adapt to life's tragedies and disasters: to the frustration of losing a limb or going blind, to the disturbance of being robbed or mutilated, or to the degradation and danger of the concentration camp. All of these are experiences from which people have emerged without being shattered and destroyed and, in many cases, with a new wisdom and compassion.

Then why is it that some people who have suffered a major bereavement find it so hard to look to the future—so difficult to stop pining for what is gone? To answer this question I think we have to understand something of the nature of grief.

Grief is seen in its simplest form in animals. Take, for example, the behavior of a lioness who has lost her cubs. She becomes alert and tense, and she moves restlessly about searching for the missing cubs and calling aloud for them. The experienced hunter knows that if anything gets in the way of the lioness, she is likely to become aggressive. Obviously this behavior helps her to find her cubs. This type of behavior applies to animals separated from the herd, and even to domestic animals separated from their masters.

Human beings who suffer a bereavement have a deep-seated need to behave just like the lioness—to search restlessly, to call out, to attack anything which gets in the way. We know that such behavior has no hope of success; we also know that society frowns upon the expression of unrestrained emotion. And so we turn our grief inward. Instead of going out and searching for the one who has gone, our minds turn again and again to the events leading up to the bereavement, as if, by so doing, we can alter what has happened. In us, the animal's unrestrained call is stifled into a sob and the anger and bitterness which we feel are either turned against ourselves for some trivial reason or directed against others, often those closest to us, whom, in some small way, we can blame for what has happened. We are sometimes surprised and shocked by the intensity of our own feelings at this time. The world, which until recently was seen as safe and secure, has suddenly become dangerous and threatening. We respond to it with bitterness and anger.

In this frame of mind, the bereaved person may refuse offers of help, turn away from the world, and try to find some way of avoiding the pain and frustration of grieving. It is sometimes necessary, for practical reasons, to postpone grieving for a while—to pretend that the disaster has not happened until after arrangements have been made and the social aspects of the funeral are over and done with. Even for the strongest, it may be difficult to believe in the reality of what has happened: we keep expecting the lost person to return; we may even hear his footstep on the stair or, in our half-waking moments, see him nearby. I mention these things because some people are alarmed by them and think they may be signs of mental illness. They are nothing of the sort. The sense of being close to the lost person, which is experienced by so many widows, is evidence of the persistence, in each one of us, of an echo of the people we love. The longer a couple are married, the more alike they tend to become. Since husband and wife share the same world, they come to view it in the same way. Each, to some extent, takes in a part of the other, and it is this shared identity which persists after one of them has died. After the tragedy has occurred, the survivor may feel as if a part of himself has gone, too, but this feeling need not persist. Eventually most bereaved people are able to realize that the part of themselves which was bound up with the lost person is not also lost; there is a very real sense in which each person leaves his imprint on the world and in the hearts of those who loved him.

Let us now return to reconsider the future prospects of the bereaved person. I think there are a number of reasons why some people find it hard to make a new life for themselves after a bereavement.

First, there are the people who, at some level or other, have never given up hope that their lost one will return. They dwell in the past because they hope somehow to bring it back. To think of a future without the loved one would be a form of unfaithfulness. They feel guilty if they stay away from home too long, and they often try to keep things exactly the same as they were when the loved one was alive.

Then there are the people who feel a need to make reparation to the dead for some wrong which they have done. Perpetual grief can become a form of self-punishment, as if one were to say, "See how much I suffer—that proves that I loved him." This form of behavior, of course, proves nothing—all it does is prevent the bereaved person from finding a new and constructive way of justifying his existence. Another mental attitude which can prevent adjustment is persistent anger. I have described how the bereaved person often turns away from the world or bitterly rejects the overtures of friends. He acts as if he had been unjustly punished for a sin which he did not commit. "If this is what the world is about, I'll have nothing more to do with it." When you talk about the future, such a person feels insulted; he will not compromise with the enemy by admitting that there may still be something left in life.

Akin to the bitter one is the person who is afraid to look forward. He seems to say, "I'm not going to run the risk of being hurt again." He is a timid person who probably depended on the lost one for many things. He feels naked and unprotected, and reacts by withdrawing into his shell and refusing to come out.

A number of bereaved people tend to have some of these attitude seven if only in minor degree. The question is, how can a person begin to take a more positive attitude? In almost all cases the answer is clear: by having the courage to face reality, by having the courage to change. All change is painful, and the change necessitated by a major bereavement is one of the most painful of all. It is hard to give up the plans and hopes of a lifetime; it is hard to sever one's links with the past; but in a paradoxical way, it is only by looking to the future that one can fulfill the promise of the past. The world can be a frightening place; there are people whom we thought friends who will let us down; we may feel ashamed of being a widow or widower instead of a married person; yet when all this is said, there is still a considerable amount left on the credit side of life. A psychologist once carried out an unusual experiment on a tortoise. He set the tortoise down in front of a plate of lettuce and sat beside it with a pencil. Each time the tortoise poked its head out of its shell, the psychologist administered a light tap on the shell with his pencil. As soon as the tortoise felt the tap, its head shot back into the shell. For several hours the experiment went on: the tortoise cautiously extended the head, the psychologist tapped it with the pencil, and the head shot back. At last the tortoise's hunger became stronger than its fear. It put out its head, the psychologist tapped with his pencil, but instead of shooting back into his shell, the tortoise lumbered over to the lettuce and ate it.

I have talked with people who have had great difficulty in coming out of their shells. Usually, when they have plucked up courage to come out, they have been surprised to find nothing frightening. One young widow told me that she was afraid to leave the house because men would whistle at her in the street. She planned to buy a large dog which she intended to train to bite any man who came near her. She never did buy the dog, for, eventually, she found the courage to go out alone. Next time I saw her, I asked her if men still whistled at her, "Oh, yes," she said, "but they don't mean any harm."

Another widow of my acquaintance, somewhat older than this girl, had never been accustomed to attending social functions without her husband. After his death she stayed at home and refused to go out. She said that she felt conspicuous in a group of people and that nobody would understand her feelings. Because she had been a regular churchgoer, I telephoned her vicar, who persuaded one of his parishioners, herself a widow, to visit my friend and take her to a church social. She was surprised to find there a number of widows of her own age, and, before very long, became an active member of their group.

The difficulty in both these cases was in taking the first step, and it may be necessary to plan this first step carefully. A vacation is often a good time. I think every widow and widower ought to take a vacation when ready to think once more of the future. This must not be too soon after the bereavement; perhaps three months, perhaps twelve, perhaps eighteen months. But sooner or later, the time for taking stock arrives. A vacation gives one leisure to think by relieving a person of the day-to-day responsibilities of life. It allows a person to get away from reminders of the past and to build up the strength and courage necessary to start afresh. Some people prefer to take such a holiday alone and others with a close friend or family member but, in either case, it is important to make the vacation a complete break with the past.

We all know how valuable a close friend can be to a bereaved person. In our work at the Laboratory of Community Psychiatry, we have often found that the person who can be most helpful to a widow is another widow. A mature person who has been through the same experience herself and has come out of it a wiser and a more tolerant human being is often able to give more real help thana busy doctor or clergyman. That is not to say that the doctor and the clergyman do not have their value. Both are likely to be well acquainted with the problems of bereaved people and will often give excellent advice.

I have written of the bereaved person's picture of the world.What is the world's picture of the bereaved person? At the time of her bereavement, the widow, for instance, is treated with sympathy but also with a measure of fear.

People are often tense and nervous in their contact with newly bereaved people and it takes some time for this embarrassment to wear off. When it does, the status of the bereaved one is not quite the same. A widow is unlikely to be invited to mixed parties, and, in a man's world, she is often treated as a second-class citizen. I do not think there is much that can be done to change these attitudes; they exist and have to be accepted.

Relationships with other people, of course, are important, and bereavement can bring people closer together. Unfortunately, it can also be a source of disruption in the first few weeks after bereavement, when everybody is in an abnormal state of mind. There is a negative side to every relationship but one of the most difficult relationships is with mothers-in-law. No matter how well one knows and loves his mother-in-law, there is always the incontrovertible fact that this is the one who took her child away. If her child dies, she has the same need to blame someone else that everyone has. It is only natural that she will direct her anger toward her child's spouse just at the time when the latter is least able to cope objectively with the situation. In the cases of six of the twenty-one widows I interviewed, this situation had occurred; words had been spoken which could not be unsaid, and a major division had appeared, the children and other relatives taking sides and the whole thing becoming a hateful mess,

When this happens both sides stop seeing each other as people and "monsterize" each other. I use the term "monsterize" as the opposite of "idealize." To idealize someone is to imagine him better than he really is, and we tend to do that after bereavement with regard to the person who has died. There is no great harm in this provided that we do not have to monsterize living people in order to preserve this ideal picture of the dead.

There is also a tendency for bereaved people to idealize the past and monsterize the future. The person who says, "I have lost everything; I can see nothing good in the world" is doing this. It is true that he may have lost a great deal, but to say that there is nothing good left in the world is untrue. I suppose we all have this tendency. If the past was so marvelous that nothing can compete with it, then what is the use of trying? We can hang up our gloves and retire from the fight with a clear conscience. We idealize the past and monsterize the present because it relieves us of the sense of shame which would normally prevent us from throwing in the sponge. This is in fact the beatnik view of the world—it is a rotten world; we cannot change it, so why try? Most adolescents go through a phase in which the enormous complexity and size of the world becomes overwhelming. As they become more mature, they discover that there is a place in this complicated world for them; they achieve a fresh identity, but as an adult, not as a child. And when they do that, their picture of the world changes. The young adult sees the world as exciting and rewarding. From being a threatening and dangerous place, it is again secure and friendly.

Would I be going too far to suggest that the bereaved man or woman also has an adolescent crisis to go through? He, too, has to find a new identity. Just as the child was protected from the responsibilities of adult life, so the married person is protected from the responsibilities of single life. Both the adolescent and the bereaved person have to stand on their own feet; both find it unpleasant, and both of them are likely to rebel against the unpleasant necessity. Occasionally a person fails to get through the adolescent crisis, and we say, "He never grew up." In the same way, some bereaved people never get through their crisis of separation.

But for those who do succeed in making this painful transition, the rewards are great. A bereaved person who has been through the fire of grief, who has looked boldly at death and accepted his loss and his new identity, is a wiser, more mature, more tolerant, and probably more compassionate human being.

Reaching Out: The Library

ROY D. MILLER, JR., M.S.

No matter how death is faced, or how its distress is resolved, the public library is an all-encompassing public institution that can offer comfort, guidance, inspiration, and escape from the oppression of grief.

The library holds an almost unique place in most communities. Because it is not a commercial institution, time can be found to guide even the most timid patron to the book, the material, or the particular kind of information which he is seeking.

In advocating the services available in the library, it is not being implied that there one can find a panacea for all ills and distress. For those of the grieving whose loss triggers an emotional disturbance requiring specialized attention, the material on the shelves in the library is clearly not a primary source of help. The self-help books, and other similar material, will be of little benefit to them and may delay their receiving expert guidance and counsel. The majority of the bereaved, however, can be supported by their own inner strength, and the self-help, inspirational, and other appropriate materials to be found in the library will bring relief and a sustaining power to augment their own resources.

The suffering of the bereaved comes not only from loss of a loved one but also from the emptiness that follows, and from the bewilderment of not knowing what to do next, or how to do it, or where to turn for help in planning for the future. With the help of family and friends, the emptiness can, at least initially, be alleviated. But there are often periods when the bereaved may want to "get away" from the role they must assume when near those who are aware of their loss. In this situation, a service can be performed by the public library which is not often considered. Specifically, it is simply a *place* where one can go.

Many seek a place where they can get lost in the anonymous "crowd" and be alone with their private grief. The library is a public service unit where one can go to be among people, but not with them. But while pointing out this quiet place into which one can retreat from the noise and confusion of daily life, this rather negative form of service must not overshadow the positive and active side.

We are speaking here of a public service unit staffed by trained specialists; a public service unit whose doors are open, and whose facilities are freely accessible to all. No matter who you are, the extent of your education, or what your specific needs may be in the way of educational or recreational reading, your local library is ready to serve you.

It is often true that outside large cities there may not be as many libraries or librarians to serve the growing public needs. And often the availability of subject specialists is quite limited. But the trained librarian, while often not a subject specialist, is a specialist by virtue of his training and experience in searching out the information you may request. And if he cannot find the answer in his own unit, he will often advise you where it might be obtained in nearby institutions or where you can write for the information.

In some states, lines of communication have been set up among various large systems to provide better service to smaller libraries not having the funds for an extensive collection. Many federated systems are being formed throughout the country working in cooperation with each other to exchange books, material, and information among its members.

There are many who appreciate what the library has to offer, and who use it frequently; but I am also sure that there are many more who, for one reason or another, do not take advantage of this convenient institution of service in their midst. It is too bad that many, because of a sense of inadequacy, or embarrassment over lack of education, fail to approach the shelves laden with the very information and guidance which will help eliminate some of these feelings.There are those, too, who consider themselves self-sufficient and it would not occur to them to go to others for help. But one must not allow the virtues of independence and self-reliance to stand in the way of seeking help when it is so readily available and so often needed. One must not be too proud to reach out for aid when it is so comfortably at hand.

Library materials are not the sole answer to solving the universal human problem of grief; there is no one answer or solution. But there is comfort in the communication possible by reading the words of one human being to another. Grief is a human condition, but it is not a permanent disability for the normal individual who consciously seeks a way out of despair. For some, relief comes from articulating thoughts, doubts, and fears to friends, relations, clergymen, or professional counselors. The mode used depends on the degree of grief, and on the availability (physical or monetary) of counselors. But the library, open to all regardless of financial or educational status, is at least able to contribute in part to a program for rehabilitation.

It is extremely difficult for many people to approach a stranger, but the librarian, though a stranger, is available and ready to help at the Reference Desk. At the time of bereavement, this reluctance to communicate with strangers is often intensified, but a visit to the library can be helpful. There is much valuable information available there, information which even close friends are often unable to provide. And especially important to remember is that even when human contact is not desired, there is the card catalog which can be of immense help if just a little time is spent learning its mysteries. Most catalogs list the books (and sometimes other materials) in the collection by title, by author or editor (if it happens to be a collection of essays, poems, etc.), and by subject. Some catalogs have all three elements of entry interfiled in one alphabet, while others may have the subject cards in a separate unit. There are often signs or cards explaining "how to use the card catalog." Particular subjects pertinent here which you might explore include: consolation, death, etiquette, wills, letter-writing, etc.

The best way to clear away the mystery which often prevents many patrons from getting the most from all that is available at the library is simply to walk up to the desk and explain to the librarian that it is your first visit and that you would like a brief explanation of its basic arrangement. When the librarian realizes that you are unfamiliar with the library, he will give you a personal tour, or a resume of the general layout. One of the most difficult problems librarians face, when serving the public at the reference desk, is trying to find out exactly what information each patron is seeking.

Because grief is such a personal experience, no one compiler could possibly offer a list of books which would meet the requirements of even a small number of those seeking help. No matter what kind of material you are looking for—inspirational, sentimental, or even cynical—there is something available to fill almost every need. The tastes and requirements of man are as widely diversified as man himself, and the public library is stocked to satisfy most of these. But do not, however, be easily satisfied. Whether your requirement is vocational, avocational, or recreational, if you choose wisely, a book can be a precious balm. Search for the book and the author who speaks to you in your own language. Looking at pages filled with type arranged in orderly rows can offer little help, except for the passing of time, unless there is a real communication between the writer and you. If there is communication, you will know it. New ideas and concepts will demand some accommodation on your part, and may spark some rethinking, whether the thought is something with which you can agree or not. For the bereaved, an active mind diverted from the thoughts of the moment can bring relief in a surprisingly effective way.

Reaching Out: Education

KARL O. BUDMEN, ED.D.

There is no panacea for the pain of grief. Perhaps it is enough to recognize that grief will run its course. We can no more retain the intensity of its pain than we can prolong the ecstasy of happiness,which eludes us even as we savor it. At first, grief strikes like a tidal wave, cutting us loose from our moorings, and all but drowning us in a private sea of sorrow. In time, however, it passes; we find ourselves exhausted and sometimes lost, but alive, and cast up on the dry beach of life. Not only must life go on, it does go on, even for the bereaved. But it is not the same. A dimension is gone, possibly a pivotal, most significant dimension. The bereaved laments,"What shall I do now? How shall I continue living without my loved one? How can my life have purpose and meaning without the dimension of that loved one? What shall I *do*? What shall I *do?*" This is the ultimate expression of loss. In that lament, however, there is the prospect not merely of solace and surcease, but of a constructive return to living. Surely there is a distinction between being *alive*—a kind of existing—and living—an involvement in the affairs of life. To exist is a passive role with a single dimension; to *live* is an *active* role implying multiple dimensions. That plaintive cry, "What shall I do?" suggests that the bereaved is reaching out, perhaps unconsciously, for *action*, for *involvement* in short, for *living*.

But what action should he take? How shall he become involved again with the world of living? That is his predicament. We search frantically, sometimes even foolishly, for a way to reconstruct our lives, a way to liberate us from the imprisonment of grief. But, in the blindness of our unhappiness, we may miss the obvious, for there is a familiar process which can develop, nurture, and enrich our lives.That process is called education, education in its broadest sense, not merely the narrow world of books and formal instruction. We accept it willingly for our children, insisting that they have the opportunity to become what they are capable of becoming. But, unfortunately, we often fail to see that the process holds as much promise for adults, and that the fruits of that process can be theirs as well.

We have in our culture an expression which perpetuates a serious misconception. It is, "You can't teach an old dog new tricks." Perhaps not, but men are not dogs; they are men, and we do know "you can teach a man new tricks." That is the foundation of American education, the underpinning of an educational structure which extends from primary education to the education of senior citizens. It is not merely a proclamation of faith; it is a reality.

As a college teacher, I have taught hundreds of parents and grand parents. They have been among my best students, bringing a kind of maturity and insight not to be expected of the typical college undergraduate. They came belatedly to school. Some were resuming an education interrupted years before by economic need or by marriage and family responsibilities. Many were just beginning the fulfillment of a dream which earlier had been put aside. Still others came looking for new skills, new directions, new possibilities. But all of them shared the desire to change their lives through education, and they shared the fear that, perhaps, they were too old to learn.

Initially, their anxieties about failure stood out almost as dramatically as the freshman caps they proudly but self-consciously wore. Yet in the long hard course of four years of college work, few dropped out and almost none were academically unsuccessful. Most adapted and served as wholesome and stabilizing influences on their younger, less mature classmates. Many graduated with honors. Looking back from the vantage point of graduation, they spoke without exception of these college years as *significant in widening their horizons, enriching their minds, and providing new dimensions and directions for their lives*. They came ready to learn, and because they were ready, they were able to learn.

College is a formal approach. But there are other kinds of educational opportunities awaiting those who are ready to learn. Across our land, in high school buildings, community centers, church basements, and grange halls, wherever people can gather, there is a growing program of adult education. But whether it is called adult education or community action, whether it is sponsored by a religious, educational, or social organization, its purpose is the same: to offer new dimensions to human life, and to reach those who are by age or condition outside the traditional channels of education. Its development and growth are evidence of its effectiveness, and its students are witnesses to its power to change and redirect life.

The offerings of such programs are as broad as the needs they try to serve from carpentry to canasta, from farming to folk dancing, from basics to business, from vocations to avocations, from earning a living to living on earnings. Faced with problems of automation, increased leisure, senior citizenship, unemployment, and poverty, society has turned to education as the golden door and has insisted that the door be kept wide open. *There are no entrance requirements but that a man walk through the door, and by his presence say, "I am here. I want to learn."* That is enough. No tests, no credentials, no previous record of achievement, no prerequisites exist for admission, only a willingness and a readiness to learn.

That open door can be an invitation to return to the living world. Its promise is not that it will fill the hours or kill time, but that through its offerings one can learn to use the hours and invest time. To learn is to be involved, to be in contact with life, and to be part of it. It is not merely to be with people; it is to be of people. If education is to be effective, it must touch the heart as well as the mind. It must stir the passions and kindle the fires of imagination and creativity. It cannot restore the dimension which is gone, but it can offer new dimensions, new interests, new involvements, and commitments for a reconstructed life. It is one of the answers to "What shall I do?" It is a place to begin.

Renewal

AUSTIN H. KUTSCHER

So closely related are the various aspects of grief and bereavement that thought can scarcely be given to any one of them without touching upon a vast number of other factors. We have reflected upon the entire subject of grief resulting from bereavement, beginning with every aspect of the human being's confrontation with the facts of life and death, from his realistic involvements through his psychologic reactions, carrying him through every ramification of his emotional response to the inevitable conclusion—final acceptance.

A time must come when one moves into the practical and tangible realm of what he can do to help himself advance further through the various stages of his grief. A beginning of reentry, however tentative or hesitant, into the pleasures of living is an essential step toward the ultimate goal of his recovery from the ordeal just past. Far from being an act of disloyalty or a sign of love forgotten, in truth, this is the greatest tribute he can pay to the memory of the lost one—a resumption of living free from the haunting pangs of past sorrow.

Before too long, therefore, the bereaved should find it possible to say with Dryden: "For all happiness mankind can gain/Is not in pleasure but in rest from pain." With the introduction of this thought, at least the thought of pleasure once again becomes tenable.

In what manner, then, can the bereaved bring himself to look, even reluctantly, upon pleasure? First of all, he must rid himself of the thought that his life at this stage should be devoid of all enjoyment. In the early stages of his grief, he doubtlessly found himself deeply troubled with guilt and self-reproach: his loved one is gone, but he is still alive and even thinking of peace, happiness, and pleasure. This is the first hurdle to cross, both with and without the added pressures imposed by one's own conscience or by relatives and the social environment in which he lives. Few people who have lost loved ones can escape the social pressures from without or subconscious pressures from within which urge them to conform to a generally accepted time table applied to grief and bereavement—regardless of his progress or lack of progress. Such obstacles can and must be overcome, and it is with the approbation of clergymen, physicians, psychiatrists, psychologists, and social scientists that one can approach these stumbling blocks.

Our world offers an inexhaustible array of diversion—reading, music, art, the theater, motion pictures, sports, travel, crafts, hobbies, television, and radio, to name only a few. It matters not how the initial disengagement from the state of bereavement is accomplished so long as the mind's total immersion in grief and bereavement is at last ended.

The bereaved must consider whether he wishes to become involved in the activity to which he is most inclined as an onlooker or as a participant. Does he wish to read, or to write? He may want to visit art museums or just one museum in particular; or perhaps he has the talent to paint; he may want to play the piano or he may prefer to listen to recordings or concerts, to hear and enjoy music as symphony, opera, ballet, or the musical theater. If he is a devotee of the sports world, many opportunities are open to him—bowling or swimming, golf or tennis, the daily sports programs to be seen on television. Some people, however, particularly if the physical activities themselves are not too taxing, may need to expend their energies by plunging as soon as possible into active participation in sports. Each individual must determine according to his own inclination whether he would prefer to watch other people in action, or whether physical participation would afford him a desirable release from the physical and emotional tensions of his bereaved state.

"But how should I begin?" The only reply is that there is no single way; there are a myriad of ways. There is an individual way for everyone—if only he will grasp it. One of my own tentative steps toward recovery from grief was to write for tickets for myself and my boys for a ball game scheduled several months later. The mere thought of taking this step was painful, but the mailing of the letter sufficed for a beginning.

Some of the bereaved may also find, as I did, that music offers comfort to the spirit. Music was the first outside influence which I was able to tolerate as an interruption of my grief. Not being a devotee of the opera or ballet, and finding the remainder of the classical repertoire inexpressibly depressing at that time, I turned to the recordings of the musical theater. For instance, *Carousel* had always seemed to be beautifully sad, and so had the theme, lyrics and music of *West Side Story*. These were music dramas which did not offend the sensitivity of the moment for me personally, and I felt that they ought not offend anyone else near me or any who might feel that my conduct was improper, unloving or disrespectful. My reintroduction to this kind of music occurred at my children's eager insistence that we watch *Carousel* on the late show. How sad and yet how exalting are the music and words, for example, of "You'll Never Walk Alone!" And thus music, the theater, and television all intruded—and, as time passed, they were to become welcome intruders.

If one has the means, travel may be the turning point. Travel has many aspects. Some regard it as an escapism, others as a search for excitement or gratification of a desire to explore new lands. Certainly, travel affords an opportunity to meet new people. It is of interest to note that most people who go on escorted tours are taking the journey that they had once contemplated taking together with the deceased loved one (usually a husband or a wife). Although now alone, the bereaved can enjoy their travels with the sense that it is under the blessing of a strong spiritual bond with the departed. Curiously enough, the friendships which are made on these journeys often last for a lifetime.

The bereaved who has an interest in a craft may find that what was once just a hobby is now a godsend. And always, there is reading. He has books in his own home to select from. If the bereaved wishes a wider variety of subjects, a trip to the public library can provide absorbing material in any area which is of interest to him. In time, these beginnings of renewal will lead to an extension of the powers of enjoyment. The senses begin to reawaken—even, for example, so elemental a sense as that of hunger. One commences to give thought not merely to the taste of food but to the breaking of bread as it once used to be. Eating at home, no doubt, has remained more or less perfunctory; as the horizon of living widens somewhat, dining with relatives or friends reminds one of the modern ritual of dining out. At first the thought of going to a restaurant poses problems. Should one go to places which have associations with the past? The question makes itself heard, "How can I eat there without him?" Should one go to new places? Will it be the same? The answer can safely be left to the decision, perhaps by trial and error, of the bereaved.

One need not search too far for additional avenues to provide surcease and renewal. Close at hand there may be means to relieve the pressure on a heavy heart: a child brings home a report card with marks that arouse pride, even if at the same time tears well up in your eyes because the loved one is not there to share your pleasure. Sometimes a friend or relative engages you in a conversation that becomes absorbing, and draws you out so that you feel like your old self again. Eventually, these pleasures cease to yield self-reproach—you no longer bring yourself up sharply with the thought that you are allowing yourself to be derailed from the main line of sorrowful thought which has been occupying your mind without relief.

Or a pet again becomes a source of comfort. People who have never cared to own a pet may now find themselves surprisingly pleased and delighted to have a puppy, for instance, demanding their care as well as their affection.

The television set provides much diversion and entertainment in every household. You may struggle against greeting the humor of a comedian with a smile, but there will come a time when the laughter from the studio audience or from your family will not intrude as harshly upon your mood. You will begin to think: Is it wrong to smile just a little even at a time of grief? Should I not welcome a smile as a sign of some recovery? Will others continue to seek me out if my sorrows are forever mirrored on my face?

And now you realize that you must think of seeking the satisfactions of companionship. Whereas until this point you have been barely able to tolerate yourself, you begin to understand that renewed sociability is imperative—that family, friends, and then perhaps new acquaintances must be accorded a place in your life. A person will gravitate naturally to whichever sex he finds more interesting, companionable, or comforting; and he will start to enjoy being among and with people for longer periods of time; and then he may enjoy and even come to love one particular person—as a companion whose presence fills him with happiness.

Whenever the bereaved can bring himself to consider the subject of remarriage, an important step in the recovery will have come to pass. Doubtless, every bereaved person initially believes this course to be an impossibility, but he must at least give thought to the possibility, difficult as it may be. He should appreciate that during his convalescence from grief, he has derived his greatest comfort from love—the love of his children, the love of his parents, and the love of his friends. And, yes, when the right person appears, once more he can experience, gain, and turn to the love of someone with whom he can share his life through remarriage.

Remarriage has the considered and authoritative approval of all groups of those who have given deep thought to the subject—the clergy, sociologists, pyschiatrists, and philosophers. The testimony of the Bible and the God-given inclinations of man attest to the reality of two basic human needs: the need for love and the need to love.

In the final analysis, whenever and however one learns anew that happiness can be *more* than the absence of pain, he will have at least modestly and perhaps profoundly regained the pleasures of living.

Part Five
NEEDS OF THE BEREAVED

Medical Needs of the Bereaved Family

GEORGE A. HYMAN, M.D.

The chief medical and psychological needs of the close members of a bereaved family must be cared for at three relevant periods: (1) shortly prior to the loss, in circumstances when death has been imminent; (2) within four weeks afterward; and (3) at a time later than four weeks.

The bereaved, as a natural reaction to their loss, tend to ignore even serious and important medical problems that may present themselves. An overt, unavoidable emergency calls forth immediate action. Excess of grief may result in accidents causing injury, and these, too, by their very nature, may require prompt care regardless of the state of mind of the grieving family.

But frequently we may encounter more serious medical problems which do not make themselves so apparent as fainting and injuries and are, therefore, ignored or brushed aside as not being of proper or of sufficient import to investigate at such a time.

Occasionally, known hypertension, diabetes, cardiac disease, and other serious ailments may exist among the mourners, and it is not unusual for medication customarily taken to be neglected and a possible crisis precipitated.

The most common lack in these periods is adequate rest, both mental and physical. It is perfectly proper to take medication to insure sleep at night, even if this must be done every night; and, during the day, for relief of nervous and emotional strain, it is often well to take a mild sedative. If sleeping problems are encountered, hypnotic drugs may be taken at night in adequate dosage.

Sometimes a tranquilizer or an antidepressant or stimulant is needed to obviate the strain of the second period.

Medical assistance should be sought when indicated, even if only to sedate the grief-stricken, and thus to avoid possible flare-ups of latent or pre-existing disorders.

It stands to reason that a bereaved person will scarcely choose such a time to undergo elective surgery. But cases are encountered in which someone facing an imminent loss may learn at the same time that he himself has developed a malignant condition which urgently requires surgery. Postponement of surgery and delay in instituting the necessary therapy may turn a possible curable situation into still

190

another disastrous source of grief for a family already saddened by the coming of, or by a current, death.

When symptoms are noticed or a serious illness is suspected in a bereaved person, it is only fair to the living for a relative to urge that the family physician be consulted. If the bereaved offers too much resistance to a visit to the doctor, the affected person can sometimes be prevailed upon to talk to the doctor on the telephone, with resultant reassurance. The complaint may be temporarily resolved with safety or, if necessary, arrangements can be made for an evaluation that would forestall a possibly dangerous delay.

The chief deterrent in situations such as this is the feeling of guilt which strikes the bereaved because he may feel he is thinking of himself at such a time. It is the duty of relatives to point out that this is not a question of selfishness; a person who is ill during a time of sorrow is in fact under an obligation not to add to the grief of the family by incurring the possibility of a further calamity to afflict them.

The appearance of disturbing symptoms, therefore, even while mourning is in progress, demands proper medical attention; and if full care *can*, in fact, be delayed until the later stages of mourning have arrived, certainly it will have been worthwhile for the sick person as well as for relatives to have found this out. Once the third period has begun, the ill person, with the support of relatives, should make regular visits to his physician to receive treatment for his condition. If there is no need for an operation and there is no severe disease, the bereaved would still be wise to review in retrospect his state of mind, and relieve both himself and his close relatives of any anxiety, doubt,or guilt feelings which may have manifested themselves during the difficult days of early bereavement. He may find that a medical consultation at this time will enormously relieve him. For instance, if a spouse has passed on, the bereaved may have fallen prey to a latent fear that an hereditary disease may afflict his children; a visit to the physician will likely prove effective in easing his mind.

Surely, if any bereaved person were to think clearly, he would realize that the loved one who has died would certainly want him to remain in good health. This simple, uncomplicated thought should go far toward eradicating unrealistic feelings about self-abnegation with respect to maintaining health during the period of bereavement. Modern civilization does not countenance the practice of suttee, either physically or symbolically, and it is to the credit of society that it tends, instead, to classify excessive grief as self-indulgence; whereas a sensible regard for the influence of the neglect of self on his relatives should move a bereaved person in the direction of seeking help when help is needed. Thus, instead of denying life, he affirms within himself that the love of the lost one has remained with him, not as a pull toward self-destruction, but as a beacon to reach for in the effort to fulfill the wish it undoubtedly expresses for his continued health and well-being.

Why You Need Your Physician Now

JOSEPH BESS, D.O.

The bereaved can profitably turn for advice to his physician. It is pertinent to set forth at this point those characteristics of the physician which qualify him as one whose counsel has its own unique validity.

First and foremost is the physician's awareness that grief for any two persons is never quite the same—nor for that matter is grief ever quite the same for any one person from moment to moment. Such a realization enables the physician to consider and prescribe for the changing needs of the bereaved throughout the process of mourning.

Secondly, and of equal importance, is his awareness of certain "normal" psychophysiological changes in the usual behavior of the bereaved ranging from disturbances of sleep and appetite to seemingly bizarre thoughts regarding the deceased. Feelings of depression, guilt, anxiety, hostility, and other symptoms, which might ordinarily have a particular meaning to the physician in some other patient, will rightly appear and be interpreted as normal or healthy reactions in the grief-stricken—in most instances. Such symptoms, he knows, are as normal in the usual work of mourning and eventual recovery from grief as fever may often be in the course of recovery from illness. Consequently, he can provide the necessary professional reassurance and encouragement so often needed during a time of crisis.

Thirdly, the physician is able to distinguish normal from pathological grief—"pathological" not in the strict sense of being merely abnormal or unusual, but rather in the sense that it is too intensive or too prolonged and which jeopardizes and finally impairs the health and well-being of the bereaved. The physician can intervene and utilize his skill, training, and experience to help avert a most serious or prolonged state of depression.

192

Fourthly, he recognizes, accepts, and encourages, the usually normal desire and need of the bereaved to communicate and thus outwardly express his innermost feelings to an individual with the capacity to comprehend his grief. Hence, as the physician listens, he also interprets the significance of the confidences he hears.

Fifthly, and of prime importance for the grief-stricken, is the bereaved's closely related need for meaningful consolation and supportive therapy—particularly in the earlier stages of grief—and the physician's ability to provide this. Such care can be meaningful because of the physician's identification and sympathy with the plight of the bereaved, and it can be supportive because of the physician's compassionate understanding of the bereaved's fears and feelings of aloneness.

Sixthly, the physician accepts as part of his professional responsibility the frequent need of the bereaved for guidance and the equally frequent dependence of the bereaved upon the physician in many matters which demand the making of decisions. Some of these questions often appear momentous in the eyes of the bereaved who has temporarily lost his usual capacity for rational decision-making. In problems of practical concern for the bereaved, especially when there are no family members at hand, the physician's advice regarding where the bereaved should live, what he should be doing, etc., can be most valuable. The physician, through his personal knowledge and evaluation of the bereaved's highly individual and uniquely different needs at any one particular moment, can often provide answers which are tailored to suit the needs of the patient.

Physiological Aspects of Depression

JEROME STEINER, JOHN F. O'CONNOR AND
LENORE O. STERN

In presenting the information which follows, neither the purpose for introducing it nor the implications should be misunderstood or misinterpreted. It is *not* intended as a layman's guide to the practice of medicine, nor as a vicarious excursion into academic medicine;

not even as an aid to the interpretation of the symptoms of bereavement—although the material verges on this.

Rather, it *is* intended to provide another insight into the full dimensions of grief and bereavement—through an understanding of which, the surmounting of the bereavement state is enhanced and the timetable of recovery from bereavement speeded. Even more specifically, the reader is encouraged to consider the information which follows as a sensible injunction against self-neglect on the part of the bereaved, who should be persuaded to seek medical advice when he displays symptoms of matching character to those described.

It is repeated emphatically: this material is not provided in lieu of a medical consultation. Also, although many types of professionals are qualified to corroborate the need for medical care and suitably direct the bereaved to a doctor, only a physician can undertake the final diagnostic step to affirm such need and prescribe the definitive therapy. Especially if there is now no one close enough to him who will urge this course, it behooves the bereaved to seek help himself as soon as he can, for there is no merit in lying supine under misfortune. All the implications of such neglect of self are deleterious in the extreme, for they can lead to unfortunate consequences that might have been prevented and which almost certainly will be later regretted.

The information here provided should serve only as an influence leading to medical consultation, the only definitive step which can help differentiate between temporary signs of a physical disorder due to grief and more serious signs of some physical deterioration that ought to be medically investigated.

The person bereaved should look upon the discussion which follows not with apprehension or alarm but with the thought that "a word to the wise is sufficient." Thus he should seek to control his grief by demanding of himself sensible behavior.

A.H.K.

The close relationship that exists between emotion and bodily function has been recognized for centuries; one sees the redness of the face which accompanies anger, the "tension" headache, the paleness which may follow fear, the weakness which may result from a sudden tragic episode. An emotion is instinctive, a state of feeling that has both physical and psychological manifestations. Physical manifestations, being more observable, are more objective in character than are the psychological. The interaction between the psychological and physical has been a subject of speculation since man learned to differentiate the effects of external events from those of his internal experiences.

Most emotional disorders have physiological accompaniments. In depression, the somatic elements are readily perceivable and are generally considered to be a reaction to what is basically a feeling state.

Depression is an internal emotional experience; generally, a response to loss. It may arise from the loss of a person or an object closely related to self; it may consist of a subjective loss of self-esteem, of love or affection. Medically, what is referred to as "depression" is the combined psychological and physical reaction to the setting up of a rather complicated set of defenses against the experience.

In one form or another, loss is a normal part of the life process. People die, loved ones are separated, relationships end, and individuals can be injured both physically and emotionally. A "normal" depression with both somatic and psychological components follows such events. The individual feels despondent, distressed, and, at times, over-irritable. There may be difficulty in eating and sleeping; there may be a loss of interest in normal activities, but usually, routine occupations and relationships are not interfered with. This type of depression is best described as a "grief reaction". It is self-limited and short-lived, disappearing within two to eight weeks and requiring little, if any, intervention by a physician. An awareness of the fact that life continues, that friends remain and that new relationships can develop goes a long way toward making a normal grief reaction tolerable. Such a reaction in varying degrees is familiar to all of us.

The "Pathologic" depressions do not resolve spontaneously and require more than time itself for their relief. They are divided into three general types: (1) a retarded depression, (2) an agitated depression, and (3) a depression characterized by somatic or behavioral manifestations, such as excessive alcohol intake, the use of drugs or anti-social conduct.

The retarded depression is best described as a generalized "slowing-down" period. The tone of the individual's feeling is one of sadness and fatigue. He moves and thinks slowly, has difficulty in sleeping and frequently finds that he awakens very early in the morning. His appetite may be poor, and there is usually a significant weight loss of from ten to twenty pounds. This group of symptoms resembles the state which occurs in some of the mammalian species when their food supply is threatened—that is, hibernation. Hibernation is a normal physiologic adaptation in animals to periodically unfavorable environmental conditions, such as cold weather. Food is not readily available, the animal's activity slows down and, therefore, he re-

195

quires less fuel. Nervous excitability decreases, as do the temperature, blood pressure, respiratory and heart rates. In human beings, one could view the retarded depression as a physiological sedation resulting from loss or injury and the ensuing inevitable threat to the satisfaction of needs: personal ambition decreases, physical movement is slowed, appetite fails, sexual desire diminishes or disappears. Insomnia develops, and the individual becomes increasingly tired, with a resulting greater desire for sleep. Unlike hibernation, this constellation of symptoms is not useful to the individual but, nevertheless, it is a coordinated pattern of body reaction which occurs often. Although coping with depressed feelings is more cerebral in the human being than in lower animals, in both there are pre-established physiological systems that come into play.

In the agitated form of a depression, an innate sense of sadness and despondency is mixed with feeling states of fear and anger. Although this syndrome, too, is characterized by autonomic dysfunction, the pattern is markedly different from that seen in the previously described retarded depression. Activity increases and body weight may either be gained or lost as the appetite fluctuates. Dyspepsia is present and, frequently, diarrhea or constipation. Women may stop menstruating and men may become impotent. On the other hand, the individual can well have a marked increase in sexual activity. It is as if there is a need for constant movement in order to discharge the great tension he feels. In the agitated depression, the basic reaction of anger is less under control and much closer to the surface than in the retarded depression. The individual is hyperirritable and tense and at times he will tell you that he is "ready to explode" or to "jump out of his skin." This form of depression typically occurs during the involutional period when sexual powers and attractiveness are felt to be on the wane.

Rene Spitz has compared the agitated state to that which is described by Hans Selye as a "general adaptation syndrome." According to this theory, a stress (which may be the emotional response to loss) upsets the balance of glandular functioning. During the first phase of the syndrome, there is great nervous tension and excitement. If this continues, it can be followed by muscular degeneration and decreased body activity. The final stage of a stress reaction might be equated with a retarded depression. However, if one considers retarded depression to be a physiologic sedative following the experience of loss, agitated depression could be seen as a state of physiological excitement.

The third major type of depression is that wherein the feeling state is hidden and is represented by various somatic symptoms or by antisocial activities. Excessive preoccupation with heart function, digestive system and other body organs is frequently apparent. Careful examination of the individual's physiological functioning and prohibition of the inappropriate behavioral outlets (alcohol, drug ingestion) will reveal the underlying sadness and depressed reactions to loss. When these phenomena substitute for what is commonly known as depression, they are called "depressive equivalents." Typically, the depressed person is felt to be an irritant by the other family members, e.g., they condemn the alcoholic for his "weakness," the middle-aged person for wearing a chip on the shoulder, and the delinquent for showing hostility. Yet all are completely unaware that they are undergoing reactions to loss. This is not to say that all persons who manifest such behavior are depressed; however, when these conditions are depressive equivalents, medical treatment must be oriented to the underlying depression. The condition can be treated by the physician with a fair chance of success.

Depression manifests itself through most organ systems:

The Skin

Most skin manifestations are secondary to changes in nerve functioning. At times there is excessive sweating. Pallor may occur. Occasionally, psychophysiological reactions such as hives, itching and other rashes are seen in susceptible individuals who are depressed.

Muscular System

Muscular coordination can be poor and there is frequently a tremor. There are variations in the speed with which the person can carry out a given act. One research scientist has measured the pattern of electrical excitability of muscles. He has developed an entire theory differentiating depression from other illnesses on the basis of the electrical potential of muscle. This author has been able to find biochemical support for his theory. Again the question might be asked whether the changes in these patterns are secondary to deranged sleep and eating or whether they are primary and definitive of the syndrome.

The depressed person tends, if he is retarded, to slump and walk slowly. There is little tone to his musculature and the response to stimuli is decreased. The opposite is true in the hyperactive, hypertonic and hyperexcitable agitated person.

Cardiorespiratory System

The depressed patient will occasionally have some breathing difficulties. These are mainly related to excessive sighing associated with feelings of shortness of breath as a result of excessive concern or concentration on the process of breathing. Most commonly, this is seen in the retarded depression or when the feeling state is being handled by denial. On the other hand, the agitated person will experience the hyperventilation syndrome. In this case, due to overbreathing, the patient. builds too high an oxygen level in the blood, causing decreased stimulation of the respiratory center in the brain, and there is a subjective feeling of shortness of breath (although the opposite is true). Dizziness, numbness of the extremities, chest pain, and occasionally unconsciousness follow. This is a self-limiting set of symptoms and is rarely dangerous to the individual.

The depressed person frequently becomes aware of a rapid, strong heart beat—"palpitations." He may at times feel that he is having a heart attack and feels as if the blood is not reaching the tips of his fingers and toes, which tingle and "fall asleep." He may become excessively concerned with his own cardiac status. Blood pressure can rise or fall depending on the individual's susceptibility. Most somatic preoccupations disappear with alleviation of the depression.

Digestive System

All depressives are subject to gastrointestinal disturbances. In the retarded depression, an individual may lose his appetite. In an agitated state, he may try to "calm his nerves" by over eating. Gastrointestinal disturbances have their own consequences—weight fluctuates, indigestion is common and, not infrequently, there are the complications of a malnourished state. Because of dietary changes or perhaps nervous and hormonal dysfunctions, the individual may either be constipated or develop diarrhea. These bowel disorders further complicate the physiological picture by upsetting the organism's salt and water balance and the ability to handle waste products.

Genitourinary System

The depressed person may complain of burning on urination or of urgency that is unrelated to any infectious process. Frequently, a woman's menstrual period becomes irregular or ceases completely.

It appears certain that these irregularities are secondary to hormonal changes.

Endocrine System

Frequently seen is a depressive reaction following the normal hormonal changes which occur in late middle-age. One also sees depression following the birth of a child. This, too, is a period of great hormonal change and readjustment. Recent work indicates that there are hormonal changes which occur during a depressive reaction. It has been shown that in severe cases there is an increase of the hormone secreted by the adrenal cortex. However, these studies have not been standardized, and research at various laboratories yields apparently contradictory results.

Disorders of thyroid function are often accompanied by depression. However, it is unlikely that depression causes thyroid dysfunction or that this is a regular accompaniment of the feeling state.

The role of endocrine imbalance in depression remains vague. Although probably not a precipitating factor, it still may be responsible for converting a grief reaction into depressive illness.

Nervous System

A sleep disturbance is always present. Early morning awakening is typically characteristic of the retarded depression. The agitated depressive is likely to have more difficulty in sleeping through the night. Careful studies using brain wave and dream patterns have shown that all depressions are accompanied by objectively observable changes. Any depressed individual is more wakeful and more responsive to sound stimulation in all stages of his sleeping than is the non-depressed individual; he sleeps less than usual, spends less time in a deep sleep, and has greater difficulty in falling asleep.

It is theorized that nerve cells, which are continually bombarded by stimuli, in this case as a result of depression, become fatigued and therefore are less able to transmit the necessary impulses for normal brain conduction. This theory would account for disturbances in memory and attention, in muscular functions, in sleep and various other manifestations.

The attention span of the depressed person is shortened. He is easily distracted and has difficulty in the interpretation of sensory impulses. Either touch, taste, hearing, and sight are bombarding him or he does not register all of their stimulation. Often he feels that he has grown hard-of-hearing, that all foods taste the same, that his eyes burn or refuse to focus and his hands cannot identify objects as readily as before.

TREATMENT

Depression is a definitely treatable entity with a good chance of successful outcome. Familiar to most persons are environmental change and counseling. Psychotherapy is frequently effective. Many new drugs are available as well as other forms of physical treatment. The role of female (estrogenic) hormones remains unclear, except, perhaps, in the management of involutional depression in the female. As an adjunctive form of treatment, the use of hormones can help to alleviate such physical manifestations as hot flashes, but they have no demonstrable effect on the psychological symptoms.

In summary, depression may be described as a feeling state of sadness, fear or fatigue, or combinations of these, accompanied by sleep disturbance, digestive disorders, nervous and muscular impairment and various other somatic complaints. This collection of symptoms is not unique, and the physician must differentiate true depression *per se* from other medical illnesses. There is no doubt that depression is not just a "state of mind." It is a generalized illness which follows the rules defining all other medical illnesses and, like others, it is both incapacitating and painful. Fortunately, there are various forms of treatment available that have proven effective in its amelioration.

Opinions of the Bereaved on Bereavement

AUSTIN H. KUTSCHER

In order to provide the bereaved and those close to them with an understanding of how others react to loss, we created a survey of attitudes of the bereaved toward problems inherent in the dying process, grief, and mourning. The following are the responses of 125 bereaved on (1) signs and symptoms of bereavement; (2) guilt and bereavement; (3) what the bereaved should be told by the physician; (4) what the bereaved should be encouraged to do; and (5) advice concerning remarriage.

SIGNS AND SYMPTOMS OF BEREAVEMENT

Regarding the appearance of grief prior to the death of the patient, 48 percent of the bereaved predict the appearance of symptoms such as loss of appetite and/or weight, sleeplessness, feelings of despair, and feelings of helplessness in the bereaved-to-be always or frequently.

Approximately 90 percent of the bereaved anticipate that dreams of the deceased will occur always or frequently. Illusions of the deceased occur at least sometimes, according to 51 percent of the bereaved, although 22 percent believe these illusions never occur.

Over half of the bereaved believe that angry thoughts and feelings toward the deceased never occur; guilt feelings are predicted to occur always or frequently by only 19 percent; feelings of infidelity are predicted to occur rarely or never by 67 percent.

That the bereaved will at least sometimes have subjective symptoms similar to the deceased is the opinion of only one-third of the group of widows and widowers.

Symptoms in the bereaved such as diminished sexual desire, impotence and greater inclination toward masturbation are reported relatively rarely by the bereaved respondents. For example, only 32 percent anticipate impotence at least sometimes; diminished sexual desire reported by 58 percent to occur at least sometimes;but 38 percent assume that it rarely or never occurs; one-third predict an inclination to masturbation will never occur.

GUILT AND BEREAVEMENT

Guilt is always or frequently less likely when there has been free expression of feelings between the dying person and the "bereaved-to-be," according to 69 percent of the bereaved. Approximately 60 percent expect that the bereaved will rarely or never experience guilt under the circumstances of beginning to function on his or her own, accepting the inevitability of the death, and then beginning to take up new interests once more. When more specific questions are asked concerning putting away pictures of the deceased, having renewed interest in members of the opposite sex, and deciding to remarry, over half of the bereaved group expects there will rarely never be such guilt feelings. They do not, however, anticipate experiences of pleasure in the bereavement state—only 19 percent expect it within a few weeks after the deceased passed away.

WHAT THE BEREAVED SHOULD BE TOLD
BY THE PHYSICIAN

It is always or frequently important to advise the bereaved how often death is faced with serenity by the dying, 41 percent of the bereaved respondents believe, and 78 percent feel that such advice is at least sometimes important. One-third of the group feels that bereaved individuals should always be made aware of the patient's right to die, although 12 percent believe this should never be the case. More than 58 percent of the bereaved believe that the practitioner should always advise the bereaved in detail that everything was done.

More than half of the bereaved group feel that physicians should encourage the bereaved to think that he will experience less fear of future tragedies following the current loss. Approximately three-fourths tend to feel that emphasis should be placed at least sometime on the bereaved's being fortunate to have a child by the departed spouse, if that is the case.

WHAT THE BEREAVED SHOULD BE ENCOURAGED TO DO

On the subject of seeking care and advice, 72 percent of the bereaved feel that regular visits to the physician during the first year should be encouraged at least sometimes; there is strong agreement that the bereaved should not be hospitalized for an elective procedure soon after or during the course of bereavement. More than two-thirds suggest that the bereaved seek advice at least soon after the funeral; however, only 29 percent suggest that such advice should, at the least, be considerable, and more than half prefer that it be minimal. The group of bereaved suggests turning to the clergyman (27 percent), the lawyer (25 percent), and the physician (21 percent). When the bereaved is religiously inclined, 79 percent of the widows and widowers suggest that at least sometimes he should be urged to attend religious services on the day(s) which have special significance with regard to the deceased. More than 74 percent agree that psychiatric advice would be of benefit at least sometimes, and 65 percent feel that this would also be true of vocational guidance at this time.

Over 88 percent of the bereaved feel that expression rather than repression of feelings, and crying, should be encouraged at least sometimes. Almost half feel that repression of distressing memories should rarely or never be encouraged. They favor encouraging the bereaved to speak about the recent bereavement: 87 percent agree that the bereaved should be encouraged to talk to old friends at least sometimes; 92 percent encourage talking with someone who has had a similar experience at least sometimes; nearly all encourage the bereaved to talk to someone about feelings related specifically to the deceased.

Over half of the widows and widowers favor keeping the deceased's wedding ring permanently. As to various other personal belongings of the deceased, there seems to be general agreement: keep some, give some to family or friends, give some to a charity. Promises made by the bereaved to the deceased during life should be followed if practical and reasonable, but hardly any bereaved indicated that such promises should be followed if not practical. The bereaved should always or frequently be encouraged to relinquish excessive attachments to the deceased, according to 72 percent of the bereaved respondents.

It was commonly felt that at least sometimes the person in grief should obtain a pet, seek a companion (if elderly), travel, go shopping, change jobs if he had long wanted to do so, move to a new living location, or seek vocational guidance. They are also predominantly in favor both of continuing old hobbies and beginning new ones at this time. About half would encourage the bereaved to resume work within a week, and three-quarters within two weeks. Some 14 percent would encourage a return to work only when the bereaved feels up to it. More than 78 percent indicate that at least sometimes this might he a time to encourage the bereaved to change jobs, if this had been his long-time desire. More than 90 percent see working as frequently or always being good for the bereaved—of those, nearly two-thirds emphasized "always." Many (37 percent) suggest that the bereaved always or frequently make major decisions as early as possible.

ADVICE CONCERNING REMARRIAGE

An impressive majority of the widows and widowers—92 percent—indicated that the bereaved should always be encouraged to remarry if age permits; 78 percent regard remarriage as the major problem of the young bereaved spouse. That those who have loved deeply and satisfyingly tend to remarry more quickly is the opinion of 59 percent of the bereaved. However, 63 percent feel that it is not desirable to encourage the bereaved to make the decision whether or not to remarry before a particular person is considered, and 80 percent also feel that it is not desirable to inform relatives and in-laws of a decision to remarry before a particular person is considered.

Part Six

STARTING OVER

A Doctor Discusses Sexuality and Bereavement

ROBERT MICHELS, M.D.

Death and sex are two topics which are extremely difficult to discuss openly in contemporary society. Both involve strong emotions, deeply rooted in the most private areas of one's life. Many individuals are unable to resolve their conflicts or diminish their anxieties related to these subjects by the usual means of discussing or sharing their thoughts with family, friends, and trusted advisors.

The problem is further compounded by a personal crisis which involves both of these areas. The death of a loved one, any loved one, invariably affects one's attitudes, feelings, and behavior insofar as sexual desire is concerned. But the death of a spouse or sexual partner produces a more direct and dramatic effect.

The death of someone we deeply love is followed by a grief that affects all personal relationships. The one who suffered the loss wants and needs emotional warmth and security but at the same time feels that he should deny himself all pleasures and enjoyments. Normal sexual behavior involves all of these: warmth, security, pleasure, and enjoyment. Thus the individual will oftentimes experience a shift in his sexual interest and behavior with a decrease in some aspects of it and an increase in others. More important than any quantitative change can be the disturbing and shattering awareness that the pleasurable aspects of sex lead to guilt, and, that greater loneliness and unhappiness accompany avoidance or abstinence.

Grief over the loss of any loved person not only affects attitudes toward personal sexual behavior but also influences basic sexual drives. An individual who has suffered a recent loss has little interest in his usual activities, including sexual activities. This diminished interest in sex is accompanied by an increased desire for tender, loving contact with the sexual partner. An understanding partner can provide this contact and, as the bereaved individual experiences a return of his normal sexual drives, he can gradually restore the relationship to its previous pattern.

The relationship between *husband and wife* is the most intimate and all-encompassing one in our society. When death severs this relationship, the surviving partner often reacts in an exaggerated form. He no longer has a sexual partner to whom he can turn. His pain is intensified since the loss has deprived him of the usual mechanism of repair. Even the thought of seeking affection or physical love elsewhere makes him feel guilty.

This problem, like death itself, seems insoluble. The individual may attempt to deny his sexual feelings or to gratify them by means of loveless relationships or masturbation. Even in the absence of bereavement such behavior may often be associated with guilt and anxiety. In the setting of grief, these responses are accentuated. The bereaved's preoccupation with his loss makes it impossible for him to take the first necessary step toward the development of another sexual relationship until, at the least, he has achieved partial recovery from the pain of the loss.

There is no easy solution. It is useful, however, to regard this problem as inevitable and face it openly. The individual must maintain his social and family relationships during this crisis. He must realize that his transiently diminished sexual impulses will be restored and that one of the problems which he faces is to find a way to gratify them. He must recognize that any possible solution may include patterns of behavior which might, consciously or unconsciously, lead to anxiety and guilt. He must strive to gratify his sexual needs with a minimum of distress and to continue his life as fruitfully as possible.

A Practical Guide for Young Widows

TAMARA FERGUSON, AUSTIN H. KUTSCHER AND
LILLIAN G. KUTSCHER

There is no blueprint for what you should do when you lose your husband. Because he was central to all of your roles, his death makes you feel that your present life is out of focus and your future precarious. Your loneliness and grief make it difficult for you to look at the situation unemotionally, trust your own judgment, and decide whether to follow the advice proferred by family, friends, and professionals.

On your own, you have to decide what your new life style will be. Conflicts between financial, occupational, sexual, and maternal needs are often the aftermath of your new status, and you may concentrate on one problem at a time, ignoring the consequences of your behavior on your other roles. For example, you may go back to live with your parents because it is less expensive than living on your own. But once you have moved you begin to realize that you resent that your mother is criticizing your children or your friends, and you regret that you have given up your independence. So before you decide on your new priorities, it may be wise to identify the problems you have in each area of behavior, foresee the consequences of your behavior, and solve any ambiguity. What is proposed here is a rescaling theory (Ferguson, et al., 1980) which we shall briefly summarize and then use to analyze the problems of the 100 young widows whom we have interviewed. This may provide a framework within which you can start coming to terms with your own problems.

RESCALING THEORY

We all have expectations about ourselves and other people. Some of these are appropriate, while others are inappropriate because they cannot be fulfilled. These expectations cover physiological as well as social aspects of behavior. The authors have entitled them "life areas."

It is proposed that a person has to achieve a balance between his self expectations and his performance, and between those expectations he anticipates of others and their performance in each life area. It is further proposed that imbalance between expectations and performance creates stress. Self-expectations include what you believe you should be doing for yourself and others, and "other expectations" include what you believe others will do for themselves and for you.

The social tragedy is that only performance is visible, and that usually there is some imbalance between expectation and performance because we live in a society where people have different norms and values. When you experience this imbalance between expectations and performance, what can you do? You can either consciously rescale your problems, or you can act automatically and have a pattern of reaction.

208

Rescaling

When you consciously modify your expectations and performance, either individually or in negotiations with others, you improve your balance and so your level of stress. For example, you
may give your child $5 a week to pay for his expenses. There is
inflation and the child asks for a $2 increase. You realize that the
cost of living has increased, but you are trying to save money to buy
life insurance. You explain this and offer to give the child $6 instead
of the requested $7. The child realizes that this offer is realistic, and
he accepts it. Both you and the child have adjusted expectations and
performance and are satisfied with your behavior.

Patterns of Reaction

You may be unable to negotiate expectations and performance
because your defense mechanisms prevent you from realizing that
your expectations and performance are inappropriate in your present
situation. For example, when bereaved you would not perceive your
son's problems because unconsciously you project on him the feelings you had for his father and expect of him a maturity beyond his
years. Instead of reassuring, you react automatically. This type of
behavior is called a pattern of reaction. There are four patterns of
reaction:

a) Brutalization: Physically or verbally you force your performance on an other. In the illustration above you would deny your
child an increase in his weekly allowance and might even accuse him
of being careless with money.

b) Self-brutalization: Physically, you force a performance upon
yourself. You are angry at your child for asking for more money, but
you do not know what to do. Therefore, you force an inappropriate
performance upon yourself, such as overeating, drinking too much,
or abusing drugs.

c) Victimization: You submit to the expectations of another,
although it negates your self expectations. You would give your child
$10 or more weekly, although it means that you have to deprive
yourself of something.

d) Insulation: You refuse to perform, either by withdrawing or
by refusing to talk about certain topics. You avoid your child or
forbid him to talk about money.

At any stage of life, you may experience an unbalance in a life
area. Through research we have identified the following life areas:

I.	Health	V.	Social Life
	Food		Love and Sex
	Motor Functions	VI.	Parenthood
II.	Speech	VII.	Politics
III.	Education		Art
	Occupation	IX.	Ethics
IV.	Finance		Religion
	Law		

The complement of life areas allows us to identify systematically whether a problem in one life area creates problems in other life areas. For example, you may give up your career to look after your young children and then realize that you do not have enough money to pay unexpected dental bills, repair the roof of your house, pay for your children's music lessons, go on a vacation. Your occupational decision has affected your financial, health, shelter, parenthood, and social life vectors. The concept of life areas makes it possible to look at the development of each area over time. You may have dropped out of school when you were a teenager, but it is only now when you are looking for a white collar job that you regret it.

Inappropriate Expectations

One of the reasons that it may be difficult for you to achieve a balance between expectations and performance in your life vectors is that you have in appropriate expectations about yourself and others. Your expectations can be:

a) Too high: It is difficult for you or other people to meet them. You want, at all costs, to keep your former life style although you have lost half of your income.

b) Too low: You do not even try to improve your situation so you disappoint others. You do not believe that you could get a job so you do not even try and have to depend on the generosity of your relatives.

c) Fluctuating: Your behavior is unpredictable. You alternate between treating your son as a responsible being to whom you turn for advice and as a child who has to be told what to do.

d) Conflicting Expectations: You are torn between two alternatives. You would like to stay home and look after your child and at the same time you want to work full time. Your conflict may be conscious or unconscious.

e) Fantasy Expectations: You cannot match expectations with a performance. You want to remain young forever.

After a great loss, it is easy to despair, but when you start looking at your situation objectively and systematically, you may find alternatives for structuring a fruitful and enjoyable life.

For each life area we shall present some inappropriate expectations and patterns of reactions that the widows in our study have experienced, and then we shall discuss how their expectations and performance could be rescaled. We have grouped some of the life areas together to emphasize the main issue at stake.

TAKING CARE OF YOUR BODY

You may be emotionally and physically exhausted after your husband's death. He may have died suddenly, and you are in a state of shock; or he may have died after a long illness, and you feel the strain of having looked after him for months, or even years.

Health, Food, and Motor Functions are three life areas which we have grouped together because sound nutrition and exercise are recognized as essential to physical and mental health. We shall discuss some of the inappropriate expectations and patterns of reactions that you may have had in these life vectors and then suggest how you could rescale some of your problems.

Health

Inappropriate Expectations
- You are exhausted but feel you should settle all your affairs immediately.
- You feel that it does not matter if you postpone everything, even simple decisions.
- You do not know whether you should immediately get a job or first give yourself time to emotionally and physically recover from your loss.
- You are so tired that you unconsciously regress and expect your parents to make all decisions for you.
- A fantasy expectation that you have is that both you and your children have the same terminal illness that your husband had.

211

Patterns of Reaction
- You quarrel with your doctor because you feel that he does not understand your problems.
- You take the tranquilizers your doctor gives you, although you have an adverse reaction to a particular type of medication.
- You start drinking too much and overeating to comfort yourself.
- You have high blood pressure but refuse to see a doctor.

Rescaling   You recognize that you need time to recover physically and emotionally from the shock of losing your husband, and that depression, anxiety, insomnia are natural physiological reactions to grief. You are angry at being left alone with so many responsibilities, and at the same time you feel you should have prevented your husband's death. But, in reality, he did not die to annoy you, and you could not have saved him because each person is responsible for his life. You both did the best you could at the time. Looking back, you may see things differently because you are more mature. But even if you had behaved differently, who knows whether it would have made a difference? This questioning is part of coming to terms with your loss. Becoming bitter will hurt you, but it will not change the course of history. Live day by day for a while until you feel ready to move on. At first, the past is too much a part of your daily preoccupations to allow you to plan your future wisely. Cherish happy memories, but do not put your husband on a pedestal. See him as he was, not perfect, but lovable—just as you are.

Your exhaustion and the difficulty you have sleeping at night may last only a short time, but it may be wise for you and your children to have a physical examination to be reassured about your state of health. If your depression persists, some professional counseling may help you to come to terms with your grief. Do not hesitate to discuss with your doctor any adverse reaction you may have to the medication he prescribes because he can adjust the dosage or change the medication.

Postpone making crucial decisions about your house, a career, remarriage, or what you want to do with your husband's life insurance benefits until you feel better and have considered the consequences of your behavior.

Food

Inappropriate Expectations
- You realize that you have put on weight and now want to lose five pounds a week, something very hard to do.

- You feel that it does not matter that you are putting on weight. A fantasy expectation that you cherish is that calories do not count—but your weight keeps going up.

Patterns of Reaction
- You force your children to eat all the food on their plate, even when they are not hungry.
- You eat the fattening foods that your parents or friends prepare for you although you are on a diet.
- You live on snacks and junk food.
- You give up trying to eat balanced meals.

Rescaling It is an effort to eat sensibly when depressed, in particular if you do not have to cook for someone else and do not have meals at a set time. But it is all the more important to have a sensible diet both for yourself and your children. This is not the time to go on a stringent diet because you are still under stress, but if you do want to diet, plan to lose or gain about one or two pounds a week. Planning ahead for your meals is a good way to remain on a diet.

You do not have to eat fattening foods to please others.

If you are concerned about a serious weight or a drinking problem, join a club like Weight Watchers or Alcoholics Anonymous instead of trying to solve it on your own. A new pride in your health, or in your appearance, is often a first step out of depression.

A basic book on sensible eating is *Overweight* (Mayer, 1969). It gives a chart of the calories, minerals and vitamin content of all foods.

Motor Functions

Inappropriate Expectations
- You set up an arduous program of jogging for yourself without consulting a doctor.
- You believe that exercise is not slimming and a waste of time.
- You would like to join an exercise class, but you feel that you should be home with your children.
- You would like to be more muscular, but in the past your apparent physical weakness has been an unconscious means to control people.

Rescaling The benefits of physical fitness are well recognized. No medication can give you good posture and muscle tone.

213

A daily walk, exercising in your home, even five minutes a day, is an inexpensive way to start taking care of your body. Joining an exercise class at the YWCA, or a health club, is relaxing. Any sport is beneficial so long as you do not start any strenuous exercise before consulting a doctor. Housework and gardening will make you feel better than if you let everything go.

You may find a babysitter for your children, or take them along. A friend may be willing to look after your children while you go out if you can reciprocate.

Good food, exercise, adequate rest, and a moderate amount of activity maybe more beneficial to your health than taking a tranquilizer each time you feel anxious, although some medication prescribed by a doctor may help you to relax during the first few weeks of your bereavement.

It takes self discipline to be healthy. Other persons will respond favorably if you look fit, and it will help you to get a job. Your children will be proud of you and your clothes will fit better. But do not go into extremes of dieting and physical exercise; keep your sense of humor about it.

LEARNING TO EXPRESS YOURSELF

Speech facilitates our interaction with others in many life vectors, and so is crucial to our ability to rescale our problems.

Speech

Inappropriate Expectations
- You believe that everyone should understand your moods, even when you remain silent.
- You are sure that no matter what you say, no one will understand how you feel.
- You are always debating whether to speak up or remain silent.
- You find it difficult to express yourself to authority figures, such as your boss or a teacher, but you do not realize that you are projecting on them the expectations that you had of your parents.

Patterns of Reaction
- You brutalize other people by telling them what they should do, ignoring that they have the right to make up their own mind.

214

- You follow blindly the advice given by others, not taking into account that their knowledge of your problems may be very limited.
- Because you find it difficult to express your feelings, you drink too much or overeat.
- You do not discuss your problems with anyone.

Rescaling   Talking about your problems to trusted friends, relatives, or professionals will help you to clear your own mind because you are listening to what you say. Moreover, their comments broaden your grasp of the alternatives you have to master your quandary.

Joining a group of persons in a situation similar to your own, such as Parents Without Partners or a group of people interested in discussing personal problems, can be helpful. You realize that you have common problems with other people, and it becomes easier to express yourself. You may get a list of organizations for widows in your area from local social service agencies or church groups.

Rehearsing an upcoming job interview with a tape recorder, or roleplaying it with a friend where first you are the employer and then the interviewer, will help you to foresee what type of questions you could be asked and will prepare you how to answer them. But do not over-rehearse any interview; remain open to answer unexpected questions. When you are in doubt about what a person means, do not hesitate to ask him to clarify his statement.

What is more important than the words you select to express yourself is that you can tolerate other people's having different opinions from yours. Being assertive is spelling out what you would like to do and expect of others but also being open to changing your expectations and performance.

DOING THE WORK THAT YOU LIKE

We have linked together education and occupation because they are both important in helping you to do the work that you want. By work we do not mean only a paid job, but looking after your children, or working as a volunteer, if this is what you want.

Education

Inappropriate Expectations
- You believe that only women with a four-year college education can get an interesting job.

215

- You believe that you are too old to learn.
- You believe that younger students will make you feel obsolete.
- You wonder whether you should spend your husband's life insurance benefits on your children's education, or on your own retraining.

Patterns of Reaction

- You accuse your teacher of being unfair because he has given you a poor grade.
- You would like to go back to school but abstain because your mother tells you that you are too old.
- To sustain yourself while studying, you eat a lot of sweets.
- Although you have studied for an examination, you decide not to take it because you are afraid to failing it.

Rescaling In our survey, we found that women who had retrained, who had gone back to school to learn a particular skill, were very satisfied with their accomplishments. They felt that not only could they get a job but also that they had made new friends and were more confident of their own capabilities.

You are never too old to learn. There will always be people who are critical; don't let them discourage you. People of all ages go back to school. Younger people will be interested in your life experience, and you may find their outlook on life stimulating.

There are different levels of retraining. You may want to study for your own pleasure without thinking of earning a diploma or a degree. This is worth while in itself, and improving your English, learning to write, draw, paint, play a musical instrument, making pottery, sewing, etc. are stimulating activities. Going back to school is an endeavor which puts you together with other people who share your interests; it allows you to develop your latent talents. You can go back to school to get a General Education Development Examination (GED) if you have not finished high school. The test consists of five parts: grammar, mathematics, literature, science, and social studies. You can take each part whenever you are ready. These courses are inexpensive—or even free—and are administered by your Board of Education. The GED is the equivalent of a high school diploma. It allows you to get a job where a high school certificate is mandatory.

The Adult and Community Education Division may offer jobs with local contractors where you can learn a skill working as an apprentice. You may earn the salary of a regular employee and attend classes. You can train to work as a carpenter, mechanic, electrician, etc. You can ask to be referred to a school counselor so that you are interviewed and given an aptitude test. In vocational high schools, courses are given on a variety of subjects such as graphic arts, commercial art, air conditioning, refrigeration, carpentry, clerical, secretarial skills, bookkeeping, upholstering, tailoring, cosmetology, cashier, checker, etc. The tuition is low.

Community colleges prepare the paraprofessional. Classes may be available during the weekend. The tuition is low, and you can study for a large number of jobs such as dental technician, medical secretary, legal secretary, school counselor, practical nurse (one year) or an associate degree in nursing or in business administration (two years). You have to be realistic about how much you like to study, what your grades were in high school; in other words, what are your qualifications and interests? Nursing requires physical fitness and enjoying looking after people, while to become an accountant you have to be accurate and learn about new techniques, such as computer skills and programming. But there are different levels of training and competence in both types of careers.

You may want to get a four year college degree, and even go to graduate school to become a lawyer, a certified public accountant, a teacher, a social worker, a clinical psychologist, and so forth. Go to your local college or university to find out what courses you would have to take, how much tuition would be, whether you could get a scholarship, or finance yourself by other means. Program of studies change over time, and new opportunities for jobs open up. You have to be careful that you do not train for a career in which there are very few jobs available so do not take advice from people who do not have up-to-date information. Go to the source itself, and talk to the college counselors in your community or to business executives and other professionals. Consulting the Occupational Outlook handbook gives you a good idea of the fields in which there is a growing demand for more staff (Bureau of Labor Statistics, 1980). Also look up the advertisements in newspapers and professional journals.

After being a housewife for many years, it may at first be a strain to write a paper or take an examination. Don't worry; practice makes it easier. It takes time to find out the requirements for an examination. Some teachers value originality; others are more concerned that you repeat what they say, or express yourself in good English. Don't let one poor grade discourage you. You will have the satisfaction of working to achieve your goals.

You may have gaps in your knowledge—so have younger students. Discuss any problems with your teacher. He may suggest what you can do to catch upon a particular subject and he will be impressed by your determination. If you get a C on a paper when you expected an A, talk it over with the teacher. He will explain to you why he gave you this particular grade, and if he has made a mistake in grading you, he can change the grade.

Spending your husband's life insurance benefits on your education does not mean that you have to deprive your children. Scholarships are available. You can also borrow money to go to school. And this makes sense because you are increasing your earning power. Find out what is available in the area where you are living. The tuition in a state school may be much cheaper than in a private school. Your employer may pay part of your tuition fees.

Occupation

Inappropriate Expectations
- You have decided to take a job only if it meets all your requirements.
- You dislike your job very much, but you are afraid to look for another job.
- You are afraid to take a full-time job because you feel it would be exhausting.
- You are unconsciously afraid to get a job because your parents always stressed that the place of a woman is in her home.
- You would like to become a physician, but you are forty-five years old, have only one year of college, and your average grade is a C.

Patterns of Reaction
- On the job, you criticize the personal life of younger workers.
- You believe that you have to work harder than anyone else because you are older.
- You work overtime but never ask to be paid for it.
- If you have a disagreement with a coworker or your boss, you give up your job.

Rescaling If you have not worked during your married life, you have to think carefully about your occupational goals. Do you want to stay home and look after your small children? Would you like to work as a volunteer one or several days a week? Do you want a job just to earn a living, or do you want to train for a career?

One important factor is, of course, your financial situation. You may not have to work until your children are eighteen years old, or twenty-two years old if they are studying full-time, but then you are not eligible for Social Security benefits until you are sixty years old, and you have to plan what you will do in the meantime. The longer you postpone getting into the job market, the more difficult it gets.

We have discussed the different types of programs available if you want to retrain. The YWCA and community colleges offer courses for the mature woman who wants to go back to work. You can learn there how to write a resume, how to be assertive at work without being aggressive. You may also get some information about the jobs available in your state. Your state Employment Office has lists of jobs available.

Questions usually asked on job applications are where and when you went to school and how much school work you have completed. You will be asked to list the jobs you have had, give the address of your employers, and reveal how long you have stayed on the job. You may be asked how much you earned in your most recent job. If you were underpaid, make it clear that now you want a salary equal to your new position. In case you have not worked for many years, mention any voluntary work that you have done or any other experience which may qualify you for the job you are seeking. You will be asked to give two or three references. You can give the name of one of your teachers if you have re-trained recently. In case you have not worked for many years, give the name of your lawyer, your doctor, or someone who has a formal position and will give you a good letter of reference. You should ask your referees if they would mind your giving their names in reference.

What clothes to wear for a job interview depends on the nature of the job you are applying for but basically be neatly dressed and confident in your ability to get a good job. Rehearsing an upcoming job interview with a friend may be helpful.

Do not have fantasy expectations about a job. Take into account your state of health before retraining or applying for a particular job. For example, if you have varicose veins, do not apply for a job which requires a lot of standing. But working full-time, talking to your co-workers, may be less tiring, less depressing, than staying home and worrying about your income. Even if at first you are not successful, keep on trying. Advertisements in newspapers, contacting employment agencies, talking to friends—all are helpful. If you have re-trained, the placement center of the school where you have retrained may help you to find a job.

It is not easy for the woman who has been a housewife for many years to behave professionally in a job. She tends to be too maternal, to be afraid to ask for a raise, or she works overtime without asking to be paid for the work she is doing. Harragan's book, *Games Mother Never Taught Me* (1977), is written for the career woman. It analyzes the pitfalls that women experience in an organization and suggests how to overcome them. One point she makes which is important is that you have to be loyal to your boss and not go over his head if you have a complaint to make. Try first to settle your grievance with the person who you think has been unfair.

LIVING WITHIN YOUR INCOME

The drop of income you experience when bereaved may be considerable. Do not panic and act hastily. You have to determine your financial situation and what you want to achieve. We have grouped the life vectors of Finance and Law together because a knowledge of the law helps you to figure out the benefits that you are entitled to receive.

Finance

Inappropriate Expectations
- You feel that you should buy a new car and also redecorate your house because for the first time in your life you have a few thousand dollars in the bank—your husband's life insurance benefits.
- You are seventy years old, have a capital of $500,000, but you feel this should not be touched even to buy a new car.
- Your husband took care of all the bills, and you feel you will never be able to make a budget.
- You cannot make up your mind whether to spend your money on re-training or on buying a new car.
- Although you have no financial expertise, you believe that by gambling on the stock market you will be able to maintain your former life style.

Patterns of Reaction
- You do not allow your children to get a loan to go to college because you are afraid they might not be able to repay it.
- You lend most of your capital to relatives or friends, although you are not sure they will repay you.
- You deprive yourself of everything because you feel the future is uncertain.
- You do not care how you spend your money.

Rescaling You may have more money in the bank than ever before because you have cashed your husband's life insurance benefits, and may even have sold your house, but what you have lost is your husband's earning power. This means not only his salary but also that, in the case of an emergency, he could work overtime, or take a second job for a period of time. What you have to realize is the *difference between income and capital*, and that a capital of $50,000 invested at 6% gives you only an income of $3,000.

You have also to think what you will do during the Social Security "blackout period" which starts after your youngest child is eighteen years old, or until he is twenty-two years old if he is going to school full-time and is unmarried. Then your Social Security benefits will stop until you are sixty years old, or until you are fifty-five years old if you are severely disabled. The Veterans benefits that you may receive for your children also stop when they are eighteen-years-old or when they are twenty-years-old if they are attending an approved course of instruction.

Before you spend your husband's life insurance benefits, you have to figure out your expenses, your annual income, and your priorities. Buying a car may be useful and cheer you up, but are you sure that you will need a car if you decide to move to a city where it may be easier for you to get the job you want? Redecorating your sitting room may be fun but you may want to spend the money converting your second floor into a self-contained apartment which you could rent. You have to take into account that you may need some money for unexpected dental bills, new clothes to go to work, or sending your son to summer camp. Take time to figure out your options.

You may feel that your first priority is to find a second husband who will take care of you financially. But an older man may have financial responsibilities of his own—a first wife or children. He may admire you all the more if you are able to live within a budget. And if you have only one alternative, remarriage, you may become too anxious about it.

First, find out how much you are spending per year. Some of your expenses may be daily, others monthly or quarterly. Figure out your expenses for the year, and then on a monthly basis. It might make you anxious to think systematically about your financial situation, in particular if you have little money and have not done it before. But this is the best way to decrease your stress and arrive at a rational decision you will not regret. The headings which follow may help you figure out your expenses. Some of them, of course, may not apply to your case. Do note which expenses are tax deductible so that they may be taken into account when your new budget is made.

Expenses

1. Rent or mortgage
2. Taxes (Federal, State, property)
3. Insurance (property, car, life ins)
4. Legal fees
5. House repairs
6. Utilities (gas, electricity, fuel, phone)
7. Transportation (car repairs, gasoline, parking)
8. Food
9. Medical and dental
10. Clothing
11. Cleaning supplies
12. Toiletries and hairdresser
13. Education (books)
14. Furniture
15. Membership in associations
16. Recreation (eating out, movies, etc.)
17. Charity
18. Savings
19. Vacation
20. Gifts (Christmas, Hanukkah, birthdays)
21. Other (debts)

You need to figure out your income to find out whether your expenses are covered. It may take time to settle your husband's estate; if this is the case, be very conservative about estimating the money you will inherit.

Income

Gross salary (less payroll deductions) If you leave the lump sum life insurance benefits with the insurance company, figure out what they will pay you in interest.

Interest from Savings Account
Interest from Bonds
Interest from Stocks
Interest from Trust
Business income
Pension
Social Security benefits
Veterans benefits
Disability benefits
Unemployment benefits
Other

If your current expenses are greater than your income, you can try to increase your income by getting a job, asking for a pay increase in your job, changing jobs, retraining, reducing your expenses, or investing your money so that you have a better rate of return. Take into account your age, your family situation, your earning power, and what you want out of life before deciding on which item you should spend money or where you should economize. If your capital is $50,000 or less and you are able to work part-time, you may have to be very cautious. But if you are in your seventies and your capital is $500,000, do not be afraid to spend some of your capital to make life more comfortable.

Some specific financial problems may be of concern to you, such as selecting a lawyer or an accountant, paying inheritance taxes, whether you should sell your house, pay off the mortgage, and how to invest money. Some general guide lines follow which you have to adjust to your particular situation.

Selecting a Lawyer Both the *honesty and expertise* of your lawyer are important. Be careful to select a lawyer who has the experience needed to deal with the problems you would like him to solve. For example, do select a corporation lawyer, and not a real estate lawyer, if the sale of your husband's share in a business requires a good grasp of corporation law. You have also to take into account how much your lawyer is going to charge you. Large established law firms are more expensive, but they are departmentalized and have lawyers who can deal with particular situations. If you have little money a younger lawyer would be less expensive. Your bank manager may recommend a respected lawyer.

Estate Tax Under Federal Tax Laws an estate of $600,000 can be inherited by the surviving spouse without having to pay Federal Estate Tax.

Selling Your House Your house may be the most valuable piece of property you own. Before you sell it, you should carefully consider where you are going to live. The value of real estate in the 1980's has increased considerably, but it may have reached a plateau when you read this book so that to keep your house as an investment may not be realistic, in particular if your district is becoming less desirable and you cannot afford to pay for maintenance, such as a new roof.

The Mortgage on Your House First, you have to decide whether you want to stay or move. You have to take into consideration the size of the mortgage on that house and the interest rate you are paying. If the rate is low, you may be better off keeping the mortgage and investing your money in Treasury Bonds or other securities that will give you a higher rate of return. A mortgage might make your house more salable because any new owner might have the benefit of a low mortgage.

Investing Your Money It all depends on how much capital you have, and whether you want a high rate of return or are more interested in increasing your capital. Selling and buying on the stock exchange is not advisable if you have no financial expertise and want financial security.

You can invest your money in:

a) Savings Account: Investing your money in a savings account is safe and the money is always accessible—sometimes too accessible—but your capital does not grow with the rate of inflation and the rate of return is low.

b) Stocks and Bonds: When you buy a stock you become a part owner in a business venture; buying a bond is lending money to a company. Some stocks in well-known established companies have growth possibilities and have been well researched. These are more desirable than others. Your capital grows with the rate of inflation, but again, this depends on the state of the economy and the severity of inflation. You should invest for a period of five or ten years. Treasury Bills are the safest, and while the rate of return may be high, it does fluctuate. The rate of return increases with inflation, but your capital does not grow. You can buy these bills for different periods of time as they mature at different dates. You pay Federal Income Tax on Treasury Bills but no State Tax. You pay no Federal income tax on Municipal Bonds.

c) Mutual Funds: The record of most mutual funds is not too successful. There are some gems, but they may be difficult to find.

d) Insurance Companies: You can leave your husband's life insurance benefits with your insurance company, but the rate of return is low. Most widows with young children tend to buy straight life insurance on themselves when their husbands die because they become fearful that they themselves may die suddenly. But your chance of dying in the future may be remote and straight life insurance is expensive. You may need only term insurance which will protect your children during the period when they are growing up and are completing their schooling. The money that you save on insurance could be used for their education, your retraining, or some other priority. You can buy renewable term insurance for five years or more. The advantage is that you will not need a physical examination to renew your insurance. After that time you may be able to convert your renewal term insurance to another type of insurance.

e) Banks, Investment Accounts, Trusts: Before going to a stockbroker, check on his reputation and the reputation of his firm because he may suggest that you buy and sell on the stock market so that he gets a commission. You can get advice from a stockbroker but leave your securities in a bank safe deposit box. Your bank manager may give you some information on what type of Municipal Bonds or Treasury Bills you could buy and do it for you. He may give you a list of reliable Mutual Funds. But just as with other types of advice you have to take into account the reputation and expertise of the person who is advising you and think carefully about what you want to do. If you have a capital of about $150,000 or more, the following types of services are offered by some banks' trust division for a percentage formula.

(1) *A Custody Account* which is a bookkeeping service. The bank holds your securities, collects interest and dividends, executes your instructions,and maintains complete financial records including information necessary for your income tax returns.

(2) *An Investment Advisory Account*. The bank will take into account your circumstances and objectives as you describe them to their Admin- istrative Officer. They will want to know if you are more interested in capital growth or in increasing your income. They may suggest that you invest 60% in stocks and 40% in bonds, but this would depend on your needs and the business outlook. They will recommend investment changes to you but will not execute them without your approval.

(3) *An Investment Management Account* can be set up. The difference between this type of account and an investment advisory account is that the bank will buy and sell securities for your account using their own discretion and notify you of any changes. These three types of accounts are revocable.

(4) *Trusts*. You can go to an attorney and have a trust drawn up. It may be a living trust which is revocable during your life or an irrevocable time trust in which you spell out how your estate will be divided after your death. By leaving your money in a trust you assure that a person receives the income of the money you set aside for him, but you deprive him of the opportunity to use the capital for some enterprise of his own choosing. You can decide, if you wish, when the trust will be dissolved and the beneficiaries get the capital.

Law

Inappropriate Expectations
- You believe that because your lawyer is your relative he has your interests at heart.

- You believe that because your lawyer is an honest man, he is competent to sell your husband's business.
- You distrust all lawyers.
- You cannot make up your mind whether or not you want to sue the factory where your husband was caught in a press.
- Because you had a domineering father, you are fighting all authority figures and are starting a law suit although you have little chance of winning.
- You hope that buying a new car for your son who has been in trouble several times for speeding, you will encourage him to drive more carefully.

Patterns of Reaction
- You drive most of the time over the 55 mile speed limit.
- You sign legal documents without reading them.
- You overeat instead of trying to find out whether your husband had group insurance.
- You give up driving becuase you had a car accident.

Rescaling
1. *Malpractice Suit.* Before you start one you need good legal advice.

2. *Lost Papers:* Go back to the source if you have lost some papers (such as the deed of your house), or you do not know whether your husband had group insurance. For example, if you believe that your husband had group insurance, but his employer denies it, check with another employee to see if all employees in his firm are insured, then confront your husband's employer again. Don't go to a lawyer before you have exhausted all other remedies.

If your son drives recklessly and has had several car accidents, let him go to work and pay for his own repairs instead of buying him a new car. When he has to pay for his own mistakes, he will become more careful. You may explain to him that he may be reckless because he is still anxious and depressed because of his father's death but he has to learn to become responsible for his own actions.

TO ENJOY THE FRIENDSHIP AND LOVE OF OTHERS

We have grouped together social life, love, and sex because if you combine love and friendship, if you respect the people you love, your relationship with them will be more fruitful.

Social Life

Inappropriate Expectations
- You believe that all of your husband's friends will go on inviting you after his death.
- You believe that your marital status is more important than you are as a person.
- Unconsciously, you are afraid to make new friends because when you were a child your parents were very critical of your friends.
- Your mother became a recluse when your father died so you feel you have to do the same.

Patterns of Reaction
- When meeting new people you can talk only about your late husband. You drop all your married friends because you feel you no longer have anything in common with them.
- You spend all of your time caring for your widowed father or mother.
- Instead of going out, you stay home and drink too much.
- You refuse all social invitations.

Rescaling The form of address when writing to a woman is Ms., which is a social recognition that you as a person are more important than your marital status. But we live in a society where the majority of persons are married and the change of status from married to single is a difficult one. Instead of interacting socially as a couple, you are interacting as a single person.

When you were married, inviting people to your home involved a division of labor. You may have cooked the meal, but your husband poured the drinks and the conversation may have ranged from fishing, politics, clothes, to your child's latest performance. Alone, it is more difficult at first to entertain. But the more you do it the easier it becomes. You can ask a friend to help you with the drinks or let people help themselves. Nowadays, many people who were married are single again through divorce or bereavement so other people can share your problems.

Talking to your close friends will be a great help because their concern will make you feel less bereft and allow you to see what is positive in your life. You may find that some of your married girlfriends invite you more often for lunch than for dinner. They may envy your independence and they, or their husbands, feel more secure with other married couples. Don't be too sensitive, we all have our idiosyncracies. Enjoy people as they are. Old friends may also introduce you to eligible bachelors, so do not limit your opportunities.

You may never have been gregarious, and it is easy to settle down with a good book or in front of the television, to retreat to the safety of your own room. But there is also a danger of becoming too absorbed in your own problems. You need new interests and activities. You can meet people with the same interests and activities by joining organizations, going back to school, getting a job, etc. However, do not go to the other extreme and be afraid to be alone.

We do not want to minimize the effort it will take to resocialize yourself. But by asserting yourself you gain a new confidence in yourself, and in others. You broaden your outlook on life.

Love and Sex

Inappropriate Expectations
- Sex should be perfect if two persons love each other.
- You feel too old to attract a man.
- You wonder whether you should have an affair or remarry.
- You would marry only a man as perfect as your first husband.
- If you remarry, what will you do in Heaven if you meet your two husbands.?

Patters of Reaction
- Your favorite son should keep you company instead of dating his girlfriend.
- You should fake an orgasm to please the man with whom you are having an affair.
- You sleep with anyone becuase you are lonely.
- Food has replaced sex for you.
- You avoid dating because you are afraid to be rejected.

Rescaling Our survey shows that the sexual needs of men and women vary a great deal. For some women and their husbands sexual intercourse was of great importance in their lives, for others this was not the case. Some women pointed out that at different periods of their lives, their sexual needs varied in intensity. For example, after having their first baby, their main preoccupation was their infant.

Physiological and social differences between women and men may explain their sexual behavior. Being too sexually involved when young, even unconsciously, with the parent of the other sex may make it all the more difficult later on to make a sexual relationship with a peer.

You may feel that you are unable to compete with younger women. But a mature man may appreciate your understanding and feel closer to you than to a younger woman who would make greater demands on him. You are never too old to experience sexual pleasure because sexuality does not always have to lead to orgasm and there is satisfaction in being held, caressed, and cherished. Oral sex and different forms of sexual stimulation can be used to arouse and satisfy you and your partner. You do not have to fake a response but, rather, explain how you feel and what you like. But even if you are on your own, you do not have to deprive yourself of sexual satisfaction as masturbation can release sexual tension.

Your opportunities to date or to remarry may depend on your age, the community in which you live, whether you make an effort to meet people as well as your own intentions. You may feel that it is better to have an affair than to remarry quickly—and this you have to decide yourself. Do not remarry only because of one particular quality that a man may have, such as his wealth, his occupation, his good looks, or because you are lonely. His health, education, ethics, religion, and whether he has children of his own will influence the life style that you lead together. Be wary of comparing your first husband and your date. They are two different persons, and your situation now is different. It is easy to embellish the past instead of accepting that there are some unique pleasures and limitations in any relationship. Remarriage in middle age is more complex, but you may have gained in maturity and understanding.

You may feel that you should devote your life to looking after your children or your widowed parent. But by doing this you prevent them from interacting with their peers and gaining confidence in themselves. By being less protective, by cherishing your own independence, you may become a role model for your family.

BEING UNREALISTIC ABOUT YOUR CHILDREN

Parenthood

Inappropriate Expectations
- You want to be both father and mother to your children.
- Because your son is bright, you believe that he can achieve anything he wants.
- You are overly concerned about your son's health.
- You are torn between marrying a man you love and rejecting him becuase your son does not like him.

- You alternate between unconsciously treating your son as a husband substitute and asking his advise or as a teenager who should be disciplined.

Patterns of Reaction
- You criticize all your son's dates.
- You discourage your daughter from dating because you are overly sensitive to her being disappointed in love.
- You do not date becuase you feel you should be home to supervise your children's behavior.
- You drink too much becuase you do not know how to discipline your children.
- You do not set any limits on your children's behavior or activities.

Rescaling The women in our survey considered that, after loneliness, the most serious problem they experienced was how to bring up their sons alone. It is difficult for the small child to understand the concept of death, that his father will not come back. The concept of heaven which is acceptable to a Catholic may be difficult for a small child to grasp, and he may want to join his father. Perhaps, explaining that if a person contracts a disease and dies does not mean that he did not love you is a suitable explanation.

Your children may feel, just as you have, that they could have prevented their father's death. At the same time, they feel rejected by him because he died. By talking to them about their feelings, you may help them to recognize that you all did the best you could and that death is one of those accidents of nature which no one can prevent. Some children find it difficult to concentrate on their school work for a period of time after they have lost their father. By sharing their loss, and giving them time to overcome it, you will help them to persevere with their studies.

Growing up is going to school, learning to interact with one's peers, deciding on a career, finding a job. Your teenage children need to be encouraged to interact with their peers and to date as a natural social experience. Talk to them about dating, sex, birth control, marriage, and having children. Discuss careers with them. Don't believe, or tell them, that they can do anything. To become competent and successful in any field requires dedication, training, and perseverance. Be supportive, recognize their problems, and do not compare them to your own.

You cannot be mother and father to your children because you cannot become a male role model for them. So it is better to be yourself. Do with them what you enjoy doing and do not feel that

230

you have to go fishing or play ball with them if you dislike it. But you can encourage your children to find male role models such as teachers, uncles, neighbors. And Scouts and summer camp may help them to learn to socialize with different people.

A major problem is that unconsciously you may alternate between treating your son as a husband substitute to whom you turn for advice and support, and as a child who is inexperienced and has to be told what to do. This is a common problem because the eldest or favorite son is the male head of the family but is still young and inexperienced. Your son, himself, may be confused as to what his relationship with you should be because he wants to replace his father but still has needs of his own. Explain to him that you can stand on your own. Enjoy your relationship, but do not ask him to become your escort.

It may be difficult at first for your children to accept your dating, that another man may replace their father. You have to make them understand that this is not the case. Each of our relationships with another human being is unique and cannot be replaced. There is no reason for you to deprive yourself of the happiness of sharing, of loving.

MAKE YOUR HOUSE WORK FOR YOU

Shelter

To make your house work for you means do not be a slave to it. Moving may be one of the first decisions that you *want* to make. It probably should be the last one, and made only after you have decided what your new life style is going to be.

Inappropriate Expectations
- You plan to move only if you find a house which meets all of your requirements.
- You believe that you will never find a suitable apartment.
- You wonder whether you should use your husband's life insurance benefits to pay for the mortgage on your house or to retrain.
- You believe that moving by itself will solve all of your emotional problems.

Patterns of Reaction
- You sell your house without consulting your children

- You do not sell your house although you cannot afford to maintain it because your children enjoy living there.
- You drink instead of trying to repaint your kitchen.
- You let the dust accumulate in your house and the weeds grow in your garden.

Rescaling The value of real estate has increased a great deal in the last 10 years. Many people bought a house as an investment, and worked hard to improve it and increase its value. But whether the value of housing will still go up so drastically in the next ten years is problematic so do not take for granted that to keep your house is the only safe investment you can make. You have to consider whether your house is convenient and whether it makes your life more enjoyable.

Before you decide whether or not to move, list your own priorities:

1. Are you staying in your house because you believe that it is an investment and that the value of your house will go on increasing?
2. Do you want to spend a minimum on housing so that you have money to retrain, buy clothes, go out, etc.?
3. Is the location of your residence important because of
   a) proximity of good schools for your children
   b) good transportation to go to work and see your friends
   c) nearness to a shopping center
   d) a safe neighborhood
   e) distance from relatives
   f) a good address?
4. How many bedrooms and bathrooms do you need?
5. Do you want a house with a garden and a basement so that your children can play?
6. Do you want to rent an apartment so that you do not have to worry about repairs?
7. Have you considered buying a cooperative apartment or a condominium?
8. Would you consider renting a room in your present house or converting your basement or second floor into a self-contained apartment?
9. Do you need a residence where you can easily entertain dates, friends, or business associates?
10. Do you want a residence where medical care is available?
11. Do you want a residence where there is a restaurant in the building?

12. Where will you park your car?
13. How long do you plan to stay in your present or future home?

TO BE COUNTED AND ENJOY THE BEAUTY
OF THIS WORLD

Politics

Women who fought for the right to vote were force-fed and imprisoned. Don't give up the right, the power, to be counted!

You may say, what does it matter—one more vote? But it is *your* vote. And a letter to your congressman, to your senator, if you believe that more re-training opportunities should be available to displaced homemakers, or on any issue of importance to you, may spur them into action.

Joining a political party and working for the candidate of your choice may help you to meet other people who share your political foresight.

Art

Is any form of art inappropriate? Now that modern paintings are decorating hospital wards, music is broadcast all day, and books on any form of art are available, our need to express and share our vision of the beauty of the world has been recognized.

When you are depressed, you become indifferent to your surroundings. But the first sign of recovery may be when the sight of flowers in bloom, the smile of your child, a familiar song moves you again. Perhaps, if everything were forever, we would not find so much meaning in being alive.

ACCEPTANCE AND FAITH

Ethics

Misunderstandings occur between people because what seems very important, very appropriate to one person, may be considered trivial by another one.

You have to find out what really matters to you. And our classification of events into inappropriate and appropriate is, of course, subjective. But we live in a social world where the expectations of others have to be taken into consideration if we want to achieve our goals. To be egocentric is to be lonely. To participate in this changing world you have to be aware of your own idiosyncracies and not let a divergence of opinion prevent you from interacting with others.

Religion

To accept that the man you love is dead is very difficult.

You may believe that it is God's will, a law of nature, or just a random accident. When we asked in our survey of bereaved women whether their loss had made them change their religiosity, some mentioned that they had become more religious, the faith of others had remained the same, and a few had rejected a religion which could not protect them from suffering.

But we are not the center of the universe, and what happens to us cannot color forever our understanding of why we are here.

So let it be. Don't become bitter. Because you have suffered, you may become more mature, more understanding, and more able to give to those around you the blessing of your courage in front of adversity.

Rescaling the Self

You are facing a period of acute social change because you are missing your husband's companionship and are now one individual facing a life style which was planned by and for two individuals. After a period of acute grief when you may question the meaning of living, it is easy to start drinking to forget, replace love with food, and soothe anxiety with tranquilizers. You may feel angry and believe that you have been singled out by fate. You may crawl back into a shell and cry, or give up trying to make a new life for yourself. But anger and sorrow will not bring back your husband and they will not help you to reconstruct your life.

You may be paralyzed by the magnitude of your problems or focus only on one problem at a time instead of seeking to gain some perspective on your new situation and identify new goals and priorities. But to solve a problem only when it has become an emergency makes life a series of crises. Between trying to achieve too much and doing nothing or drifting, there is a middle path.

This theory provides you with a framework to rescale the self. You alone can do it because each person has different values and what means a great deal to you may be of little importance to another person. As a first step, we would like to identify how important each of the following life areas is for you. You have four choices and may check each of them as very important, important, unimportant, or very unimportant.

		Very Important	Important	Unimportant	Very Unimportant
1.	Health	—	—	—	—
2.	Nutrition	—	—	—	—
3.	Shelter	—	—	—	—
4.	Sports	—	—	—	—
5.	Speech	—	—	—	—
6.	Social Life	—	—	—	—
7.	Politics	—	—	—	—
8.	Art	—	—	—	—
9.	Education	—	—	—	—
10.	Occupation	—	—	—	—
11.	Finance	—	—	—	—
12.	Love and Sex	—	—	—	—
13.	Parenthood	—	—	—	—
14.	Religion	—	—	—	—
15.	Law	—	—	—	—
16.	Ethics	—	—	—	—

Secondly, check any of the life areas in which you believe you have a serious problem:

_____	Health	_____	Education
_____	Nutrition	_____	Occupation
_____	Shelter	_____	Finance
_____	Sports	_____	Love and Sex
_____	Speech	_____	Parenthood
_____	Social Life	_____	Religion
_____	Politics	_____	Law
_____	Art	_____	Ethics

And, finally, if you are worrying which of two or several alternatives you should select when facing a particular problem, write them on the following lines. Your dilemma may be in one life area such as whether you should buy or sell an apartment. It may be between life areas such as whether to stay home and look after your young children or to take a job.

Problem	Alternative 1	Alternative 2	Alternative 3

This identification of your problems makes you realize what is of greatest concern to you. We suggest that it is in those life areas you consider very important and in which you have serious problems that you should start rescaling your problems.

In our discussion of life areas we have grouped together several life areas under one heading such as "Taking Care of Your Body," "Doing the Work You Like." The chart shows you how, under one heading, you can see at a glance the consequences of your behavior in life areas which are closely related.

To rescale your life, you have to identify what type of imbalance you experience between expectations and performances, and in which life area. Basically, do you feel that you are not achieving your goals because of your own shortcomings or that other people are not helpful?

To show you how to proceed, let us say that one of your problems is that you would like to lose 5 pounds weekly but are not achieving this goal. In that case on the chart in the life area of "Food" under "Present Behavior," write down that your expectations are to lose 5 pounds weekly. Under "Performance," write down that your weight remains stationary. Thinking about your expectations of others makes you realize that you have asked your mother many times to stop giving you her home-baked cakes but that she does not comply with your wishes. You write this down under "Expectations" and "Performance."

In the second column under *Evaluation of Present Behavior,* you analyze why you are not reaching a balance between expectations and performances. This makes you aware that your self expectations are too high and your other expectations too low and to please your mother is more important than your own satisfaction. Losing 5 pounds a week means going on a stringent diet, and you are too tired just now to do anything so drastic. You diet and lose a pound during the week and on the weekend you get discouraged and you gorge on your mother's pies and regain the weight you lost.

So in the third column under *Rescaling* you put down your new self expectations which are to be satisfied with a weekly loss of a pound and not to overeat during the weekend. Under other expectations you write down that you will not try to stop your mother from baking but will eat some fruit instead of her pies.

On the same page are listed two life areas that you have to consider when taking care of your body: Health and Motor Functioning. Excessive dieting or lack of exercise can undermine your health. You may decide to have a medical checkup and ask your doctor for a sensible diet. You may also decide to increase your physical activity as it is a healthy way to burn calories. However, your main problem may not be one of health or weight; it may be a financial one or your relationship with your son. Proceed in the same manner. Make your own chart, write down what you expect of yourself and others, and then try to rescale the problems.

You have experienced a serious loss, have faced the limitations of being alive, and realized the brutal fact that what we can do for those we love, for our selves, is limited. So you need to recover, to rescale your problems. But do not go to the other extreme and drift instead of rebuilding your life, step-by-step. Depression often occurs because a person magnifies a particular problem and minimizes his blessings and strength. Do not focus on one problem: your financial situation, your relationship with your son, finding a new home. Looking at your behavior in other life areas helps you to realize the consequences of your behavior and to count your blessings. Be proud of what you have accomplished in the past. Instead of money you may have wonderful children, good friends, or sound health.

Rescaling is teaming to know your own idiosyncracies. Your expectations, in general, may tend to be too high, too low, fluctuating, conflicting, or belong to a world of fantasy. In your pattern or patterns of reaction you may tend to become depressed or angry when frustrated. You act on the spur of the moment, procrastinate instead of acting, give up too soon, or take refuge in oral gratification instead of seeking new alternatives.

Knowing who you are, what you want, what your strengths and limitations are will help you to be more realistic about other people and understand their values. Each person has problems that relate to their situation, background, and idiosyncracies. You cannot change other people, you are not responsible for the whole world, but you can make a contribution, enjoy life, negotiate with others, and be free to select your own friends.

Most of the widows we interviewed complained about their situation. One widow, whose husband had died after a prolonged battle with cancer, was working full-time as a telephone operator. She was forty-five years old, had two teenage sons, and was renting the top flat of her house which she had converted into a self-contained apartment. When asked why she did not complain, this woman replied, "There are greater problems in life than becoming a widow."

ACKNOWLEDGMENTS

We are very indebted to the following people: Jack D. Ferguson, Elliot D. Luby, Calvin E. Schorer, and Garfield Tourney for their help in developing the theory on which this paper is based. Saroj Parasuramani whose help identified the different educational programs available to a woman who would like to retrain, Kay Abbot for supplying information on the different services provided by the Y.W.C.A.; and Lewis A. Helphand and Robert A. Hackathorn for clarifying the different financial options available to a widow.

The Authors

SELECTED BIBLIOGRAPHY

Caine, L. 1974. *Widow*. New York: William Morrow & Co. New York: Bantam, 1975.

A professional woman explains the problems she encountered when combining a career and bringing up her children after her husband's death.

Cammer, L. 1969. *Up From Depression*. New York: Simon & Schuster. 1971. New York: Pocket Book.

Helps you to distinguish between depression as a grief reaction and as an illness which requires medical care.

It gives information about what to do when depression strikes a member of your family.

Dyer, W.W. 1976. *Your Erroneous Zones*. New York: Funk & Wagnalls Publishing Division of T.Y. Crowell. 1977. New York: Avon.

How to overcome self-defeating behavior.

Ferguson, T., J. Ferguson, C.E. Schorer and G. Tourney. "Bereavement, Stress, and Rescaling Therapy." In *Acute Grief. Counseling the Bereaved*, eds.

0. Margolis et al., New York: Columbia University Press, 1981.

Defense mechanisms are translated into expectations and performances to explain how a person can regress unconsciously to prior states when bereaved.

Ferguson, T. 1973. "Decision Making and Tranquilizers in Widowhood." In *Psychopharmacologic Agents for the Terminally Ill and Bereaved*, eds. I.K. Goldberg, S. Malitz, and A.H. Kutscher. New York: Columbia University Press, Ill 1973.

A steady diet of tranquilizers may lull a widow into a false sense of security although her basic problems still remain unsolved.

Fulton, R. (with assistance of J. Carlson, K. Krohn, E. Markusen, and E. Owen). *Death, Grief and Bereavement—A Bibliography, 1845-1975*. New York: Arno Press, 1977.

An excellent reference volume prepared by a prominent sociologist in the field of thanatology.

Furman, E. *A Child's Parent Dies (Studies in Childhood Bereavement)*. New Haven: Yale University Press, 1974.

A study of grief, loss and mourning in childhood based on case studies.

Glick, I.O., R.S. Weiss, and C. Murray Parkes. *The First Year of Bereavement*. New York: John Wiley and Sons, 1974.

A follow-up study of the emotional and social problems of widows and widowers forty-five years old or younger.

Grollman, E.A. *Talking About Death: A Dialogue Between Parent and Child*. Boston: Beacon Press, 1976.

A book explaining death to children with an extensive guide for parents including a list of pertinent books and tapes.

Harragan, B.L. *Games Mother Never Taught You: Corporate Gamesmanship for Women*. New York: Warner Books, 1977.

Identifies the traditional feminine attitudes that handicap you, confuse and discourage you when you try to cope with daily challenges.

Harris, T.A. 1967. *I'm OK—You're OK (A Practical Guide to Transactional Analysis)*. New York: Harper and Row. 1976. New York: Avon.

To function in a society the mature adult has to learn to respect himself and others.

Kutscher, M. et al. *A Comprehensive Bibliography of the Thanatology Literature*. New York. Arno Press, 1975.

A compendium of references covering publications in the periodical literature, as well as books covering many related disciplines.

Masters, W.H. and V.E. Johnson. 1970. *Human Sexual Inadequacy*. Boston: Little Brown and Company. 1980. New York: Bantam.

Based on their own research, authors provide information on sexual function and dysfunction. New forms of treatment are outlined.

Mayer, Jean. *Overweight*. Englewood Cliffs, N.J.: Prentice-Hall, Inc.

The goal of weight reduction is not only to lose weight but to keep it off; a well balanced diet is advised. The book contains a table of food values, 1968.

Parkes, C.M. *Bereavement (Studies of Grief in Adult Life.)* London: Tavistock publications, 1972.

This book describes the effects of bereavement upon physical and mental health. Discusses several factors that are thought to affect the course of grief. Gives the names of organizations in England and in the U.S. which help bereaved persons.

Porter, S. *New Money Book*. New York: Doubleday, 1979.

How to earn it, spend it, save it, invest it and borrow it. And use it to better your information. Gives a great deal of information on everyday matters and managing your money.

Silverman, P.R. "The Widow to Widow Program: An Experiment in Preventive Intervention." *Mental Hygiene*, 53: 333–337.

Widows can give helpful advice, information, and support to other widows.

Simpson, M.A. *Dying, Death, and Grief*. A Critically annotated Bibliography and Source Book of Thanatology and Terminal Care. New York: Plenum Press, 1979.

An extensive annotated bibliography.

U.S. Bureau of Labor Statistics. *Occupational Outlook Handbook, 1980–81 Edition*, 1980.

Finding Fulfillment in Remarriage

CHAPLAIN DAVID B. MAXWELL

To a person who is experiencing the anguish of grief at the loss of his spouse, the idea of remarriage may seem not only disloyal but also almost blasphemous. Yet, such a consideration may be inevitable for the sake of children or because of one's own basic need for intimate companionship. The conflict of these two considerations makes a careful scrutiny of this subject imperative for a person attempting to struggle through the grief of such a loss. To deal fully with this question, an exploration of the possible origins of these feelings of disloyalty, as well as an analysis of one's personal and most basic concepts of love and life, is necessary.

It is altogether possible that behind the fear of being disloyal to the deceased partner may lie feelings of which the individual is completely unaware. Beneath these feelings may be an unsuspected undercurrent of resentment toward the deceased spouse. A revelation of the presence of such feelings to the person facing this dilemma would usually come as a complete surprise and be met with disbelief. This is so because in the living relationship there had never been a hint of such resentment. Any dissatisfied emotions were instinctively hidden and never admitted to consciousness.

The question of disloyalty seems to arise most often in marriages in which the relationship took on an unrealistic quality of perfection; in which no anger or resentment was ever apparent; in which the basic and natural aggressive human drives were never expressed; and where any unpleasant confrontation was avoided. All efforts were made to maintain "peace" and to avoid disturbances and expressions of disagreement.

For some of these reasons, and of course there may be many others, the person troubled by thoughts of disloyalty may want to explore these feelings in depth with someone qualified to help. Only then can he overcome his inhibitions and undertake a new relationship such as marriage. Needless to say, if such an exploration does take place and the individual is able to come to terms with his natural, aggressive human drives, then the new marriage relationship may be even more fulfilling than the former one.

But the consideration of remarriage may go beyond the question of disloyalty: it may touch on the person's basic concept of life itself. It may touch on his concept of himself as a human being who can have, he may very possibly discover, a tremendous potential to love again and to grow in the experience of loving.

To some, the concept of love may appear in terms of an emotion which can be measured quantitatively, an emotion which is limited and subject to diminution. Love may be conceived of as having already been "bestowed" on someone, precluding any possibility of being "bestowed" on another. Behind such a concept must also lie the parallel idea that the human potential is limited and that existence itself is circumscribed and set; that nothing can change the boundaries of what we now are or are capable of becoming. If this is our concept of life, then it would follow that once we have bestowed our love, we are thereafter depleted of it and have no more to bestow on someone else. It would also follow that such an individual would enter into a new marriage relationship with a skeptical attitude, convinced that he or she did not have anything to give, but hoping to make the new marriage work—somehow.

Parents who are considering the possibility of having a second child often experience this kind of self-questioning of their potential to love. Very often they feel that, since they have loved their first child with such intensity, they will never be able to feel comparable depths of love for another child. It comes as a complete surprise to find that, not only are they capable of loving the second child as much as they did the first, but that their love for the first child may even be enriched and deepened. It comes as a complete surprise, too, that the more they love, the more they are capable of loving; that any newly realized capacity to love only increases the capacity for love, and that this resource does not suffer from any effects of depletion.

The New Testament, it seems to me, specifically directs us toward such depth and potential. Christ beckoned mankind toward such a concept of life when he said to the woman at the well, "The water I shall give . . . shall be . . . a well of water springing up." He was describing to her the inexhaustible nature of the true potential of life and of love. It is as though he were saying that the person who is really in touch with life is in touch with inexhaustible sources of love, and that such inexhaustible resources cannot be confined, circumscribed, and limited as would be a commodity.

Perhaps it was this underlying assumption about the true nature of life and the potential to love which prompted Christ to respond as He did to those who questioned whose wife a woman would be in the afterlife if she had married again. In explaining that, in the afterlife, this would not be God's concern, He may have been suggesting to his questioners that they were concentrating on the lesser of two good things—the narrower hope of reunification with the loved

242

one, as against the development of a broad view of that quality in life which is inexhaustible in its potential to relate to other human beings in the giving of love.

All of this is particularly valid in any attempt to help a person who grieves at the loss of his spouse. Such a person must realize that although the wish to be rejoined with the loved one is worthy, the wish to devote oneself completely to the task of the development of one's full potential to love during life is far greater. Once this is assimilated, the task of emerging from a state of grief may be speeded, since emphasis is then on life and not on death. This emphasis may also help the bereaved partner to see remarriage not as disloyalty but as a further step toward the real challenges of life: the development of the full capacity to love and of the human's full potential to relate to others in love.

Remarriage: A Psychologist's Advice

ROSE N. FRANZBLAU, PH.D.

Where there has been a good first marriage, the chances for a good remarriage are greater. In the original loving relationship, tensions, disagreements and hurts are worked out amicably. Differences are taken in stride because the love for the other is great and real, and guilt over unresolved conflicts is minimal. When this guilt is not properly resolved, it may stand in the way of a new relationship. All sins of omission and commission must be expiated while the survivor lives alone with tortured memories of the departed one, fearing that remarriage will only bring a repetition of past failures and unhappinesses.

Sometimes, this fear of remarrying is countered, paradoxically, by entering into a precipitous marriage. The couple may not know each other very well, or very long, but suddenly they seem to feel some kind of basic attraction for one another, and they rush into marriage.

This kind of marriage, when wrongly motivated, is not likely to last or be a happy one. It may be an escape from a reality they cannot face, or a heroic effort to gain reassurance that the death of their

243

mate does not mean that their life is over, too. When the couple later begin to face each other realistically, they may react just like youngsters who marry too early and accuse the other of not being the same person they represented themselves to be. If the couple ultimately separate, they can thereafter remain single, as they really wanted to originally. They can say to the world that at least they did try, even if they failed.

Religions show deep psychological insight when they set one year as the customary period of mourning. It takes this length of time, emotionally, to work out one's grief and to let the wounds heal. When remarriage takes place precipitously, while the wounds are still fresh and open, the grief may be taken out undeservedly on the new spouse. Disagreeable comparisons may be made with the deceased's mate, and the new home may become a "menage a trois," where the memory of the departed one is ever-present as a hurdle in the life of the couple, whether in their loving or their fighting. The person needs to adjust step by step and area by area to a life without the departed loved one. When the reality that the beloved partner will never return has been accepted, the bereaved can feel free to face life again and to want a new love and a new marriage. It can be like a cherished theme of love, played now as a reprise.

In the choice of a new love, there is naturally a question as to how the new mate would be as a parent to the survivor's children. When there are little ones, this consideration is basic, for the success of the new marriage may depend on how the new mate is accepted by the children, and vice versa. Otherwise they may be so busy fighting the children's rejection of the new mate that they haven't the time or the energy to build the good life they want.

Sometimes, remarried partners go into competition for the attention and affection of the other's children. This competition not only adulterates the romantic and tender love of the couple for each other but can have adverse effects upon the children of both, whose relation ship can become complicated by inordinate jealousies and resentments.

Sometimes, the new mate will go out of her way to prove to the children of the other what a good and loving mother she is. She expects the children to feel in their hearts toward her as they did toward their own parent. Such an expectation may be doomed to disappointment. To children it seems to say that parents can be replaced, and if that is the case, then children can be replaced, too. They also feel they would be disloyal to the memory of the deceased parent. The guilt from such feelings of disloyalty would be converted into hostility, which sooner or later would explode into disobedient or disrespectful behavior, calling forth recriminations from the new mate. An unrealistic approach can thus make things more difficult, and a happy adjustment all the harder to achieve.

Where the pair have had good relations with their own children, there is usually more compassion for the other's children. Each of the pair can face their role in the new family realistically. Neither expects the other to be an exact counterpart of the original parent. This gives them free rein to exercise the necessary authority and to impose necessary restrictions, even though they are not the real parent. They may also give themselves permission to go all out in anger when the situation calls for it, without fearing loss of the stepchildren's favor.

The pain of bereavement has its roots in common experience dating from the very beginnings of life, and varying from age to age.

The weakness and helplessness of the infant highlights the fear of abandonment as the greatest of all terrors. The little one's frantic cry says that with no one around to help, disaster must ensue. The child going off to school for the first time fears that his home and the beloved people in it will not be there when he returns.

Even later, when a life-dream like going off to college or getting married finally comes true, there is still fear of giving up the known and familiar. Tears are not always of happiness or gratitude, but may express the anxiety accompanying separation, which is equated with abandonment.

Fears related to death partake of the same phenomenon. No one, not even adults, can really conceive of their own personal death. As children, in moments of anger, they may see themselves lying in their coffin, surrounded by the repentant mourners, especially their parents. The child does not see himself as really dead, for he is fully aware of all the weeping and wailing going on and expects it to end with a great reconciliation scene, in which the parents take him up into their loving arms and promise never to behave so badly to him again. The thought of one's own death is in such cases merely a way of punishing an offending loved one. By so abandoning them they are doing to the other what they fear might be done to them.

The concept of death in childhood, as well as in adulthood, is thus seen basically to relate to the greatest fear of all—being left out and left behind, all alone on the face of the earth. The great hurt and grief in bereavement, no matter what our age, when a loved one departs, is always a phenomenon of being deserted or exiled. Even the rationalization that death was a release for one who suffered greatly, or that the departed one may have had a long, happy, and fulfilled life, is only of passing comfort. Sorrow is as much for one's own loss and what one has been deprived of, as for the departed whose life has come to an end and who can feel nothing more. Grieving may also be used to show how much the departed meant to the bereaved, and how alone and deprived they now feel.

Whenever a loved one departs, the living always experience guilt feelings. They feel grateful for having survived, but their guilt over this thought makes them go through all kinds of self-flagellation. There are flashbacks about what more they could have done, or things they shouldn't have done that might have made the departed happier or prolonged his life.

Since the conscience of a child is still in the process of growing and developing, it isn't strong enough as yet to generate the kind of guilt with which adults plague themselves. The child may even feel that if the parent had loved him enough, he would have found some-way of remaining alive. The parent's departure, therefore, becomes for the little one a statement of his unworthiness, and is accompanied by a loss of self-esteem.

This is one reason why the bereaved child often practices the mechanism of denial while the wound is still raw, and goes about his usual activities, behaving as if nothing had changed in his life. This kind of magical thinking is a built-in protective device which helps the child to face a reality which is truly unbearable. It is as if "wishing will make it so," and will make the parent return to life. When the child finally reaches the point where he can face reality, he begins to mourn, and begins to call for constant attention and care. This is a reversion to childish behavior, which in the past always evoked loving parental care. The surviving parent is often shocked by the youngster's withdrawal at the time of tragedy, and then outraged by his demands to be given total attention, as if nobody else had been hurt.

But the surviving parent will often times behave very much the same way, and will use the same mechanism of denial and escape, not letting their sorrow show in the presence of their children, with the rationalization that they must be protected. However, the real reason may be that they are afraid to lose control over their feelings in their child's presence. This might adulterate their image as the one who knows all and can do all. To a certain point, this has validity. To see parents totally overcome by their emotions might make a child feel forsaken again, with no one around who is strong enough either to survive or to protect him.

However, when the emotion of the adult is totally controlled, the youngster may begin to wonder whether the surviving parent really cared for the one who died. Such super control and withdrawal from all emotion only makes it harder for the child to accept the reality of death and prolongs the period of mourning.

It can be a great comfort to a child to be allowed to grieve with the adults who are bereaved. By the loving sympathy they show to others, they comfort themselves, and when they see that they are of help to the adults, it helps them to become a bit more confident that they will find some consolation themselves.

During the height and newness of the period of grief and mourning, grownups, just like children, may have moments of escapism when they fantasy that this was just a nightmare from which they will awaken to find that their beloved is still there. But sooner or later, they accept the sad reality and return to the stream of life, thinking of establishing a new pattern of living again.

Children will sometimes take the lead directly, or in a roundabout way, by asking the surviving parent when a new "mommy" or "daddy" will be brought into the home. This is the child's way of saying that he is gradually accepting the irrevocability of death. He misses his beloved parent, but feels different from other children because he has only one parent. He wants to be like everyone else again, with two parents. It is easier for the child to reach this point than it is for the surviving parent.

There are, nevertheless, some hurdles in the way which are peculiar to the child's stage of development. In the early years the child has the wish to possess exclusively the parent of the opposite sex. When the parent of the same sex dies, the child feels somehow that his wish to get the parent out of the way was responsible for the death. Having the desired parent all to himself is like a dream come true. If the parent should find a new mate, the child sees him as an intruder and trespasser. Whereas, with his own father there was enough love to compensate and overcome any hostile competitiveness, this is not true in the relationship with the newcomer.

Yet a little boy likes to have a man around the house who can take him out and engage in many manly activities with him. In time, this proves to be a force exerting pressure in a positive direction and if the new substitute father-figure is at all sympathetic, a good relationship will ensue.

As for the little girl, the fantasy that her father was taken away from her because she wanted to take him away from her mother makes her somewhat hesitant and apprehensive about showing any affection, at first, for the new man in her mother's life. She fears that the same thing may happen all over again.

Even when the children are fond of the newcomer, they sometimes see in the remarriage a second desertion of them. Part of the extra love and concern that was given to them by the survivor after the death of their parent is now being taken away from them and given to the new mate. The children may be envious of the loving

247

expressions of the newly married couple and the mindfulness and consideration that they show to each other. It is reassuring to the children, in that it forecasts a rounded and happy home for them. But it takes some time for the adjustment to be achieved by all the parties involved.

The situation is even more complicated, naturally, when each of the couple brings children from their first marriage with them into the new marriage. In addition to establishing a relationship with the new substitute-parent, the children from each side have to adjust to the newcomers into the family who aren't really siblings. But they are required to treat them as if they were.

The cross-parents, too, have a special problem of adjustment to the children of the new mate. Each of the couple is at first apt to be somewhat overly defensive or overly punitive when their own child acts up. They may want to show their own child that the others will not be allowed to take advantage of the situation. Or else, to show how fair they are, they will punish their own child much more than his misbehavior deserves. The child blames the other children for the parent's unfair behavior and they become the targets for his aggressiveness and hostility.

The handling of two sets of children in such situations requires a great deal of skill on the part of both parents. There can be a broken home with two families living under the same roof but not together. However, when the children felt loved during the first marriage and got along reasonably well with each other, and when the second marriage is a love-match, too, the hurdles are not so great and, with time and patience, the aware couple can surmount them. The results make it well worth while.

During adolescence, when a boy needs his father and at the same time rebels against his authority and supervision, the death of this parent is a great loss. It comes at a time in his life when he is searching for his own identity. Sometimes it opens the door for the youngster to take over and become the man of the house, in a sense, and the responsible person the father always had wanted him to be. This is a great testimonial to the memory of the departed. But sometimes the youngster is not capable of meeting the challenge and either falls apart or falls into bad habits as a symptom of his rebellion and frustration. The mother can be a tower of strength to her adolescent orphan son or a seductive clinging vine, who holds back his development to maturity.

To a girl, the death of a father at this age represents the departure of the first man in her life and can intensify her normal doubts about whether she will ever find a good and loving man of her own. At such a time, an adolescent girl will often feel guilty about leaving the house to go on a date when her mother is home, all alone and lonely. Such sympathy, carried to extremes, can keep both mother and daughter grieving too long, and can delay their return to normal living patterns.

The death of a mother often requires the adolescent girl to take over the management of the household and the care of the younger siblings. Doing good for the living, she feels less guilty about any competitiveness which she may have had in her relationship with her deceased mother. She can also play the little substitute wife and mother to her father in a realistic fashion, without feeling guilty about it. The realities give her fantasy fulfillments full sway and she gets applause, not criticism, for filling her mother's shoes. If this situation prevails too long, it can do her a great disservice and hurt her fitness for marriage to a man of her own generation. The remarriage of the father during this phase represents a second rejection to the adolescent girl, and also a lack of appreciation on her father's part for what she is, and what she did for him.

But perhaps the greatest impact of a parent's remarriage on the adolescent is with regard to the youngster's fantasies about sex. Every child has the secret wish to view what the parents are doing in the privacy of their bedroom. With the remarriage of the parent, the old curiosity is re-evoked with regard to the relations with the new partner. Now the fantasying, which can run the gamut from A to Z, is more permissible emotionally because it doesn't involve two parents—but only one parent, who married a stranger. The adolescent girl whose mother remarries may see in her a discouraging rival and competitor who always seems to win out and get her man. The girl may feel that the mother should act her age, and stay in the background and let her daughter take the center of the stage. She may become very demanding of material possessions, clothing, and freedoms, on the grounds that this will enable her to attract and win a man of her own.

The adolescent male may feel somewhat the same way when his father remarries. He may see the new wife, especially if she is younger than his mother was, as more of a peer or older girl friend than an authority figure. After all, if the parent is young enough to remarry and start a new sex life, then this is really coming down to his own level, or one which he aspires to reach very soon. Having demoted the couple to his own level and promoted himself into their class, he now talks more blatantly and openly about sex. He will make kidding, insinuating remarks about the couple's new sex life or tell too much about his plans for his own sex life. To allow this kind of behavior to continue only says to the boy that it is all right for him to compete with the husband for the new mother's love and attention. Playing into his fantasy that he is the other man in his mother's life only stands in his way of his achieving mature manhood.

In many ways, a new wife may have an even harder time with her husband's daughter. The adolescent girl may feel deprived and excluded when a new woman comes into her father's life. With this new competitor, she can never win out. It is even worse than it was in the case of her mother, because there, at least, she was sure of her love, while here, she must curry favor from a rival to win her love. It seems manifestly unfair. What is worse, the new mother lays down the law and has the authority of the father behind her to put it into action. She may, therefore, become the open target of the adolescent daughter's rebellion.

The new wife has some other hurdles to overcome in regard to the daughter. She sees in her not only a beautiful young competitor who is the darling of her husband's former life but also a living reminder of the first wife. This is particularly so if the daughter resembles her mother physically.

One might think that this competitiveness and rivalry with the newcomer in the family would be absent when the sons and daughters are married and off on their own, but sometimes it is even greater than in childhood. They may feel burdened having to spend time looking after an older parent, but often they see the remarriage of this parent as an act of disloyalty to the departed one. It also seems to them like a lack of appreciation and gratitude for all that has been done for them by the grown children.

The grown child, taking over the role of parent to the parent, now wants the right to approve of the person the parent is dating. A grown son may not express disapproval as openly as a daughter-in-law. She may reject the newcomer because of some real or imagined personal characteristic, thereby expressing for her husband the disapproval he feels but cannot express for himself. The daughter-in-law may also use the newcomer in the family as a target for expressing old angers toward the parent who has departed. Since there is no blood relationship, she feels freer to express her hostility.

Grown children on either side may not welcome the younger new siblings who are brought into their lives by the remarriage. They may accept the parent's new mate and even be sympathetic to the new life that the parent has begun to live, but that is often as far as they are willing to go. They don't relish the idea of having to spend time with any additional newcomers or of expanding the family circle to include them. They often feel this to be an imposition and an intrusion on their own lives and those of their children. It may seem too great a price to pay to be relieved of responsibilities.

When the parents have passed 65, grown children's objections to their remarriage are sometimes even greater, for they fear they may have two old people to look after instead of one. It is hard for them emotionally to conceive of caring for this stranger in their midst, should the newcomer survive their parent, despite the love and companionship that this one gave the parent.

Sometimes, also, the children's feelings are complicated by financial considerations. On the parent's remarriage, they may worry about what will happen to their inheritance. When the newcomer survives the parent and is provided for in the will, children may feel they were robbed to provide for a stranger. It helps to clear the atmosphere for the future when a prenuptial marriage contract is entered into by the old couple, and the children know their interests are protected.

To adult children, the remarriage of a mother is usually more acceptable than that of a father. A woman alone feels self-conscious about moving in the social stream of life without a male companion.They fear also that the mother will become increasingly dependent and demanding if she remains alone. When a man comes along who is willing to take on the support of their mother, it relieves them of the burden that they would otherwise have to bear.

But they are not as sympathetic in the case of a father. Somehow, a father who is not supposed to be able to look after himself, run his house, and prepare his meals is suddenly expected to manage all this without the ministrations of a loving wife. They often mind when he starts dating or socializing, as if it were treasonable to them and to the memory of their mother.

Another reason why the remarriage of the mother is looked upon more favorably by a daughter or a daughter-in-law is by contrast they find it less intrusive and burdensome to have a father or a father-in-law who is a widower live with them; hence, the pressures for his remarriage are less. A widowed mother may be more helpful around the house, but she is also apt to be more bossy and interfering, telling her how to run her life and raise her children. This is sure to arouse resentments, so that when the widowed mother finds a new husband, it may occasion rejoicing and relief.

There is no greater loss than the death of a child, and the bereaved parents may look to their grandchildren to fill the great void in their lives. For the grandchildren, it is good to be surrounded at such a time by loving relatives, and there is no one with whom they can feel more secure than their grandparents.

However, when the survivor remarries, the grandparents often feel that they are suffering a second loss. It reopens the wound all over again. They fear that their grandchildren will be taken away from them by the new parent who has come to replace the loved one in their lives. They will sometimes act like a divorced parent and insist on their visitation rights. The in-laws cannot help seeing in there marriage a desertion of their departed child. In subtle and circuitous ways, they may keep reminding the children about the parent who died, which may prevent them from accepting the finality of death and adjusting to the new parent. Such an attitude on the part of the grandparents makes it even harder for all to adjust to the new family constellation. The surviving parent may withdraw the children from the grandparents in self-protection, until certain that they accept the new spouse wholeheartedly.

Naturally, the parents of the other one, who has remained alive, want their son or daughter to remarry, and they are much more accepting of a new mate, more cooperative and less intrusive.

Adolescents sometimes use the remarriage of a parent, about which they have conflicting feelings, to justify their feelings of rebellion and hostility. They feel that they have no one now to turn to, with one parent dead and the other remarried. They may then use the grandparents as their confidantes, to whom they can express annoyances and criticisms of the parent's new spouse. When the grandparents listen, or worse, invite this kind of gossip and tattling behind the parent's back, they only increase the youngster's guilt. In the end, it makes it more difficult for such a young person to grow up and away from his parents healthily.

The marriage of older people is becoming increasingly common as the life span grows longer and longer. From the standpoint of society, this must be reckoned as definitely on the positive side of the ledger, but to grown children, it may not appear so clean-cut. When the old parent begins to act like a young colt, sexy and in love, the younger generation may think it is a sign of senility, and like "second childhood."

The older couple may have to prove themselves all over again in order to be accepted by the younger generation, which they cared for and reared, but which now feels it has to supervise, guide, and discipline the older ones, and tries to effect a reversal of roles. Such so-called parental care coming from their children only makes the elderly couple feel as if they are deteriorating rather than rejuvenating. It makes them feel they are going back to the helpless, dependent state of the child, which precedes departing this life for good.

This is contrary to all the facts of the case, and also runs counter to the new life-expectancy statistics. More and more older people now fashion their lives so that they can continue to live, love, and learn. But these three "L's" must meet the needs of the older couple on their own level. Engaging once again in a love-life gives them a reason for living and strengthens their drive to survive.

In a remarriage, each brings a lot of the past—old memories, feelings, and attitudes relating to the first marriage—into the new union. Often a most important living part and symbol of the past is the children of their first marriage. These are constant reminders of the first love in the other's life. Sometimes, however, the couple feel as if ghosts of the past are present constantly.

When they begin their new sex life, they may be haunted by a feeling of infidelity to the old partner, almost as if they were committing adultery. If the intimacy proves to be satisfying and rewarding, they may begin to make comparisons, judging the past mate to have been inadequate. If it is less gratifying than before, they may feel that they are being punished by the fates for wanting to relate to another in love. They may rationalize that, after all, the second time around cannot be expected to be as good as the first. On a deeper level, they may feel they are being faithful and loyal to their first love, since no one else can truly be a replacement.

In the extreme cases, one partner will want to keep pictures or other memorabilia of the departed around the house, even in their bedroom, on the grounds that the children should not be made to feel as if the memory of their parent was completely wiped out and no longer had any meaning. When the new spouse finds this objectionable, they answer that if their love was great enough, such minor details would be overlooked. Sometimes the close friends or relatives of the departed one want to be included in the circle of the new relationship, on the same basis as all others. When this unrealistic demand is not granted, they react with great hurt. The real message they are transmitting by this is that they are hurt that the mate of the deceased remarried. By the tensions they create, they punish the newcomer.

A pair who remarry feel that life has favored them, and that they are fortunate to be wanted in love, all over again. After all, to the couple it is a new and gratifying experience which is expressed physically, emotionally, and psychologically. But to the relatives and family, such gratifications and satisfactions cannot be expected to be present as compensations.

Awareness of the normal problems that take place in such are marriage is the first step toward happy adjustment. The second is acceptance of these problems as characteristic of such situations, and not implying any reflection upon themselves or others. The third and final step is putting this awareness and acceptance into action, by working out all difficulties lovingly and patiently.

Just as the new couple are adjusting to each other, the family and friends must adjust to them. They, too, need time to do so.

When the youngsters in the family see their parent's new life continuing and blossoming, their faith in the continuity in life and happiness is reaffirmed. Then they can give up the feeling, born of their tragedy, that when the life of their beloved parent ended, all hope of happiness in their own life came to an end as well. In giving renewal to each other, the couple also gives new hope and a love of life to their children.

Thoughts about Remarriage

FREDERIC P. HERTER, M.D.

It has been my observation that the happily married individual is the first to become remarried after the loss of husband or wife. This appears at first paradoxical, but I think the explanation can be found in the fact that these people have become dependent on a totally shared existence for their happiness. Grief at their loss is soon supplanted by a renewed need for both giving and accepting love, and it is not surprising to find that these second marriages are usually extremely happy ones. It is also not surprising that a certain degree of guilt accompanies the second courtship and the initial phases of their marriage. Months before, it seemed quite inconceivable that any further personal relationships could ever be entered into. To love another, fully and with intensity, appeared impossible. Did not such a new relationship, in fact, lessen or negate the validity of the shared happiness of the first marriage? Was not that first love a hollow and transitory liaison, to be forgotten and violated at the first opportunity? Could not a new attachment be construed as gross infidelity? The answer of course lies in the fact that the capacity for love is infinite in its scope and must find some vehicle for expression; it does not die with the death of a loved one, but rather reroutes itself into other channels. Such is the essential nature of man.

Etiquette and Remarriage

ELIZABETH L. POST

The question of whether a bereaved person wishes to marry again is, of course, a purely personal one. Many people cannot conceive of living with anyone other than the one they have lost. Others feel this way at the moment of bereavement, but gradually change their minds as time heals their wounds or their loneliness increases. Still others realize shortly after the death occurs, or even beforehand in the case of a prolonged illness, that they undoubtedly will want to marry again. This is often true of people who have been very happily married and enjoyed a relationship of mutual trust and understanding. Although they realize that a second marriage may not provide exactly the same relationship as the first, they are fully aware of the joy and companionship that a good marriage brings, and do not wish to go through the rest of their lives alone.

There is no longer any objection, as far as etiquette is concerned, to a widow's or widower's starting to see members of the opposite sex as soon as he, or she, wishes. It may be with remarriage in mind, or it may be that one enjoys the company of the opposite sex. But to become publicly engaged very shortly after a bereavement would show little respect for the deceased. In ordinary circumstances, a bereaved person should wait nine or ten months before announcing an engagement, and approximately a year before remarrying. Of course, there are perfectly acceptable reasons for shortening these times, such as the imminent departure of one or the other for overseas military service. But under normal circumstances, a reasonable wait serves several purposes: it softens the shock which the family of the deceased may feel when they are told of the proposed remarriage; it allows any children involved to come to know the future step-parent; it indicates a respect for the deceased; and most important, it allows the bereaved person sufficient time to be sure of his, or her, own emotional stability and rational approach to remarriage.

Part Seven
FINANCIAL PRAGMATICS OF BEREAVEMENT

Counseling the Bereaved: A Financial Primer for the Widow, Widower, and Surviving Children

GERALD ROSNER

The emotional trauma of a death in the family is often accompanied by the shock of financial reckoning. For an estate plan the true test lies in the ease or difficulty of working through the probate and estate administrative process.

The circumstances of dying, the length and severity of the terminal illness and the mental conditioning of the dying person's family all play significant roles. My major purpose here is to examine some of these variables and discuss how each affects and is affected by financial considerations.

SUDDEN DEATH

When death results from accident, stroke or heart attack, it has a numbing effect on survivors. They themselves are often in shock and unable to function normally. Such routine matters as funeral arrangements, posting obituary notices, ordering death certificates, notifying close friends and distant relatives are best left to a third party, such as a friend or a competent funeral director. If the deceased was a member of a religious group, the minister, priest or rabbi can usually be counted on for assistance.

Once the conventions have been observed, however, a terrifying period can follow immediately after the formal week or two of mourning when everyone returns to his own family, job and home and the surviving spouse and or children find themselves alone. Neighbors and friends may continue to call, console and occasionally visit, but the aloneness caused by death may continue through bereavement and may be particularly noticeable in a spouse or child who has survived a sudden death. The sense of aloneness is chilling and unrelenting. The period of mourning is extended and can create an awful feeling of impotence in dealing with everyday matters.

ACUTE TERMINAL ILLNESS

Certain cancers, AIDS, and ALS are a few examples of diseases which can lead to death after a relatively short spell of illness. Disbelief is probably the most prevalent response of survivors, particularly if surgical intervention was tried but proved ineffective. Much time and energy is expended in clinical post-mortem analysis and anger is often directed at the physician and surgeon. Modern medical "miracles" have been so hyped and touted that survivors often think a different doctor or a different hospital or the use of exotic drugs would have prolonged the life of the deceased.

The pursuit of elusive cures is publicized almost daily in the press. Each new hope leads to a new disappointment and the cycle repeats itself, causing increasing frustration and anguish.

A friend of mine whose 45-year-old wife has been diagnosed as an ALS victim follows up every possibility, no matter how remote, for a cure or arresting agent wherever in the world it may take them. He has neglected his work, clients and children in frantic pursuit of these chimeras and will surely impoverish the family in the futile hope of success. No one can gainsay his efforts; he is a man possessed.

My friend's behavior is, alas, not unusual. Hosts of quacks and con men prey on the victims of incurable disease and reap huge financial gains at the expense of family members who simply cannot accept the notion that death is inevitable. Outrage is closely akin to disbelief and both reactions impede rational behavior.

CHRONIC TERMINAL ILLNESS

Certain ailments such as the various scleroses, dystrophies and juvenile diabetes produce physical changes over long periods of time. To the patient, each episode of pain or disability is a jarring reminder that the disease is still there and is not going away. Diet, medication and behavioral prescriptions are helpful in controlling the symptoms but do nothing to eradicate the cause.

Since the episodes tend to be sporadic and often mild, family members may not even be aware of them. Nonetheless, awareness that the sword could fall any moment is chilling. Parents of diabetic children often console themselves with the thought that they will probably die before their afflicted child and thus be spared the torture of seeing their child go blind or lose a leg.

My daughter-in-law was diagnosed as an MS victim when she was 28. At first, neither she nor her parents would accept the diagnosis. She lived in New York at the time and was able to indulge the luxury of seeking alternative diagnoses from a variety of prominent neurologists throughout the city. Ultimately, after repeated testing and re-testing, the original dread diagnosis was confirmed and re-confirmed and she had to accept the fact that her life was irreparably changed. Once she accepted the incontrovertible nature of her condition, she settled on one physician, followed his advice, joined a support group and, despite her occasional terror, continued to be a model wife and mother and to maintain an active career as well.

AGING

Only in the second half of this century have we as a society been confronted with the fact that of a large segment (11% in 1980) of our population live into their eighties and nineties. The causes have been carefully explored in numerous papers, books and forums and there is no need to repeat them here. The financial problems of aging are, however, very much our concern and, we will deal with them from the point of view of society as a whole and specifically from a perspective which accepts aging as a terminal condition of living with certain effects on the survivors.

PRE-MORTEM ESTATE AND FINANCIAL PLANNING

Planning for one's death is in large measure a function of time. Since the time of death is uncertain, the best estate plan is one which is constantly updated and revised as if death could occur tomorrow. Sudden death certainly validates the wisdom of frequently updating one's estate plan.

But most of us don't live that way. Preoccupation with one's death is not conducive to a joyous life, though arguments could be advanced that on creative forces are intensified by a sense of impending death.

Laws governing the distribution of property after death do not recognize differences based upon cause of death or the time it takes to die. Each person is permitted to give away up to $600,000 either during life or after death without incurring a federal gift or estate tax. State laws differ.

A married couple can shift ownership of property back and forth to each other with tax impunity. They can also join in gift making during their lifetimes, giving up to $20,000 to each of as many donees as they choose each year without invading their lifetime exemptions. The annual exclusion is non-cumulative. Trusts, foundations and charities as well as individuals may be considered valid recipients. In fact, even larger amounts can be donated to educational and charitable organizations.

Hence, one can readily see that large estates can be reduced to no-tax status if there is enough time to embark upon and implement a gift-giving program over a long period. Economic life being what it is, however, large accumulations of wealth tend not to occur until late in life. The most obvious exception is, of course, inherited wealth. Despite this, proper planning, established early in life and reviewed periodically, can not only enhance the amounts one may give away during life and after death, but can also reduce dramatically the percentage of an estate which is lost forever to taxes and administrative costs.

EXAMPLE: Let us assume husband age 60, and wife, 57, each own $1,000,000 of assets. Both are in good health although the husband's family shows a history of cardiovascular disease and the wife's mother and aunt died of cancer. Their progeny consists of three grown children, all prospering, and one grandchild, age 8.

The husband's normal expectancy is about 18 years and the wife's is 24. During the expectancy periods, if they added no additional capital and earned no more than 5% net of taxes and subtracted nothing, each would have $2,407,000 at the first death. Then, if the unlimited marital deduction were utilized, the survivor would be worth $4,814,000, ignoring any state taxes, administrative and probate costs. This amount, in turn, would grow to $6,450,000 at the second death, passing as the gross estate of the second person to die.

Estimated costs of passing an estate of this size would be: Administrative and probate costs: $325,000. Federal estate taxes: $2,996,300, for a total wastage of $3,321,300, leaving the net distributable estate at $3,128,700.

In other words, failure to plan can result in an ultimate payment of transfer costs which exceeds the net estate passing to heirs. Despite the curtailment of several important estate planning devices through recent tax-law changes, ample opportunity still exists for the judicious arrangement of one's assets and their disposition.

Time, as always, is a key factor. Time to plan, time to try and time to change. When terminal illness strikes, time is no longer an ally. Relief is still available, even when time is short, but expert assistance is required.

POST-MORTEM ESTATE AND FINANCIAL PLANNING

What can be done after the patient dies? Is post-mortem estate planning feasible? The answer is yes, but ...

261

Of paramount importance is whether or not the testator had ever written and signed a will, whether the will is of recent date, whether it truly expresses the testator's intent at the time of death, and whether the document complies with state law and will be accepted for probate. If no will exists, the deceased's property, will pass by operation of the laws of intestacy. The court will appoint an administrator to see that those laws are complied with. The court will also appoint a guardian to protect the interests of minor children, if there are any. Although the surrogate by definition is supposed to stand in the shoes of a will-appointed executor, there is little likelihood that the descendent's survivors will receive the consideration they think they deserve.

The best course for the survivors to follow is a cooperative effort to work with the administrator in locating and evaluating assets, searching through drawers, closets, file and safe deposit boxes and all of the decedent's financial advisors and contacts. This is a tedious, thankless and often unrewarding job but unless it is done, and done thoroughly, chances are excellent that items of value will be forever lost and some beneficiary will be denied his or her inheritance. Following are some of the items the administrator will look for:

- Income tax returns (last three years)
- Titles to automobiles, boats, other vehicles
- Any trust documents that may exist
- Stockbroker's statements, bond and stock certificates
- Bank statements and canceled checks
- Life insurance and other insurance policies
- Group insurance certificates
- Notes, mortgages, other evidence of loans by or due to decedent
- List of debts of decedent
- Statements of any companies in which decedent had an interest
- Coin and stamp collections
- Valuable objects of art, and so on

An improperly drawn will can be as bad as no will at all, and one which does not meet the requirements of law (for example, lacks witnesses or is defective) will not be accepted for probate and appointments under such a will would be deemed invalid.

Then there are those cases where a will exists and is valid but was written and signed many years before. Named beneficiaries are no longer alive, assets listed no longer exist, specific bequests cannot be satisfied, charitable bequests cannot be honored, the executor appointed cannot be found, and the attorney who drafted the will has been disbarred. This is called a mess and there is very little anyone can do except to muddle through the probate process and get rid of it.

Death of a loved one is traumatic enough; we don't need legal and administrative entanglements to add to our grief. And this is where post-mortem counseling and planning can prove invaluable to the bereaved's family. A counselor can guide them at their own pace, keep them informed of the steps taken and to be taken, complete and file claim forms, feed a stream of information to the accountant and attorney for the estate, deal with the bureaucracies, prioritize bill-paying, examine the claims of creditors, and so on.

Even when an estate appears at first glance to be simple and straightforward, unforeseen complications invariably arise. Rarely is an estate of any size closed in less than a year; typically, it takes at least twice that long. And this is during a time when survivors are lonely, insecure, depressed and often very angry. Clearly, this is a time when outside assistance is needed. If the decedent was a partner in a closely-held business, many nasty successive ownership issues can emerge. If no buy-sell agreement had been entered into prior to death, the problems of valuation and ownership have to be faced by the successors. One side will be dealing from weakness; that side is usually the surviving spouse. In such cases, a skilled outside counselor can prove extremely helpful as an advocate and relieve the family of many pressures.

Probate is the process of completing the unfinished business of the decedent. As such, it can help the family 'let go' and get on with their own lives.

The Multiple Roles of an Estate Lawyer

RICHARD H. BERNSTEIN

The broad technical role of a lawyer handling an estate is to help the family marshal the decedent's assets, pay the creditors, file the appropriate tax returns and distribute what is left. Except in the case of very modest estates, this process typically occupies two to three years, sometimes longer. Furthermore, in many estates there are sensitive family issues to deal with which are inextricably tied to the legal decisions which must be made. As a result, the estates lawyer is likely to be closely involved with, and have a substantial impact on, the family of the deceased—and especially the surviving spouse for the immediate as well as the extended period of bereavement.

Because of the significant role the estates lawyer will play, the choice of the "right" lawyer is critical. In many cases that choice will have been made long before the death of the first spouse. If not, the anxiety of having to select an attorney to handle the estate will only add to the built-in anxieties and stress to be faced by the surviving spouse. [4]

In the unfortunate situation where the attorney to handle the estate has not been pre-selected or where it is clear that the choice was not a good one, it is imperative that the "right" lawyer be found. Given the myriad details and filing deadlines which must be met in a typical estate, the selection process should begin without delay.

But who is the "right" lawyer? Certainly, it is someone who is at least technically competent in the area of estates law. With the assistance of relatives, friends, accountants and other personal advisers and local bar associations, it should not be difficult to find a number of attorneys who meet this criterion.

Technical competence, however, should not be the only factor in choosing an attorney, especially an estates attorney. Because he will perform so many sensitive roles, the attorney should be someone with whom the surviving spouse feels a natural rapport and whose judgment is trusted in both legal and non-legal matters. These non-legal skills of the attorney will be critical in giving the spouse a positive attitude toward the entire probate process and in helping her or him surmount the emotional hurdles in the post-mortem period.

Also, unless the spouse already has trusted professional advisers, she or he will be inclined to turn to the attorney for guidance on the choice of accountants, stockbrokers and investment advisers, among others. Furthermore, especially in estates where there are delicate family relationships, the choice of the right counsel is critical. For example, there may be children of a prior marriage whose feelings and relationship with the surviving spouse must be considered. A careless remark or a tactless letter by the attorney or his client could damage or destroy a relationship and possibly trigger otherwise avoidable litigation.

Even assuming the children are the offspring of the marriage between the deceased and the surviving spouse, there is no guarantee that they will be happy with the testamentary plan of their deceased parent. Here again, an astute and sensitive attorney can play an invaluable role in attempting to maintain family harmony.

Finally, no matter what the circumstances of the death of the first spouse, the survivor is likely to experience stress at various levels. Part of the attorney's job, as I view it, is to minimize the stress for the surviving spouse as much as possible. For example, depending on the circumstances of the spouse's death, and the medical and mental condition of the survivor as perceived by the attorney, it may be advisable for the attorney to screen the surviving spouse from making certain decisions until he thinks the survivor is emotionally prepared. This might even mean holding off discussing or taking certain legal steps until he feels the surviving spouse is ready to cope with the subject matter of the discussions.

Naturally, one hopes that an attorney who felt his client was having difficulty coping emotionally would guide his client to a psychiatrist, psychologist or social worker for professional treatment or guidance. Wholly apart from his humanitarian motives in doing so, an experienced estates attorney would know that unless his client was functioning properly, the administration of the estate could be seriously impeded.

Once selected, the attorney has several major jobs to do right away. The first, and perhaps the most important, is to educate the surviving spouse as to the key elements of the estate administration process, in language the spouse can understand. While the use of technical terms may be indispensable to a thorough explanation, the attorney *must* make every effort to state matters in the simplest language possible. It is all too easy to slip into legal jargon, either inadvertently or consciously (as a way to "impress" a client). The danger is that the client will not know what the attorney is talking about, feel too embarrassed to ask, and will, to the attorney's subsequent amazement, remain mystified about what is happening for the duration of the estate.

The solution to the problem is fairly simple. The attorney must continue to explain until he is convinced the client understands him, and the client should continue to ask questions as long as she or he does not understand what the attorney is talking about. If possible, the attorney should not try to spell out the whole story at once, and the client should not insist that it be done that way. Furthermore, the attorney should be aware that any technical explanation he gives to a surviving spouse early in the bereavement period will fall on inattentive, if not deaf, ears. A grieving wife or husband may not be attuned to listening to legal explanation, no matter how simplified they may be. Thus, it is the attorney's obligation to repeat and reinforce information and to pick carefully his times for important discussions with the surviving spouse.

The second major job for the attorney is to explain to the surviving spouse as soon as possible the attorney's function in the administration of the estate. It is important to give a specific account of the matters that he will be taking care of for example, preparation and filing of the probate papers; collection and consolidation of estate assets; preparation of any state estate tax or inheritance tax returns and the Federal estate tax returns, if necessary; filing an inventory of assets with the local probate or surrogate's court and the preparation of the estate's final accounting.

The third key task that the attorney must perform early in administration is to explain to the surviving spouse precisely what his or her role will be. Assuming the spouse is an executor or co-executor of the estate, the spouse will not only be required to sign virtually all legal documents on behalf of the estate, but also will have a number of decisions to make. For example, should a suit be instituted to recover money lent to a third party by the deceased spouse? Should a piece of real estate owned by the estate be sold and, if so, on what terms? Should the estate settle a will contest filed by a disappointed heir? All of these are executorial decisions, but the attorney's opinion ought to be sought in each case.

Many other functions performed during estate administration are customarily done by the estate's attorney, even though the functions themselves are more executorial in nature than legal. Among these are the transferring of assets from the decedent's name to the estate's name; the keeping of the estate's checkbook and other records; and applying for social security benefits on behalf of the surviving spouse. Whether one or more of these or other executorial functions is to be done by the attorney or the spouse-fiduciary should be clarified early in administration.

In my experience, even the tasks which may appear very simple to a lay person can become extremely complicated in the context of an estate and are better left to the attorney. For example, the transfer of bank accounts or securities from a decedent's name into the estate's name often requires supporting documentation that a non-lawyer would ordinarily be unable to obtain without an attorney's help. As a result, I have often found that it takes less time and cost for my office to handle certain executorial chores from start to finish than to let the spouse-executor try to do it alone. On the other hand, I have often been told by surviving widows that they need a greater sense of involvement in their husbands' estates, and that despite the risk of inefficiency, errors and greater cost, they would prefer to do something themselves rather than have our office handle it. Obvi-

266

ously, these are sometimes difficult decisions for the spouse and the attorney to make, and occasionally the decision is changed in midstream. In any event, the key is to make sure that the attorney and the spouse-fiduciary know what the trade-offs are before the work is started.

One further thought about the role of the estates lawyer: Because of his close involvement in the lives of the bereaved, he is very much a care giver and often feels that he is practicing everything but the law. Early in my career I was advised of this phenomenon by a colleague who quoted someone else as saying that "being an estates lawyer is as close as you can come to being the family doctor without having a license to practice medicine." I have no quarrel with that statement.

NOTES

1. This article is addressed principally to surviving spouses who presumably have been made the primary beneficiaries of heir deceased spouses estates and who will be serving as Executors of Administrators of those estates.
2. Under Federal law, any estate of $600,000 or more is required to file a Federal estate tax return within nine months of date of death. For good cause shown the filing period can be extended up to 15 months from date of death. In either event, the Internal Revenue Service has two years from the filing of the return to audit the return and assess any additional tax. As a result, in estates where Federal estate tax returns are required, it is unusual for estates to be closed out in less than two years from date of death.
3. In many states outside New York, an estate lawyer is commonly referred to as being a probate lawyer. Also, in many states other than New York, the court having primary jurisdiction over a decedent's estate is called the Probate Court. In New York the court having primary jurisdiction of a decedent's estate is officially called the Surrogate's Court.
4. Wholly apart from the need for a lawyer capable of handling the administration of the deceased spouse's estate, it is essential for the family to have a lawyer with the expertise to do the proper pre-mortem planning. This planning includes the preparation of wills, trust agreements, powers of attorney and, in appropriate cases, shareholders agreements for the orderly transfer of closely held family businesses. It may also include the lifetime shifting of assets from one spouse to the other or to third parties. In any case, much of what the lawyer will be called upon to do will frequently be tax oriented. Thus, in choosing an attorney to do the pre-mortem planning, the family should seek out an attorney with a thorough knowledge of estate planning and the complex estate, gift and income tax laws that govern estates.

267

Family Assistance and the Probate Process

MILTON MILLER

After the death of a family member, it is frequently helpful to have one of the close relatives involved in the probate process. The understanding of the process and involvement can give a sense of direction and accomplishment which can ease the mourning period.

Many of the probate tasks are time consuming. With the assistance of the attorney and the accountant, a family member who has the time and the inclination can complete tasks which would otherwise have to be done by the professionals. The involved family member is thus participating and also reducing the fees of the professionals. More can be retained for the family.

Tasks which can be accomplished by a family member:

1. Make funeral and burial arrangements.
2. Deposit original will, any codicil and separate writing with the clerk of the Circuit Court.
3. Determine preliminary probate information and compile summary of assets and liabilities.
4. Furnish copy of will to all beneficiaries.
5. Inventory the safe deposit box.
6. Sort and locate all informational documents required, such as the following:
   a) All signed copies of Decedent's wills and codicils, decedent's death certificate and obituary notice.
   b) Decedent's military identification number and V.A. identification number, if any. Dates of military service and branch of service and certificate of discharge or separation from service.
   c) Income tax returns for the last 3 years for decedent and decedent's spouse and decedent's business or any partnership or trust in which decedent was a partner, beneficiary or trustee; State of Florida or other state intangible tax returns (if any) for the last 3 years for decedent and decedent's spouse; declaration of estimated tax due (IRS Form 1040 ES) for year of dece-

dent's death, if filed; all gift tax returns (IRS Form 709) ever filed by decedent's spouse.

d) Titles to all automobiles, boats, airplanes, or other vehicles registered in the name of decedent or decedent's spouse, and if subject to a lien, the loan number, payment book, name and address of each lien holder.

e) General description of all personal property owned by decedent or decedent's spouse including livestock, farm products, jewelry, art, household goods and personal effects. With respect to jewelry, household goods and personal effects, itemize only those items of considerable value ($1,000 or more) with the balance being lumped under a general description.

f) Copies of all trusts created by or for the benefit of decedent or descendent's spouse and inventory or valuation of each trust, copies of wills, trusts, state and federal inheritance and estate tax returns, and audit adjustments, and orders or reports of distribution for estates of persons from whom decedent inherited property within 10 years prior to decedent's death.

g) Assemble original stock certificates, bonds (except bearer bonds) including Series E Savings Bonds, mutual fund certificates or statements, and all broker's statements for the past 3 years.

h) Certificates of deposit, savings passbooks or statements and checking account statements and canceled checks for 36 months preceding death, (and when received) for the month of death, and subsequent month as well, and the checkbook stubs for each account on which decedent was a signatory, whether joint or individual. Copy of the most recent financial statement available for decedent and decedent's spouse.

i) Life insurance policies or certificates of group insurance, health or disability insurance policies or certificates, life insurance connected with credit cards, auto and real estate mortgages and other debts.

j) Homeowner's property, fire, jewelry, auto, casualty, liability, theft and miscellaneous property insurance polices.

k) Real estate and tangible personal property tax receipts for the last three years (if any). Deeds, contracts, title insurance policies, surveys, and contracts for purchase and sale pertaining to real estate and all other matters in which decedent has an interest, whether completed or pending.

l) Notes, mortgages, and security agreements payable to decedent.

m) List of debts owed by decedent, including funeral bill and available last illness expenses, hospital bill, doctor bills, and all other debts owed by decedent, including information regarding the name and address of the person to whom the debt is owed, when the debt is due, whether interest is accruing on the debt, and the amount.

n) Financial statements and tax returns of closely held businesses and partnerships and other items relating to value of and income for such businesses and partnerships.

o) Agreements to which decedent or decedent's spouse was a party such as leases, partnership agreements, buy-sell agreements, employment agreements, stock purchase agreements, stock options, pension agreements, profit sharing plans, annuities, franchises, patents, copyrights, leases, and other such agreements.

p) Decedent's occupation at date of death, the name address and telephone number of the employer and the person to contact concerning any death or survivor's benefits available. If decedent was self-employed, decedent's trade name, business address, telephone number, and federal tax employer identification number for the business. Copies of financial statements for the past 3 years for the business. If retired, give decedent's former occupation, employer and nature of business.

q) Marriage certificate, birth certificate for decedent and decedent's children, divorce, judgments, property settlement agreements, the date and place and decedent's marriage to and name, address, age and Social Security number of decedent's surviving spouse and for any prior spouse, including date of termination of prior marriage and whether terminated by death or divorce.

r) Name, address, age, date of birth, marital status and Social Security number of all children ever born to or adopted by decedent, whether presently living or not, and if not living, death certificate for deceased child and furnish all information previously requested. If decedent was married more than once, indicate the other parent of the child or lineal descendent.

s)   Club, fraternal and lodge memberships of decedent.

t)   Names and addresses of all hospitals in which decedent was confined in the last 3 years, and of decedent's personal physician and the physicians attending decedent during decedent's last illness.

7. Arrange to and take possession of, protect and preserve real and personal property.

8. Determine adequacy of insurance coverage for estate liability, real property and personal property and arrange for needed insurance.

9. Financial arrangements:

    a)   Open checking and savings account for estate.

    b)   Pay all periodic obligations such as mortgages, property taxes, condo, assessments, etc.

    c)   Maintain estate check book.

    d)   Pay administrative expenses.

    e)   Pay claims. Note: If done by other than attorney, the attorney should prepare satisfaction and release of claim forms simultaneous with claim payment.

    f)   Pay miscellaneous items.

    g)   Maintain estate accounting. Note: The final account or optional interim accountings, if elected, must be prepared in pleading form, filed and served by the attorney.

    h)   Make principal and income accounting allocations of income and expense items. Note: This is particularly critical regarding items originating close to the date of death. Some single items must be prorated between principal and income.

    i)   Collect periodic receivables and deposit. Note: If this matter is accomplished by the executor, xerox copies of checks and cash receipt vouchers and deposit slips must be retained.

    j)   Initial responsibility for investment decisions regarding sale of assets and investment proceeds.

    k)   Disburse partial and final cash distributions.

10. Bank dealings:

    a)   Transfer funds from decedent's individual checking and/or savings accounts to estate accounts.

    b)   Advise banks holding decedent's individual checking accounts of death with instructions not to pay checks after 10 days.

    c)   Maintain, renew, convert, cancel or re-register CD's.

d) Direct inquiries to banks regarding deposits, loans, or safe deposit box.
11. Collections
Undertake to collect or to assist in the collection of:
a) Mortgages, leases or other periodic receivables.
b) V.A. death and burial benefits.
c) Employer, fraternal or professional organization death benefit.
d) Benefits receivable from qualified retirement, IRA or Keogh plans and unqualified plans, if any.
e) Life insurance payable to the estate and premium refunds.
f) Life insurance payable to beneficiaries.
g) Medicare claims and collections (coordinate with doctors and other who accept assignment).
h) Health insurance claims and collections (coordinate with doctors and others who accept assignment).
i) Credit union account.
j) Prepaid newspaper and magazine subscriptions.
k) Prepaid membership refunds.
l) Prepaid health or disability or other insurance premiums.
m) Personal injury or accident claims.
n) Pending tax refunds.
12. Arrange for evaluation and appraisal (and alternate 6 months re-evaluation when applicable). Note: The valuations must comply with regulations issued pursuant to Internal Revenue Code on:
a) Real property.
b) Tangible personal property
(furniture, furnishings, personal effects, jewelry, antiques, automobiles, etc.).
c) Series E bonds.
d) Stocks and corporate or municipal bonds.
e) Other intangibles (mortgages, etc.)
f) All other property.
13. Continuation or cancellation of services and maintenance contracts such as: utilities, telephone, lawn, pool, exterminator or other services.
14. Management and operation of any rental properties owned by decedent.
15. Management and operation of any business owned by decedent.

16. Arrange to forward decedent's mail to executor and advise Post Office of change of address.

17. Determine whether to surrender property to persons presumably entitled thereto, and timing of transfer.

18. Transfer title to vehicles.

19. Prepare and file SS4 *Request for Employer's I.D. Number* for each testamentary trust and for estate.

20. Transfer securities through stock brokers.

A Confidential Family Financial Checklist

EDWIN NADEL AND JOHN J. PARKER

The facts in this checklist will help the patient, his advisors and family members coordinate affairs of financial concern. It has been broken down into 15 different sections dealing with personal data, income requirements, various questions, disability, insurance, life insurance details, other assets, storage of papers, investment plans, estate objectives, taxes, distribution considerations, discussions about maturing trusts and anticipating inheritances, other pertinent data, and a check list for other documents needed for analysis.

I

Date _____

Name	Company
Residence Address	Business Address
Phone _____ Years there	Phone _____ Years there
Date of Marriage	Nature of Business _____ Title

273

FAMILY DATA

Name   Relationship   Birth Date   Birth Place   M or S   Health*   S.S. No.

_____

_____

_____

_____

Family Information   Stepchildren—Adopted

Earning Ability of all (Use separate sheet if necessary)

Other Dependents—Parents, In-laws, etc.   Extent of Support

Previous Marriage   Divorce   Separation Agreement   Date

Physician

HOME OWNERSHIP

1. Mortgage Date _____ Amount _____ Interest _____ % Term _____
   Monthly charges _____ Unpaid balance _____ Prepayment privilege _____
2. Do you wish home free and clear? _____ Or extra monthly payments? _____
3. Any Home improvements: _____
4. Can you make a list of costs, dates, and descriptions? _____

_____

_____

II
FAMILY CASH AND INCOME REQUIREMENTS

A. Monthly Income

1. Dependency period $ _____
2. Readjustment for _____ yrs. _____
3. Life Income   _____
   (Outside income $ _____)

C. Settlement Funds

1. Current expenses $ _____
2. Obligations   _____
3. Final expenses   _____
4. Taxes: a) Income   _____
   (quarterly estimate)
   b) Property   _____
   c) Death   _____

B. Special Cash Needs

1. Mortgage $ _____
2. Emergency fund   _____
3. Educational fund   _____
4. Any litigation?   _____
5. Any special bequest?   _____
6. Charity   _____
7. _____ _____

D. Special Income Needs

1. Parents? _____ _____
2. _____ _____
3. _____ _____

III
QUESTIONS

1. What is the managerial and business ability of spouse? _____
2. What is the managerial and business ability of children? _____
3. What is their business experience? _____
4. Can spouse or other family members draw income from business at death of principal? _____

5. What Group Insurance does your company offer? _____
6. Does your company have a $5,000.00 tax-free death benefit? _____
7. Does your company have a pension or profit-sharing plan? _____
       What are your benefits if you:
                  Terminate: _____ Become Disabled: _____
                  Die: _____
                  Can Life Insurance be added to the plan? _____
8. Are you able to borrow? _____
   _____ (Discuss in Detail.)
9. Burial arrangements? _____
10. Obituary? _____
11. Do you own any Flower Bonds? _____
12. Do you have Annuity Payments? _____ Will they continue to others? _____

IV
YOUR CAREER—JOB—BUSINESS

Describe: _____

Should you change jobs? _____
Income: _____ Benefits: _____

V
DISABILITY INCOME

1. Total Income required during disability? _____
2. Professional Overhead Expense or Business Overhead Expense:

Rent	$ ___	Periodicals	$ ___	Elec., Oil, $	
Property Taxes	___	Maintenance		Gas, etc.	___
Properety Inx. Prem.	___	Service	___	Dues:	___
Property Mtge. Int.	___	Equipment		Other Fixed	
Employees' Salaries	___	Depreciation	___	Expense	___
		Liability Insurance			
		Premiums	___		
Sub-Total	$ ___	Sub-Total	$ ___	TOTAL $	___

3. Are you covered by a State Disability Program? _____

275

V
DISABILITY INCOME (cont'd)

4. a) Major Medical Plan? _____ b) Hospitalization? _____

    c) Will company pay medical bills? _____ d) Can Major Medical be continued by family? _____

5. How long secy./nurse/or key employee working for you? _____

6. To what societies do you belong? _____

7. Termination clause in lease? _____

8. Any Disability Buy and Sell Agreements? _____

9. What is the company's policy with respect to paying executives who become disabled permanently or for a long period of time? _____

10. Where are disability insurance policies stored? _____

VI
LIFE INSURANCE DETAILS

Where are insurance policies stored? _____ Who owns them? _____

Are there any loans? _____ Are they insured? _____

What are you doing with your dividends? _____ Any with company? _____

What are you doing with your paid-up additions? _____

Do you have your last premium notices? _____

Do you have any group insurance? _____

Is there insurance on your wife or children? _____ Why? _____

    Why Not? _____

Is your life insurance beneficiary the same as your will? _____

    Has this been checked? _____

What are your insurance objectives? _____

Any Group Creditors Insurance? _____

    Any Convertible Decreasing Term? _____

Should Business Insurance become personal insurance? _____

Purchase Options? _____ Family Agreements? _____

	Date Acq.	cost Values	Situs. state	Gross Values			Loans**	Income	Hard to Sell***	Liquid
				Husb.	Wife	joint				
Real Estate										
Saving Acct's										
Checking Acct's										
Gov't Bonds										
Mutual Funds										
Stocks										
Bonds										
Personal Effects										
Special Equip, etc. Art—Antiques										
Notes										
Mortgages										
Patents & Royalties										
Life Ins. Face Amount										
Ins. Cash Values Other Lives										
Pension/Profit-Sharing										
Interest in Trusts										
Deferred Comp. Stock Option										
Vested Interests										
Business Int.										
Power of Ap-pointments										
Children's Assets (Owned by H. or W.)										
Total										
Any Loans Separate H.W. Joint										
Net Assets at Death										

*Percentage of Gift   **Insured

**Indicate Husband, Wife or Joint   ***Should assets be sold NOW—Discuss

VIII
STORAGE OF IMPORTANT PAPERS OR DOCUMENTS

1. Assets on Previous Page _____
2. Wills _____
3. Marriage Certificate _____
4. Birth Certificate _____
5. Divorce Decree _____
6. Tax Returns _____
7. Discharge Papers _____

8. Trust Instrument _____
9. Children's Bankbooks _____
10. Travelers Checks _____
11. Stamp Collection _____
12. Coin Collection _____
13. Agreements _____
14. _____

IX
INVESTMENT PLANS

1. Investment Plans _____ Surplus for Investment _____
2. Special program for children? _____
3. Investment ability of wife? _____

X
ESTATE OBJECTIVES

_____

_____

XI
TAXES

Income Tax paid last year—State $ _____ Federal $ _____ City $ _____
Please furnish copies of last year's tax returns.

XII
DISTRIBUTION CONSIDERATIONS

1. Special Family needs:
2. Charitable bequests:
3. Trusts (Describe): Past:
   Contemplated:
4. Should current assets of children be used for education or living expenses?
5. Disposition of Business Interests (Retention or Sale)
6. Gifts: Past: Present or   Return   Total Exemp.
7. Gifts: Past: To Whom When Future Value Submitted Used
   Contemplated:

XIII
MATURING TRUSTS, ANTICIPATED INHERITANCES, LEGACIES

1. Self:
2. Other Family Members:
3. Review estate plan of other family members: